'OUR LITTLE GANG'

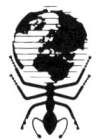

'OUR LITTLE GANG'

The Lives of the Vorticists

JAMES KING

REAKTION BOOKS

For Brigid Peppin

Published by
REAKTION BOOKS LTD
Unit 32, Waterside
44–48 Wharf Road
London N1 7UX, UK
www.reaktionbooks.co.uk

First published 2025
Copyright © James King 2025

EU GPSR Authorised Representative LOGOS EUROPE,
9 rue Nicolas Poussin, 17000, La Rochelle, France
email: contact@logoseurope.eu

Printed and bound in India by Replika Press Pvt. Ltd

A catalogue record for this book is available from the British Library

ISBN 978 1 83639 055 8

CONTENTS

INTRODUCTION

'We are getting our little gang together after five years of waiting,' Ezra Pound informed the poet William Carlos Williams in December 1913.[1] The 'little gang' to which he referred were the Vorticists, a group of like-minded visual artists of which he was not a member but the unofficial promoter. Pound's use of the word 'gang' suggests that he saw the Vorticists as a group of outsiders to the literary and artistic establishments. The word 'gang' can also imply that the group might be capable of committing unlawful acts. And this is certainly how the group was sometimes seen by their contemporaries. 'Of waiting' indicates that something had been delayed and had finally arrived.[2]

Pound was the first person to apply the term 'vortex' to the 'little gang'. By definition, the vortex is a whirlwind sucking in everything it encounters, whether animate or inanimate. As a metaphor, the word describes a world in chaos. Wyndham Lewis described the word more specifically: 'At the heart of the whirlpool is a great silent place where all the energy is concentrated. And there at that point is the Vorticist.'[3] The Vorticist is therefore positioned on the narrow border between order and chaos.

Vorticist art inhabits a realm where chaotic energy is harnessed. At the core of the vortex, there can be moments of epiphany or ecstasy – this is what the Vorticists believed could only be pictured in abstraction rather than representational art. However, they practised a precise form of abstraction. There is a branch that never correlates to objective reality and there is a programmatic variation that uses various strategies to reference reality. Vorticist art – with significant exemptions – is programmatic.

The twentieth century had entered the world of machines, and Vorticism had to deal with this phenomenon. Although the 'new art' did not have to embrace the machine (unlike its arch-rival, Futurism), it had to take it into account. This can be seen in the Vorticist partiality for depicting mechanical-looking diagonals juxtaposed to the still centre of the vortex. The poet and critic T. E. Hulme spoke warmly about the use of 'machine forms': 'A whole picture is sometimes dominated by a composition based on hard, mechanical shapes in a way which previous art would have shrunk from. It is not the emphasis on form which is the distinguishing characteristic of the new movement, then, but the emphasis on this particular kind of form.'[4] Vorticist art depicted machines and recognized their importance but was never pro-machine.

In its brief existence from 1913 to 1915, Vorticism was the first attempt by English artists to practice a form of abstraction that was distinct from all the other manifestations on the Continent. Most accounts tend to place Wyndham Lewis at the centre. There are good reasons to do so because of his ability as a leader – although a self-serving one – and his considerable skills as an artist. This results in a story about one person who controlled a group of his colleagues rather than, more accurately, a narrative about a group whose members had very different personalities, aims and ways of making art. Vorticism, moreover, is not a single style, although these artists often riff on each other's work. There were moments when their works were very similar.

Vorticism has long been a curiosity in the history of modern British art. Despite its short existence, it has much to tell us about how England proved a hostile environment. It is also a movement that was stifled by war: in a very real way, it simply ran out of time. However, the drift of this narrative is concerned with why Vorticism came into being, its accomplishments and, especially, its practitioners.

There has been outstanding work on Vorticism by scholars such as Richard Cork, William Lipke and William Wees. There are also superb articles on specialized aspects of the movement. Although building upon this excellent scholarship, this book takes an entirely different approach by taking the form of a group biography centred on the vivid interactions among seven Vorticists: five men – William Roberts, David Bomberg, Edward Wadsworth, Wyndham Lewis and Henri Gaudier-Brzeska (referred to as Gaudier throughout this book) – and two women: Jessica (sometimes Jessie) Dismorr and Helen Saunders. Of the seven, only Gaudier did not train at the

Slade. Apart from Saunders and Dismorr, all were at some point employed at the Omega Workshops. There were other artists who produced significant Vorticist work (Cuthbert Hamilton, Frederick Etchells and Lawrence Atkinson), and I describe their contributions during the course of my narrative.

I emphasize how relations within the group influenced the making of their art. Roberts and Bomberg were resistant to be labelled Vorticists. Wadsworth supported Lewis, but they had significant aesthetic divergences. Lewis and Bomberg despised each other. Dismorr and Saunders quietly bided their time in a testosterone-filled environment.

Part One is centred on the early lives of the seven – especially their nascent artistic sensibilities; the seven are thrown into the vortex in Part Two; Part Three emphasizes their post-Vorticist existences.

Some misconceptions are corrected in my account. For example, Dismorr and Saunders are often described as ladies-in-waiting who existed on the margins of Vorticism. This is misleading and incorrect. Their contributions were both extensive and crucial in Vorticism's brief life.

Another major theme is emphasized. As Karin Orchard has argued, Vorticism encapsulates one of the great dilemmas of visual modernist art. There is a 'constantly shifting to-and-fro struggle for predominance between abstraction and illustration, between pure form and literal representation. This conflict was particularly plain in the vision and experiments of the Vorticists.'[5] The Vorticists believed in abstraction, but they were almost always dependent upon some form of representation.

In addition to recreating the personalities of the artists, I also pay close attention to their works and their exhibition history. Their lives were filled with power struggles, missed opportunities, violent encounters and heart-breaking mishaps. Their story is about fledgling artists striving passionately to make the world a better place.

PART ONE: TYROS

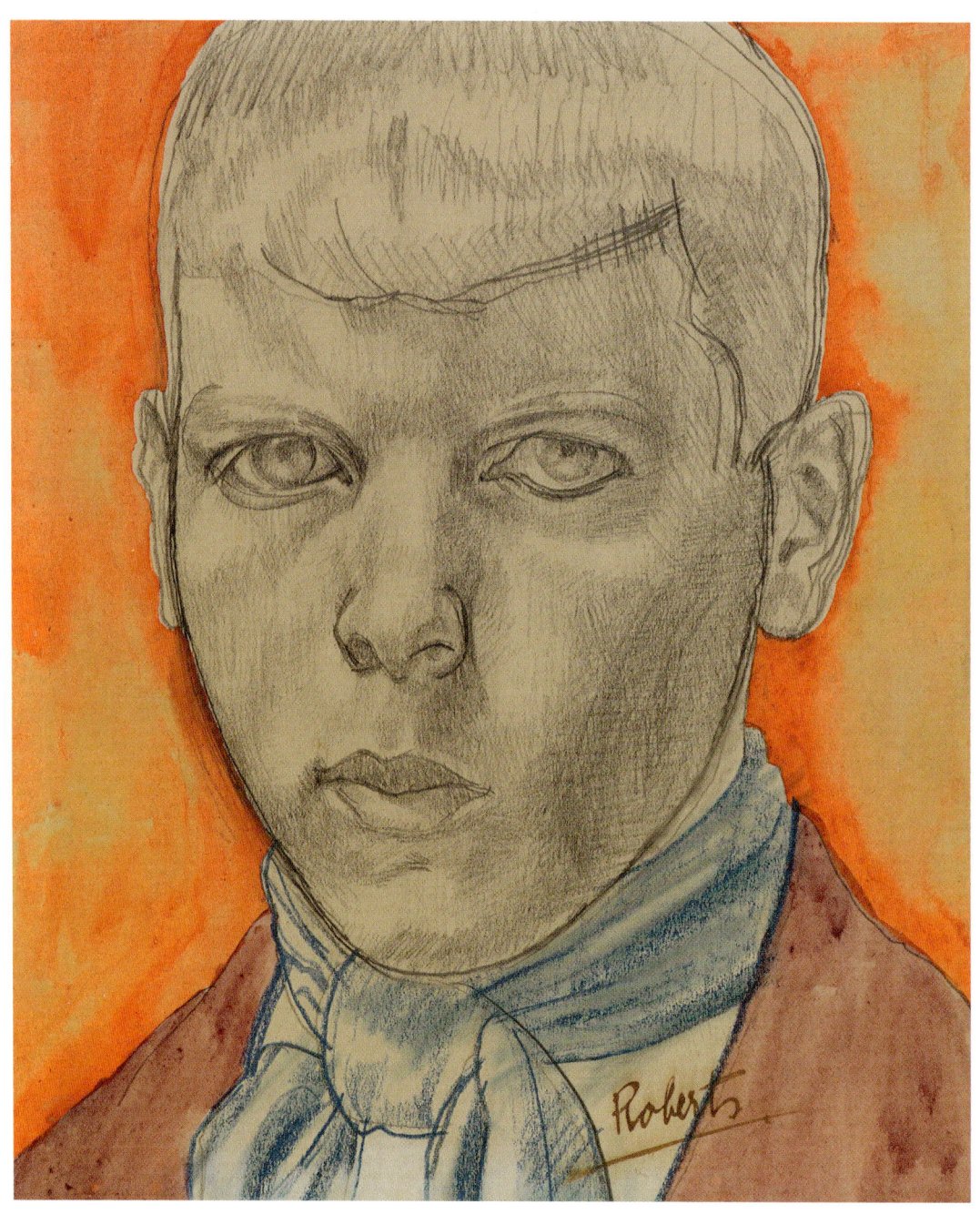

William Roberts, *Self-Portrait*, *c.* 1912–13, pencil, crayon and watercolour.

1

THE WOULD-BE CUBIST: WILLIAM ROBERTS

From childhood, William Roberts felt destined to become an artist. 'It was about my twelfth year that my interest in drawing began to attract the notice of my teachers.' He was born in the working-class section of the inner London borough of Hackney on 5 June 1895 and was the third of four children (two brothers, one sister) of Edward (Ted) Roberts, a carpenter, and his wife, Emma.

The artist's boyhood memories were tainted by the end of the four-year Boer War in 1902, when he was seven. Inspired by that conflict, he remembered, he and his friends played soldiers, 'form[ed ourselves] into groups, and armed with sticks, or their caps rolled tight at the end of pieces of string, went to war with each other'. Unemployed, returned soldiers roamed the streets. 'Outside the pubs, fights were frequent, and as the blood and beer mingled, the children danced to the tunes of a wheezy barrel organ.'[1]

In the summer in nearby London Fields, boys from that neighbourhood could earn spending money by retrieving stray balls that came leaping across the tennis courts. During the winter, Roberts and his playmates escaped the cold by standing on the iron grids over the basement of a bakery.

At the age of three, he attended Gayhurst Road School, a couple of streets away from his home. He remembered little of his education there in the next nine years. What he distinctly recalled is that, at the age of twelve, his drawing attracted the attention of his teachers. He was allowed to miss some of his regular lessons so that he could concentrate on art. At about this time, the headmaster decided that the youngster should attend art classes at nearby Queen's Road School, where art classes were held two days a week. Through this connection, William Robins, a teacher at St Martin's School of Art, offered him evening lessons.

Some days at Gayhurst, he stood 'at an easel in a corner of my regular classroom and painted in water-colour'. He made some still-lifes, but he was also very ambitious. He once undertook a large-sized copy of a Venetian scene by Turner. A bit later, Roberts drew an accomplished self-portrait in which defiant eyes confront the viewer. This is the face of a very determined teenager, someone keenly aware of his own nascent talent. An unwavering, often obstreperous belief in himself remained the cornerstone of Roberts's personality.

When Ted Roberts became aware of his precocious son's fascination with art, he made an easel for him and accompanied him at six one morning to deliver it to Gayhurst. He supported his son's ambitions, but, nevertheless, at the age of fourteen, William had to find a job. After several missteps, he was taken on as an apprentice at Sir Joseph Causton's in Eastcheap near the Billingsgate fish market. This firm, although also a law stationer, produced posters and all manner of commercial art. Twelve artists were employed at Causton's. As the lowly apprentice, Roberts mixed paints with a large palette knife on an old litho stone; he also had to ensure that buckets of water, used for gouache, were always filled.

Inside the shop, there was merriment among the underlings. The water Roberts fetched was used by two of the artists to 'attempt with considerable splash' to put a colleague into one of the buckets headfirst. There was indoor golf whereby yardsticks were used as clubs to knock a ball of tightly wrapped paper into rings chalked on the floor.

Eastcheap, especially in the morning, was 'animated'. Roberts witnessed 'long lines of horse drawn carts and vans of the fishmongers packed by the kerbs', awaiting their consignments of haddock, herring and codfish while the 'porters, wearing their queer hats for carrying the heavy crates of fish on their heads, hurried around shouting'. Nearby, down by the side of the Thames, 'was a scene, if not of crime, certainly of toil, glitter and wealth'.

After his ten-hour workday ended at six, he walked through Cheapside and Holborn to St Martin's in Endell Street, near Drury Lane. There, for three hours, he drew from plaster casts of Greek and Renaissance sculpture. He seldom reached home before ten.

Sixteen-year-old Robert's break came in 1911 when the drawings he made at St Martin's won him a London County Council scholarship to the Slade. 'This event', he rejoiced, 'brought me release – after one year – from the seven years apprenticeship contracted with Causton's.'

The 'release' introduced Roberts to a new roster of teachers, including Frederick Brown and Henry Tonks, and to a group of extremely talented students like himself. The Slade School of Fine Art was named after the collector Felix Slade, who endowed chairs of fine art at Oxford, Cambridge and the University of London. In London, Slade had also provided funds for scholarships, and, in recognition of this largesse, the college established a teaching institution. From the outset, students at the Slade were so thoroughly vetted that they were not examined on admission. Also, all instructors (usually referred to as tutors) had to be practising artists.

The first head of the Slade School in 1875 was Sir Edward Poynter, followed by Alphonse Legros and, in 1892, Brown. These three were opposed to the moribund teaching methods at the Royal College of Art in South Kensington, where drawing was taught by copying casts of ancient sculpture. In contrast, Brown emphasized the individuality of his pupils and promoted expertise in draughtsmanship as the cornerstone in his dedication to forming artists. Both he and Henry Tonks, his principal assistant, were heavily influenced by French Impressionism; as such, they focused in their own work on the ways in which light created fleeting, momentary impressions.

Trained as a doctor, Tonks stressed anatomy in teaching life drawing. He required his students to study old master drawings at the British Museum and underscored sight size (measuring at arm's length) in the rendering of models. One student recalled him as 'physically . . . a towering, dominating figure, about 6ft. 4in. tall, lean and ascetic looking, with large ears, hooded eyes, a nose dropping vertically from the bridge like an eagle's beak and quivering camel-like mouth'.[2] His belief in drawing was the basis of his teaching philosophy: those 'of great [artists] are like lines in Shakespeare, the beauty of which are beyond explanation'.[3] He instructed students: 'Don't copy, but try and express the shape you draw; don't think about the paper and the flatness of it; think of the form and the roundness of form . . . Think of those bones, those beautiful sweeps and curves they have.'[4]

The doctor-turned-artist was rigid in his conviction about how to train his charges. He once told a friend: 'I cannot teach what I don't believe in . . . this talk about Cubism [must] cease; it is killing me.'[5] Many of Tonks's students remembered him as a gifted teacher, a person of wit and charm, although when displeased he resorted to ridicule and sarcasm. Once, disgusted with a student's work, he asked him: 'I suppose you think you can draw.' The student, with suppressed fury, replied: '*If* I thought I could draw – I shouldn't come here, should I?"[6]

Roberts's skill in draughtsmanship was so evident that he moved quickly from the Antique to the Life Room. 'Toward the end of my first morning there,' he remembered, 'the female model fainted and collapsed.' A fellow student 'took off his jacket, covered the prostrate naked form with it, then strolled off unconcernedly to lunch' after performing this chivalrous act.

Realizing that Roberts was exceptionally proficient, Tonks encouraged him and about a half a dozen of his peers to learn mural painting. They decorated the walls of a girls' club in Fulham using egg tempera on paper stretched on the walls. Roberts's panel showed carpenters, like his father, at work. In the summer of 1911, he was among a select group invited to stay at a country mansion owned by a friend of Tonks. That year, Roberts would have attended some of the lectures given at the Slade by Roger Fry. For Brown and Tonks, inviting Fry to speak was the equivalent of setting a snarling cat among innocent pigeons.

Up to 1909, Fry had been stalled in his career as an artist and a connoisseur. After studying painting in England and in Paris at the Académie Julian, his path forward was clouded. He tried his hand at classical landscapes, deplored Impressionism and was suspicious of Whistler's innovations in painting light and colour. His epiphany occurred when he became fascinated by Cézanne's revolutionary emphasis on form in line, mass and colour. According to him, the French artist had discovered a 'modern vision with the constructive design of the old masters'.[7] After his conversion, Fry became an ardent proselytiser of Post-Impressionism. He organized 'Manet and the Post-Impressionists' at the Grafton Galleries in 1910 and, two years later, the 'Second Post-Impressionist Exhibition', devoted in part to English artists who had adopted Post-Impressionist techniques.

In 'Manet and the Post-Impressionists', Fry attempted to display the advances in art on the Continent. The critic Desmond MacCarthy dubbed this much reviled show the 'Art Quake of 1910'. Works by Cézanne (21), Van Gogh (25) and Gauguin (46) were heavily featured, although some by both Matisse (two paintings and drawings) and Picasso (three paintings and drawings) were represented. Manet was not a Post-Impressionist but his *Bar at the Folies-Bergère* was placed in the first exhibition room across from two canvases by Cézanne. In this way, Fry was indicating that Manet was of the

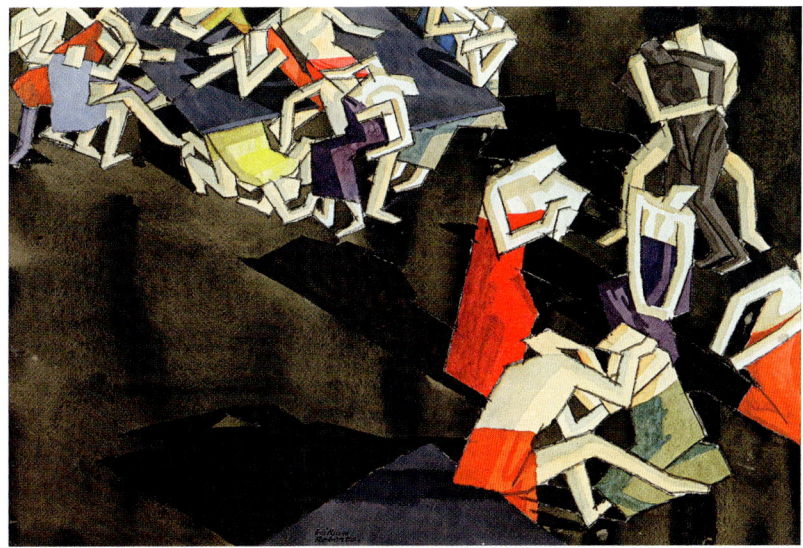

William Roberts, *Study for 'The Return of Ulysses'*, 1913, chalk and watercolour on paper.

past and proclaiming Cézanne as the founder of Post-Impressionism and, therefore, modernism.

There were 257 works in the 'Second Post-Impressionist Exhibition' divided into three sections: English chosen by the critic Clive Bell, Russian by the artist Boris Anrep and French by Fry. Cubist works by Picasso were on display. Bell's mission was to display the works of modernist English artists whose work had been inspired by the 1910 exhibition. He chose Vanessa Bell, Frederick Etchells, Jessie Etchells, Eric Gill, Henry Lamb, Duncan Grant, Spencer Gore, Stanley Spencer and Wyndham Lewis. In January 1913, when the exhibition was rehung, Edward Wadsworth was added.

For Tonks especially, Post-Impressionism was heresy. Moreover, he deplored the ways in which a once classically inspired artist like Fry became, almost overnight, an advocate for a dangerous form of modernism. Tonks's belief system and Fry's transformation, Roberts and his peers realized, were part of a dramatic shake-up rocking contemporary English art. Would it remain insular, or did it look to the School of Paris to reinvent itself?

At the time of the first Post-Impressionist show, there was in London an assortment of competing (but often overlapping) groups. In 1893 Fry joined the New English Art Club (founded 1886) and exhibited there on a regular basis until 1908. Like Brown and Tonks, it favoured Impressionist art whereas the Royal Academy remained hidebound. In 1907 Walter Sickert began the Fitzroy Street Group, which merged with the Camden Town Group in 1911. Some members of the latter group welcomed Post-Impressionism. In 1908 Frank Rutter of the *Sunday Times* founded the Allied Artists' Association to promote modernist art. He wanted to stage exhibitions modelled on the Societé in Paris and the European Secessionist exhibitions.

The men and women at the Slade wanted to become modern, up-to-date artists but there remained a quandary. To which group should they pledge allegiance? Against the advice of their elders, they were anxious to explore the various kinds of modernism making their appearance.

In the summer of 1913 when his last term at the Slade had come to an end, Roberts holidayed in Italy and France. That stay influenced the direction in which he headed: 'I became an abstract painter through the influence of French Cubists; this influence was further strengthened' by his trip to the Continent. Armed with a strong letter of support from Lawrence Binyon, the keeper of the British Museum Print Room, he called on Fry, who had recently founded the Omega Workshops. There, he obtained work painting designs on paper knives, lampshades, tabletops and silk scarves. He was employed three mornings a week and received a half sovereign each time. He fondly recalled: 'With no rent to pay, and a salary of thirty shillings – in those days that was independence.'[8]

When he opened the Omega Workshops in July 1913, Roger Fry was attempting to find another way of revitalizing English art. In the 'Second Post-Impressionist Exhibition' he had included English artists who had embraced that movement – or, in the case of Lewis, were moving even further in the direction of abstraction.

He had another agenda, as Richard Cork has pointed out: 'The more Fry saw of the young English painters involved with the Post-Impressionist cause, the more convinced he became that they were indeed capable of meeting the challenge of applied art. In [a] 1912 essay he maintained that a sane and unoppressive socialist system would encourage artists to earn their living by making "objects of daily use and ornament". Their abilities as artists would thereby be deployed even as they were enabled to subsidize their own painting and sculpture.'[9]

Roberts's tasks at the Omega Workshops were entirely in accord with his leanings since he probably first saw examples of Cubist oils and watercolours, including some by Picasso and Braque, at the 'Second Post-Impressionist Exhibition'. Moreover, he understood that Fry's definition of modernism was wide-ranging. Many of the items for sale at the Omega were brought in unadorned so that the artists could experiment with their embellishments. Many were done in the highly saturated colours favoured by most Post-Impressionists; they were also indebted to the bright costumes and sets of the Ballets Russes.

His notion of Cubism was – and remained – vastly different from that of others in that he showed no interest in its analytical or synthetic manifestations. Roberts's first surviving oil, *The Return of Ulysses* (1913), at first glance seems representational.[10] It shows Ulysses, assisted by his son Telemachus and two other followers, slaying Penelope's suitors. She appears in the right-hand portion of the composition positioned between the fighting warriors. Roberts leaves much of the left-hand foreground empty of action and shadow-like forms are rendered in brown against a black background. This is a Cubist-inspired work in its use of straight lines in rendering figures to give them an abstract-like quality. Space in this composition is so flattened that the absence of any sense of perspective also bestows an abstract-like quality to the entire composition. The scene looks elaborately choreographed so that any sense of action or movement has been erased – here, Roberts's idiosyncrasy and originality can be clearly seen. In 1913 he was searching eagerly for ways – on his own terms – to become a Cubist.

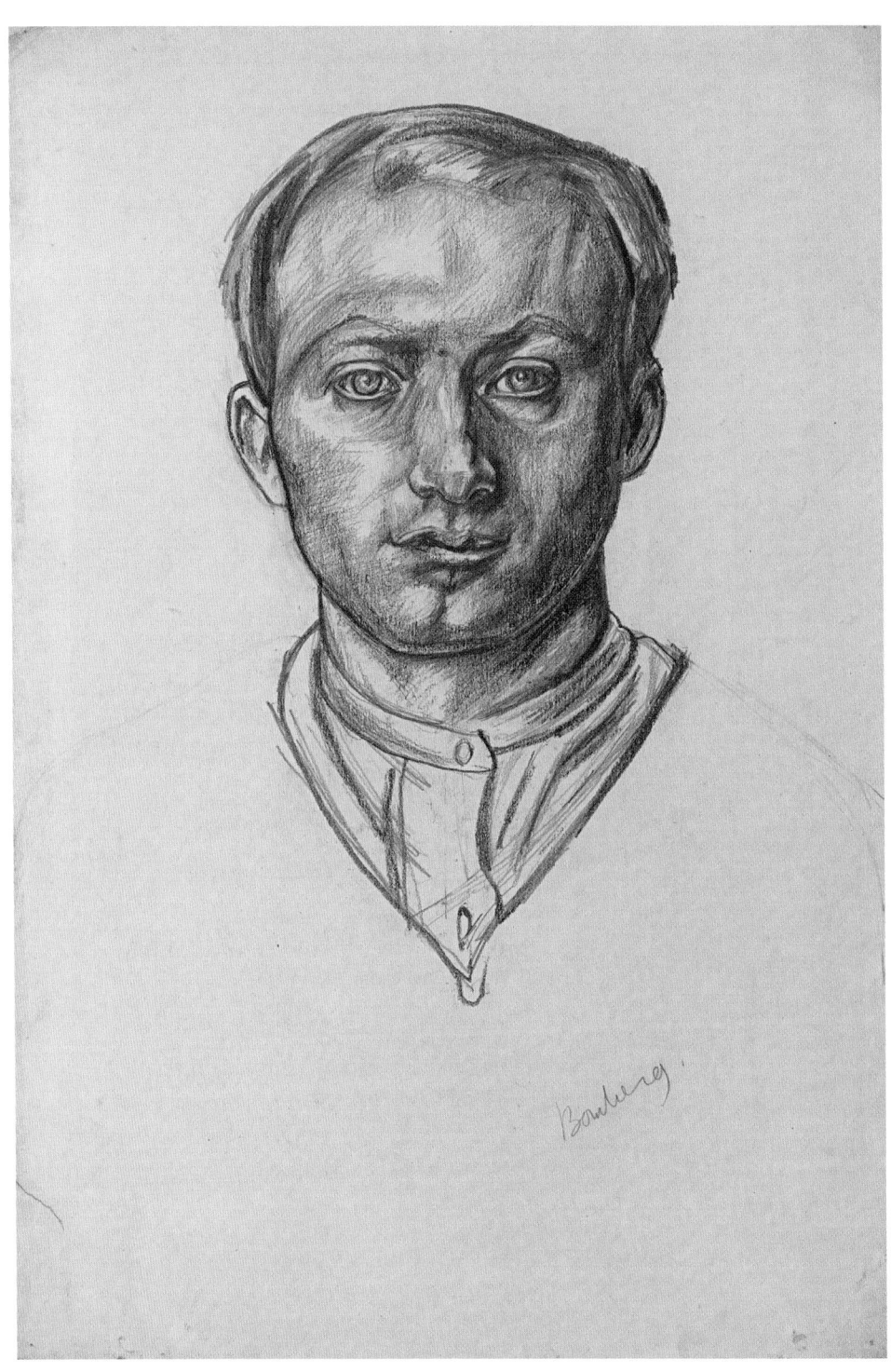

David Bomberg, *Self-Portrait*, c. 1913–14, chalk.

2

THE DISSIDENT:
DAVID BOMBERG

One evening when Roberts was at his drawing class at St Martin's, his teacher came up to him. 'Take a look in the Life Room. There is a male model posing there with a marvellous figure.' Roberts later expressed his astonishment: 'I did not know that the model was David Bomberg, or that in a year's time I would be drawing him as he posed in the Life Room of the Slade.'[1]

Five years older than Roberts, Bomberg was born in December 1890 on Florence Street in Birmingham. Roberts was from a family of artisans who struggled to survive, Bomberg from one of crushing poverty. His father, Abraham, a saddle-maker, emigrated from Warsaw to London to escape the pogroms. The move was motivated by the hope that a wealthy uncle of his wife, Rebecca, would assist them to settle in Whitechapel, the area in the East End of the city where many Jewish and Irish immigrants lived. When Rebecca's uncle did not provide the anticipated help, Abraham, whose profession was very specialized, felt he could not make a living there. In hope of better prospects, the couple and their four children moved to Florence Street, 'where one drain [served] 12 houses. [It was] situated so near the back door of one of the front houses . . . that in summer especially the effluvia is very unpleasant, and the door has to be kept shut.'[2] There was no green space, and the back-to-back houses were situated in a heavily industrial section of the city.[3]

When the family's fortunes did not improve on Florence Street, the seven moved to Cardiff, where their luck was no better. In 1895, now a family of eight, they returned to Whitechapel. Living conditions in this section of London were deplorable, but the ghetto-like atmosphere created a strong sense of community. The family – which consisted eventually of eleven children – squeezed in uncomfortably in a top-floor flat with no bathroom or lavatory of its own in a tenement on St Mark Street. The Bomberg children

– like all the others in that neighbourhood – wandered the streets and, in the process, encountered a great deal of antisemitism. The insults hurled at them hardened them – being disbarred by poverty and race created a strong sense of solidarity.

The Bomberg household was dysfunctional. At the beginning of the new century, Abraham received commissions from several leather goods merchants in the West End. His improved circumstances led to gambling. When he lost, as often happened, he lashed out at his wife and children. One of the children recalled, 'when he smacked my mother one day, [one of my brothers] hit him back and so the other brothers took [him] out to the back room and pretended they'd beaten him to placate my father.'[4] In response to his violent behaviour, Rebecca protected the children and rejected her husband's Orthodox observances.

Probably on Abraham's insistence, most of the Bomberg children attended the Jews' Free School in Spitalfields. David did not go there – probably because no space was available – and went instead to the Old Castle Street School, where many of the teachers were Jews. At that school, David's love of drawing emerged. One of his sisters recalled, 'All I ever saw David do was draw, and he didn't even join us at meals.'[5] He inherited his fiery father's temperament, but they had little in common apart from that. One of his brothers recalled, 'David must have been affected by the strain of living with a father who gambled and a mother who resisted him. My father didn't understand David's interest in art, and no pictures were ever hung in the family flat. But David was a special child for his mother.'[6] She did everything in her power to encourage him in his determination to become an artist.

Like Roberts, Bomberg had to find a way to make a living. His parents decided – probably late in 1906 – that he would become an apprentice in chromolithography in the workshop of Paul Fischer in Islington. This decision did not sit well with the son, who had already taken on at the age of fifteen a variety of short-lived jobs to pay for his tuition at the evening life classes taught by Walter Bayes at the City and Guilds Institute.

Whenever he could steal away from Fischer's shop, Bomberg copied old masters at the major collections to which he could gain entrance. One Saturday afternoon at the Victoria and Albert Museum when he was focused on drawing a cast on Michelangelo's *The Bound Slave*, a stranger asked if he could inspect the drawing. The man was the celebrated painter John Singer Sargent, who took steps to obtain admission for Bomberg to the Slade by approaching the Royal Academician Solomon J. Solomon, a prominent member of the Jewish community, to assist him. Solomon contacted Fred Brown, who inspected Bomberg's work and spoke to him at length. An invitation to the Slade was not forthcoming. Despite this setback, Bomberg, like Roberts, abandoned his apprenticeship.

He took on a few jobs to support himself. He posed for Sargent, and Roberts saw him when he did so at the Slade. Bomberg kept himself relentlessly busy. He took a course in book production and lithography at the Central School of Art and Design. He also attended evening classes at the Westminster School of Art from Sickert, who specialized in working from life-class models.

Twenty-five years before, while staying in Paris, Sickert had met Edgar Degas and incorporated the French's artist's penchant for sombre colour values and emphasis on structure. Sickert was the teacher from whom Bomberg learned the most; his later interest in dancers as a subject may have been inspired by Degas. Sickert, one of the founders of the representationally inclined Camden Town Group, was open to a wide variety of other modernist styles.

Bomberg's time with Sickert prepared him for what he was exposed to in 1910 at 'Manet and the Post-Impressionists'. He had never seen a Cézanne and the attention to both volume and form he witnessed in the work of that artist must have struck him deeply. He would also have noticed that Van Gogh and Gauguin incorporated similar values in their art but used more vivid colours.

A boyhood friend recalled that Bomberg became 'very "blasty" – pugnacious is too mild a word. He wanted to dynamite the whole of English painting.' At the same time, his left-wing leanings came to the fore. 'We used to mooch around the streets of Whitechapel completely wrapped up in our own misery,' a friend recalled.[7] Bomberg was also acutely aware of how far outside the social order Jews were perceived. As he became more and more conscious of how his poverty and his race placed him on the margins of society, his anger and resentment came to the fore.

When he was finally admitted to the Slade in April 1911 with the financial assistance of the Jewish Education Aid Society, Bomberg was already a

well-trained, very opinionated artist who realized that the Slade was a necessary stepping stone for advancement in his profession. He needed the Slade,
but he was angry that its doors had been closed to him for so long.

Bomberg quickly became 'the official wit of the Life Class' with an 'aggressive style'. Roberts recalled a particularly dramatic episode when Bomberg
walked 'into the Life Room, a board under his arm, bestride a donkey [draw-
ing bench] and started to draw'. That led to a 'punch-up' when a French
student proclaimed how strong he was. Bomberg responded that he was
equally strong. The Frenchman approached Bomberg, and a fight ensued.
Bomberg's opponent landed on the floor, 'scrambling up, he seized a drawing board and hurled it at Bomberg, who promptly jumped clear in time.
Quiet was restored with the arrival of Tonks to find out the cause of the
disturbance.'[8] Another time, Bomberg and an Italian male model wrestled.
After rolling about a good deal on the dusty floor of the Life Room, locked
together in a tight embrace, Bomberg finally managed to come up on top.
He also blackened the eye of a classmate who attempted to bully the Jewish
students with antisemitic invectives. One day in 1912 when Fred Brown
made a derogatory remark about one of his paintings, Bomberg 'brought his
palette down on' his teacher's head.[9]

Bomberg remained desperately short of money. He and his Jewish com-
patriots 'brought food from home, and perhaps could find a halfpenny for a
cup of coffee . . . Most spare cash was rigorously saved to be spent on mate-
rials, charcoal, paints, brushes, canvas.'[10] Bomberg was also a tough customer
in appearance. His clothing was outré, his stance menacing and his overall
compartment defiant. In many ways, he turned out very much like his father
in temperament. His saving grace was his art.

From boyhood, Bomberg was an outstanding draughtman, especially in his
self-portraits and portraits. During his Slade years, his repertoire expanded
to include the entire human figure. This fascination with the form of the
body and how to reduce it to its essence would later find expression in his
fascination with dancers and dancing.

At the 'Second Post-Impressionist Exhibition' in 1912, Bomberg saw
examples of Cubism such as Picasso's *Woman and Mustard Pot* (1909–10). Like
Roberts, he began to construct his own adaptations of this new 'ism'. In 1913
he made his own version of *The Return of Ulysses* – the subject-matter had

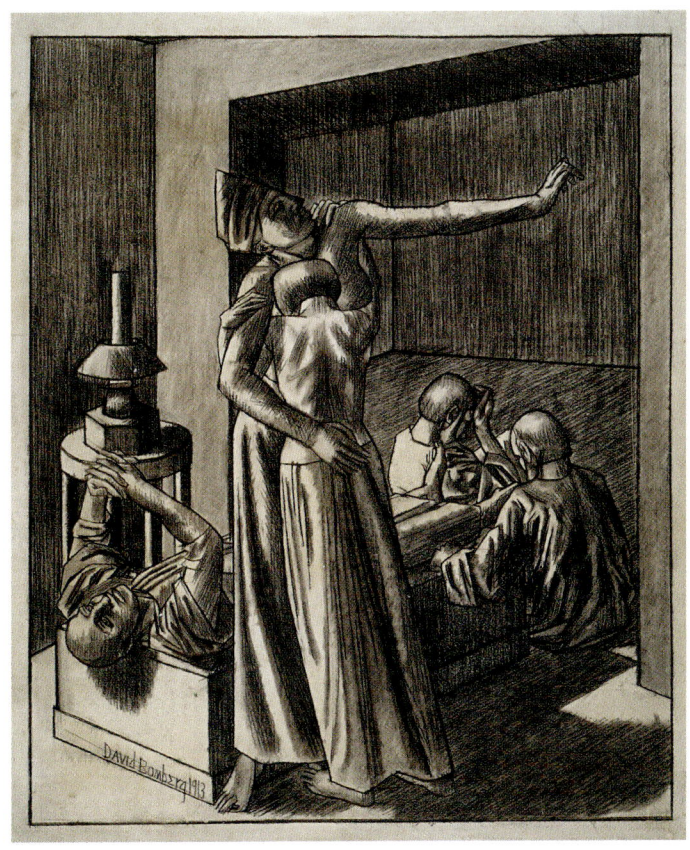

David Bomberg, *Family Bereavement*, 1913, Conté crayon on paper.

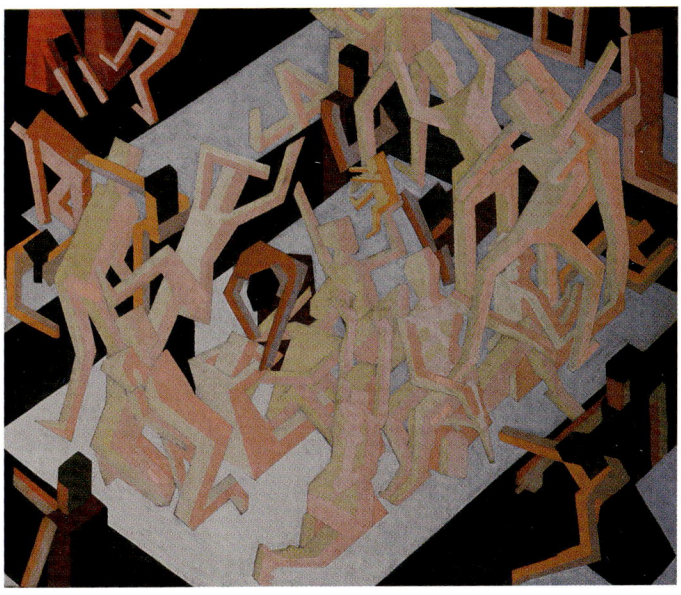

David Bomberg, *Vision of Ezekiel*, 1912, oil on canvas.

probably been assigned by one of their tutors to both Roberts and Bomberg. In a preliminary drawing, Bomberg arranged his figures in a static composition showing the soon-to-be-slain suitors. In his watercolour of the same subject, any sense of lethargy has vanished because the figures have been transmuted into elaborate swatches of colour interacting with each other.[11] Bomberg's knowledge of contemporary art on the Continent was further enhanced when he accompanied the sculptor Jacob Epstein to Paris in May 1913 to select work for the Whitechapel Art Gallery's 'Twentieth Century Art: A Review of Modern Movements', an exhibition that took place in the summer of 1914.

Shortly after his mother died in 1912, Bomberg drew *Family Bereavement*, in which five mourners are shown; in *Vision of Ezekiel* (also 1912) a similar configuration is rendered into stylized geometric abstract shapes. Almost all Vorticist works can be linked to a similar methodology whereby elements of representation are merged with abstraction. The conversion of anatomical representation into geometric shapes, a trait shared by Roberts and Bomberg, may have been inspired by the Cubist fragmentation of space by Picasso and Picabia or similar experiments by Gino Severini that disrupted the visual field by dividing it into fragments.

Vision of Ezekiel is a particularly good example of Bomberg's passion for uncovering essential truths beyond representation. In the Old Testament narrative, the prophet Ezekiel is conveyed to a valley of bones. There, God commands him to order the bones to hear the word of the Lord. 'So I prophesied as he commanded me, and breath came unto them, and they lived, and stood upon their feet' (Ezekiel 37:10). *Family Bereavement* is about the finality of death. Bomberg may have constructed *Vision of Ezekiel* to comfort himself in the wake of his mother's passing and to suggest some sort of after-life existence. To discard conventional notions of death, he discarded traditional notions of representation.

In 1912–13 Bomberg, having discovered ways of channelling his boundless energy and aggressiveness into his compositions and hearing that Roberts had been hired at the Omega, applied and obtained work. Like his friend, he soon felt bored and out of sympathy with the tasks he was asked to perform. Not surprisingly, he made his dissatisfaction known. In so doing, he created a great deal of tension at the Workshops.

On 26 December 1913 Vanessa Bell bluntly cautioned Fry: 'I think Bomberg and Co. are intolerable. You must simply treat them in a perfectly cold business-like way. After all it is purely a business matter and you haven't really any choice . . . I believe you will be able to get hold of all sorts of quite good people and it's absurd that they should give themselves these airs.'[12] Bell was experimenting with Post-Impressionism at this time in her art. Moreover, many of her designs for the Omega allowed her to introduce abstract elements. She was responding not to Bomberg's art but rather to his frequent displays of frustration and annoyance.

He found it difficult to contain his 'airs' – he did not attempt to tame them. Those same 'airs' explain in part the inventiveness that had taken over his work. He was possessed with thrusting himself forward, daring himself to reach further heights of inventiveness.

Even more so than Roberts, Bomberg would resolutely sit on the margins of Vorticism. He did not like the term to be applied to his art that is extremely different from that of the other artists in the group, but in spirit – and his initial willingness to be co-opted – he was as rebellious as the other participants.

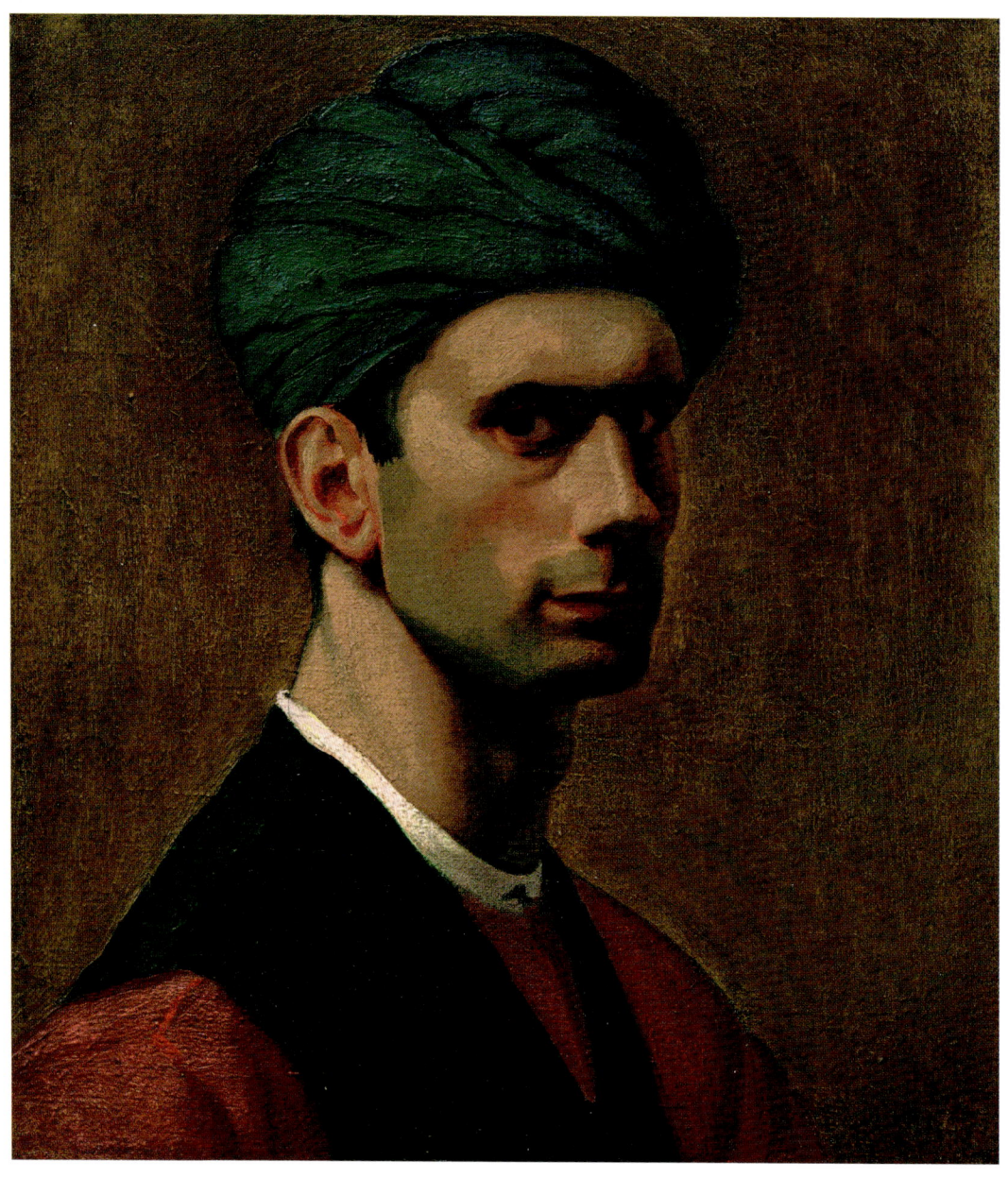

Edward Wadsworth, *Self-Portrait Wearing a Turban*, 1911, oil on canvas.

3

THE COSTER:
EDWARD WADSWORTH

Unlike Roberts and Bomberg, Edward Wadsworth's early life was one of privilege. But it was marked by heartbreak. He was born on Prospect Street, Whitcliffe, Clekheaton, Yorkshire, on 29 October 1889, the only child of Fred and Hannah Wadsworth. Fred was from a family that owned wool mills; Hannah's family were worsted spinners. From the outset, the match seemed perfect: the couple were in love and their union cemented the relationship between two families with shared business interests. Tragedy struck nine days after the baby's birth when Hannah died of puerperal fever.

At first, Fred resented the child who had taken his wife's life. Being around the infant brought him excruciating pain. 'He could not even bear to look at him, and the child was banished from his presence. It was five weeks before he could even get himself to register the birth.' By the time the toddler was three, the recalcitrant father had come to dote on him – but in an undemonstrative way. When photographs were taken of father and son together, Fred is seated 'whilst Edward stands beside him, an almost fortuitous figure, as if he were a stranger lad taken in off the street to act as a stand-in for the real son'. As a child, a keen observer noted, when Edward would walk around a factory with Fred, 'he liked to pick up cut-out bits of metal, the curious shapes of which stimulated his invention.'[1]

In later life, Edward's daughter Barbara recalled, 'he disliked the evocation of childhood memories, and, when, on rare occasions in his presence, the family albums were taken out, a tight, disapproving expression would come over his face. Only very seldom did he touch upon or reminisce about the past.'[2]

From 1899 Wadsworth became a boarder at Godby's School at Ilkley, where he was an exceptionally good student. Father–son relations became even more convoluted in 1903 when Mary Owen became Fred's housekeeper. Family legend has it that this gorgon-like woman had designs on becoming the second Mrs Fred Wadsworth. When Edward was home, she persistently sat, ate and walked with father and son. In this arrangement, Edward felt he had become an unwanted third wheel.

In 1903 thin-skinned Edward was sent to Fettes College, the celebrated public school in Edinburgh. In his memoir, Bruce Lockhart, a fellow student, observed: 'Fettes was not a picture palace for aesthetes nor a happy home for poets . . . It is true that the sensitive boy who excelled neither at games nor at work must have suffered, especially if he had musical or artistic tastes.' Lockhart did not wish to create the 'impression that . . . Fettes was a hot-bed of bullying . . . There were one or two sadistic fellows.' He also recounted: 'Occasionally the big boy overshot his mark, and once a small boy's nose was broken.'[3] Edward was the small boy.

Once his son finished at Fettes in 1906, Fred decided to send him to Munich to study machine draughtsmanship and to learn German. Those two skills he felt would be valuable to him when he took over the running of the mill. With considerable reservations, the son carried out his father's wishes. Unbeknownst to Fred, during his stay in Germany, Edward took instruction in printing, woodcutting, drawing and painting at the Knirr Art School. 'There he transformed from a provincial schoolboy into a cosmopolitan.' He found 'himself surrounded by people so immersed in matters of the intellect, who created for him a world within a world of such stimulus that it was hard to go to bed at night and force oneself to sleep.' Unfortunately, that 'romantic and violently exhilarating Continental episode . . . came to an end during Christmas 1907, when Fred paid him a visit'.

How much Fred knew at this point about Edward's resolve to become an artist is unknown. The son was 'not by nature a front-line fighter, and always had to have some outside influence to push him into open confrontation'. During that stay, Edward finally informed his father: he wanted to study art, and, moreover, he intended to become a painter. Having declared himself, Edward did not back down even though he anticipated his father's reaction, which was unequivocal: 'Very well then, you can do what you want, but you won't get a penny from me to do it on.' When he uttered that threat, Fred was probably aware that his sister, Annie, had provided her nephew with a beneficiary (allowance) of £250 a year.

Finally free of paternal constraints, in 1908 Edward enrolled at the Bradford School of Art. He spent the following summer in Le Havre, where he made watercolours of the main streets. At the end of that year, he received a scholarship to the Slade, where he registered on 15 May 1909 in the Fine Arts course that took place six days a week. He had brought his ambitions to fruition.

At the Slade, Wadsworth was, as to be expected, an outstanding student: in 1911 he won a prize for *Nude in the Life Room*, an oil painting that evidenced outstanding skills in the kind of draughtsmanship preached by Tonks. However, he found that instructor rude and arrogant – he summed him up as 'awful' and 'simply bloody'. Wadsworth considered the other members of the teaching staff dull. On the other hand, he was inspired by his fellow students.

Although Wadsworth was a reticent person, he may have cut loose in Munich. He certainly did so at the Slade. The introvert came out of his shell through his association with the Slade Coster Gang (later, they called themselves 'the Neo-Primitives'). This group acquired the label 'costers' because they 'wore black jerseys, scarlet mufflers, and black caps or hats' identical to the men who hawked vegetables and fruit on the street. With considerable exuberance, the gang was devoted to various kinds of mischief. They fought with medical students for possession of 'Phineas, the bekilted dummy which stood outside a tobacconist's shop in Tottenham Court Road and was rightly or wrongly considered the mascot of University College, London'. The police were tolerant of the group's schoolboy pranks, although these renegade art students were sometimes attacked by rival groups who thought they were 'foreigners'.

There were affairs of the heart between members of the gang and female students. Wadsworth pursued a woman dubbed Ann Somebody. One wag recalled: 'They were grand girls, junior in years, but really much too old for us. In some things we were so young and stupid, and we never hesitated to indulge in every form of dalliance.' As a group, they 'represented a reaction against the priggishness, posturing, and posing' of the previous generation of students at the Slade: 'we [one recalled] must have been a trial to poor virgin Tonks.'[4] Although he was contemptuous of that instructor, the excitable, high-strung Wadsworth remained calm when upbraided by him.

Despite the high jinks in which he eagerly took part, Wadsworth remained a dedicated, precocious student. In March 1910 he exhibited examples of his

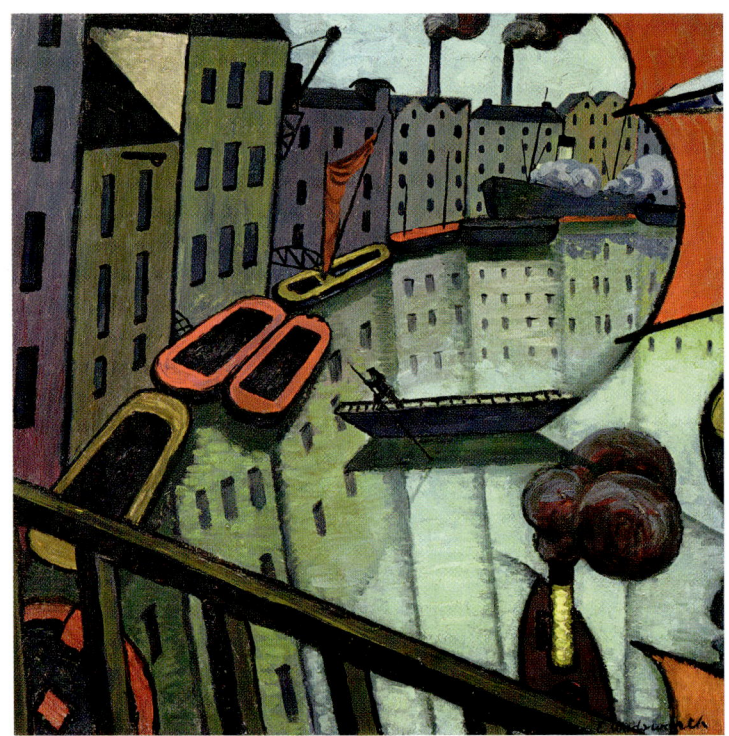

Edward Wadsworth, *Rotherhithe*, *c.* 1913, oil on canvas.

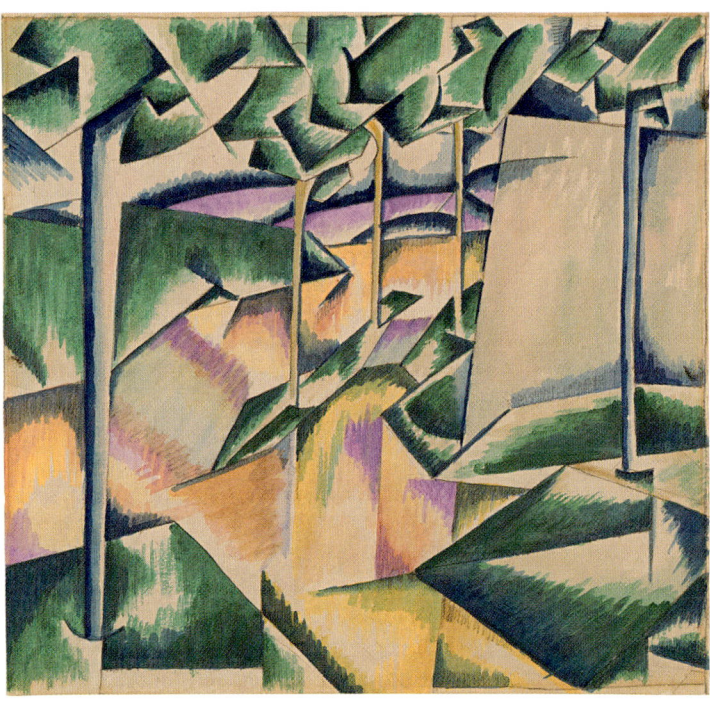

Edward Wadsworth, *Landscape*, *c.* 1913, gouache and graphite on paper.

work at the Bradford Art Club. A year later, he painted the accomplished *Self-Portrait Wearing a Turban*. Such works had long been a staple in Western art by the likes of Van Eyck and Rembrandt. Wadsworth, in engaging in this form of orientalism, was following that tradition.[5] In this rendition of himself, he stares out from the canvas with a dash of malice and arrogance. His defiant countenance shows how much the naive young man had gained in self-assurance. The artist's sometimes phlegmatic temperament belied his strong sense of himself. He seemed compliant, but this was protective covering.

During Wadsworth's last two years at the Slade, Roger Fry served as a lecturer in fine art. Through him, Wadsworth became aware of Cézanne, Van Gogh, Gauguin and the other Post-Impressionists. Like Roberts and Bomberg before him, Wadsworth in late 1912 or early 1913 – before the Omega Workshops opened – called upon Roger Fry to obtain work. He was assigned to the restoration of the Mantegna cartoons at Hampton Court. Years later, he saw his work there as pointless, although he somewhat sarcastically but accurately observed, 'Personally I have to thank [Fry] for introducing me to egg-tempera.'[6]

By 1913, Wadsworth had become a skilful artist in his chosen profession, although he did not know the direction he wished to pursue. Several landscapes, like *Rotherhithe* (*c*. 1913), employ highly saturated colours that show indebtedness to Post-Impressionism; they also demonstrate his early penchant towards abstraction. At the opening of the Omega Workshops in July 1913, he contributed geometrical designs – not dissimilar from Vanessa Bell's – suitable for carpets, curtains and tapestries. At about the same time, he extended those designs into bold semi-abstract landscapes as in *Landscape* (1913). Unlike Roberts and Bomberg, Wadsworth, at this time, favoured straight, only slightly undulating geometrical lines. A more cautious person than either Roberts or Bomberg, he took his time in allowing further experiments with abstraction to dominate his drawings and paintings. He was still an artist-in-waiting.

4

THE UNSEEN:
HELEN SAUNDERS

The Slade's Session Calendar for 1910–11 reveals a perplexing statistic: 253 students were enrolled – 189 were women. Admission standards were high, and these women met them. Despite their accomplishments, many were putting in time before marrying; a sizeable percentage simply wanted to obtain a teaching qualification. There were no female teachers with whom the women students could identify and emulate – or by whom they could be inspired. The institution did not encourage them to think of themselves as becoming full-time artists. Men were to become 'professionals', women were not. However, among some of these women, despite the barriers erected, there was a constituency that recognized that society was in flux – the world was changing and so was the definition of art.[1]

Complacent Edwardian society was threatened with upheavals in a manner not completely different from the new modernisms that had infiltrated the art world. The suffragettes vehemently demanded that women be given the right to vote. In doing so, they were also challenging the notion of women as the second sex. It was a time of turbulence in which women fought for equality. Virginia Woolf put it this way: 'The cruel thing was that while we could see the future, we were completely in the power of the past.'[2]

In this perilous milieu, nevertheless, a small number of women at the Slade determined to become professional artists were in large part successful. They exhibited widely, formed exhibition societies and established their own networks. History has not completely clouded their achievements, but it has often treated them cavalierly because a male-centred paradigm has been imposed upon their accomplishments. They may have been invited to train as artists, but they found themselves uninvited by the patriarchy.

Although the lives of some English women artists at the beginning of the twentieth century are recorded in detail (Vanessa Bell, Gwen John and Dora Carrington), factual details about many others (in comparison to their male counterparts) are hard to uncover because they were considered unworthy of serious attention. Deborah Cherry has observed, 'professionalism was most vociferously claimed as masculine by the upper strata of middle-classmen. In the language and institutions of art, femininity was positioned as the very antithesis of the professional artist.'[3]

The career of Helen Saunders illustrates this claim. The daughter of Alfred Saunders, a solicitor, and his wife Annie, she was born in 1885, two years after her only sibling, Ethel. The family lived in a spacious house in Ealing. Her parents may have anticipated that both their daughters would marry, but they had role models in their father's four unmarried sisters – one established a District Nursing service, a second provided shelter for 'fallen' women, the third was an Anglican deaconess and the fourth a missionary.

At the age of eighteen, Saunders determined to become an artist and began her training in Ealing at the studio of Rosa Waugh, who had studied at the Slade. As at the Slade, Waugh's students progressed from the antique to the life class. Saunders remained for three years with Waugh, who was partial to Impressionism. In her teaching, Waugh emphasized what she called 'Natural Perspective', a doctrine that maintained that 'a wandering field of vision' was more relevant than a fixed vantage point.[4]

In 1906 Waugh, struggling to enlist students, asked Fred Brown for permission to advertise that she prepared her students for the Slade, her alma mater. The following year Saunders gained admission to the Slade as a part-time student and regularly attended three days a week until the conclusion of the spring term (the signing book indicates that she was there a total of 25 days). Years later she told a relative that she had not gained much from her brief stay. Why Saunders left the Slade prematurely is unknown, but she may have been averse to making drawings from plaster casts since she had been so trained at Rosa Waugh's.

Much has been written to suggest that Tonks was overly critical of women, condescended to them and treated them harshly. There is no evidence that Saunders was subjected to bad behaviour from her teachers or fellow students. Diana Manners, later Lady Cooper, had an unpleasant experience

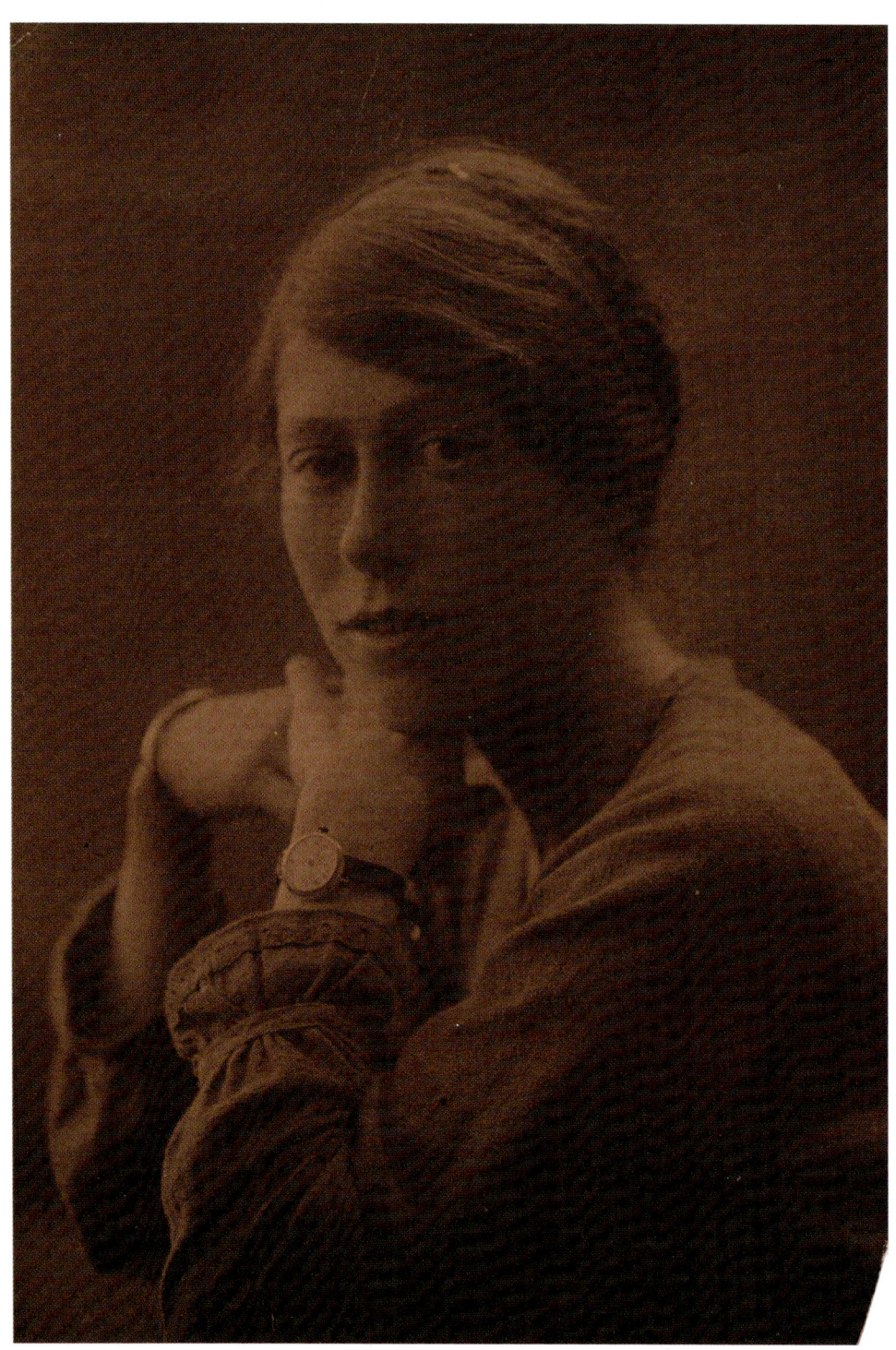

Helen Saunders, *c.* 1906.

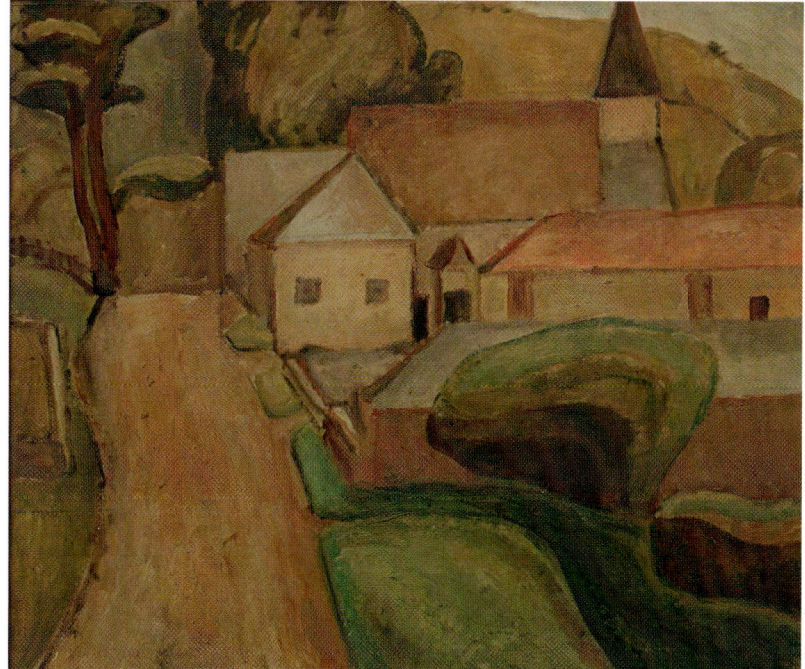

Helen Saunders, *Barn and Road* (formerly known as *Litlington*), *c.* 1911–12, oil on canvas.

when she visited the life room: she found the nude models 'very cold and livid [with their] goose-fleshed bodies'. She was also disturbed by the alarming figure of Professor Tonks, who 'set me trembling as though he were Justice itself'. On this point, Waugh had told a friend in about 1898: 'The Life Class is like Hades!!!' This may be a guarded reference to Tonks. However, Waugh's sister, Edna Clarke Hall, recalled: 'He never made me cry. I adored him when he was kind and still loved him when he was unkind. But he never told me to go home and do my knitting as he had done to some other girls.'[5]

The available documentation suggests that the irascible but often kindly Tonks was friendly or unfriendly to all his students regardless of their gender. At some point between 1907 and 1912, Saunders, obviously disappointed by the Slade, attended the Central School of Arts and Crafts. At about this time, she moved from Ealing to Phené Street in Chelsea.

At the Central School, she may have encountered friends of Vanessa Bell and, probably through that connection, exhibited at the Friday Club in February 1912 and four months later at the Galerie Barbazanges in Paris in the 'Quelques indépendants anglais' (an exhibition curated by Roger Fry).

That July, she showed three paintings at the Fifth Allied Artists' Association's London Salon. In March 1913 Fry invited her to contribute to the first Grafton Gallery exhibition at the Alpine Gallery, where he concealed the identity of the contributors 'to try the experiment of exhibiting the pictures anonymously in order to invite the spectator to gain at least a first impression of the several works without [an] almost predilection which a name generally arouses'.[6] As Brigid Peppin has argued, 'Part of Fry's purpose in concealing the authorship of individual works may have been to counter the prevailing prejudice against women artists.'[7] The canvas Saunders showed was probably *Barn and Road*.[8]

Later in life, Saunders stated that her early work had been heavily influenced by the 'Second Post-Impressionist Exhibition'. Like Roberts and Bomberg, she responded to the exhibition by redefining her concept of what a work of art could be. The exhibition aroused her interest in abstract and semi-abstract work uncommon in England at that time.

Semi-abstract is the correct word to describe *Barn and Road* (*c.* 1911–12), where the church and farm are converted into brightly coloured, highly stylized flattened blocks reminiscent of Gauguin and the Fauvists. Although almost none of her works before 1912 have survived, it would be safe to assume that this oil painting was, for her, a breakthrough. A bit later, she attempted more daring experiments with 'ideas' originating in Paris. When, in 1913, she showed a now lost painting at the Sixth Allied Artists' Association London Salon, it was described by one visitor to the exhibition as 'Cubist'.[9]

5

THE OVERLOOKED:
JESSICA DISMORR

Jessie Stewart Dismorr – who later chose to be called Jessica – was born on 2 March 1885 to James Stewart Dismorr and his wife Rebecca at Gravesend, Kent. James and Rebecca – first cousins – were born to well-to-do families in Australia; the couple immigrated to England so that James could pursue his career as a sugar broker and colonial agent. The family moved to Hampstead when Jessica was a child. There, from about the age of twelve until she turned sixteen, she was educated at the Kingsley School, which advertised itself as a 'School for the Daughters of Gentlemen'.

Like Jessica, her sisters had ambition beyond the domestic: Violet studied German and Beatrice Egyptology at University College, London. From April 1903 to December 1905 Dismorr registered as a student at the Slade. No information survives about her experience there.

Since her parents were wealthy and provided her with an allowance, Jessica had the means to pursue her interests. Determined to become an artist, from about 1906 to 1908 she lived in France, in the fishing village Étaples, about 30 miles from Calais, to study at the atelier of the American-born artist Max Bohm, whom Sargent regarded as an excellent teacher. There, she did not find the stimulus she needed.

She might have simply travelled in 1909 but settled in Paris from 1910 to 1912 to attend the Académie de la Palette. Her personal life in Paris may have been arduous and lonely. Female artists, especially those from abroad, tended to lead solitary lives interrupted only by their attendance at ateliers.

Dismorr's new school, where classes were given in English and French by a large assortment of instructors, had gained a stellar reputation under the direction of Jacques-Émile Blanche from 1902 to 1911; he promoted his academy as offering instruction in avant-garde techniques and, in the

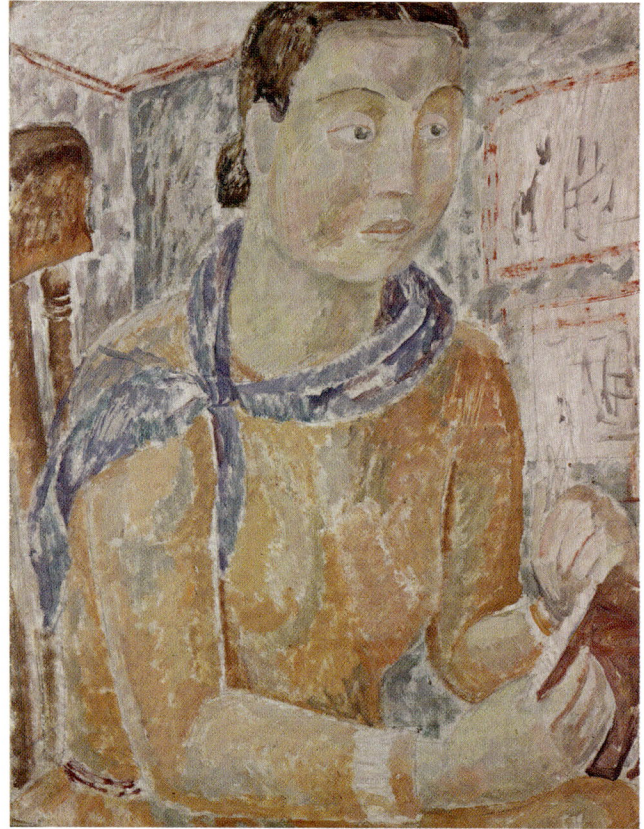

Jessica Dismorr, *Self-Portrait, c.* 1929, oil on gesso board.

process, attracted many foreign students. Blanche was an Impressionist but other teachers, like André Dunoyer de Segonzac and Jean Metzinger, were Cubists. Dismorr gravitated towards a part-time teacher, the Scotsman John Duncan Fergusson, a Fauvist, who was known to offer his assistance to students struggling against the mainstream. Through him, she began experimenting with that form of modernism, and by 1912 her work demonstrated her strong affinities with that style.

In 1911 Dismorr became involved with *Rhythm*, a magazine begun in London in 1911 by John Middleton Murry and Michael Sadleir. Ferguson was the art editor. The editors never defined clearly what they meant by 'rhythm', but for Ferguson it was the essential quality in any work of art. As such, it may refer to 'significant form' – as defined by Bell and Fry – allied to dancing, as popularized by the Ballets Russes and Isadora Duncan.

In the autumn issue of *Rhythm*, Dismorr portrayed the celebrated dancer in white against a black stage curtain. The curtain billows downwards whereas Duncan triumphantly raises her hands and sleeves backwards; in so doing, she throws off bonds of oppression.[1] Throughout her career, Duncan sought to liberate the dance as a site of male power and, in so doing, she revolutionized her chosen form of art. In a similar way, Dismorr would attempt to liberate visual art from male supremacy. Like her, Lewis, Bomberg, Roberts and Gaudier were fascinated by dance and how its physical dynamism could be captured in two- and three-dimensional works of art.

The artists in the *Rhythm* circle were often overlooked. In November 1912 an exhibition of *Rhythm* art was held at the St Catherine Press on Norfolk Street in London. Since it overlapped with the 'Second Post-Impressionist Exhibition', one critic asked: 'Why was this branch of British Post-Impressionism ignored by the directors of the Grafton Gallery – this branch that is so alive and fresh?'[2] Another reviewer, P. G. Konody, was startled: 'It is very difficult to understand why no place should have been found in Grafton Street for the very interesting work of artists like . . . Fergusson and Miss Jessie Dismorr.' Although Konody was sympathetic to *Rhythm* art, he was critical: 'With all their faults – and their chief fault is a monotonous liveliness of pattern and bright colour which defeats its own end through

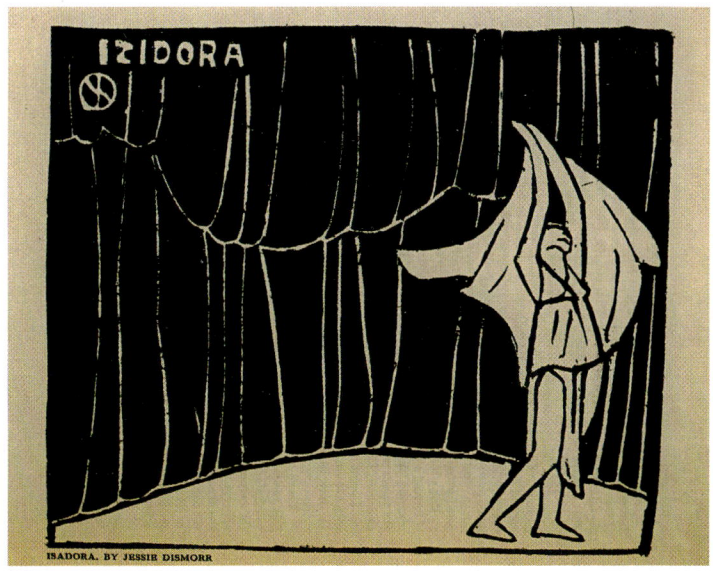

Jessica Dismorr, *Izidora*, illustration in *Rhythm* (1911).

lack of contrasting repose – they at least have made up their minds to work in two dimensions, whereas the Grafton Post-Impressionists still frequently waver between the two and the three dimensions.'[3]

Dismorr's *Sunlight, Martigues* (1911) shows some of the faults Konody highlighted: the colours are bright but outlined (and confined) in such a way as to suggest they are pieces of stained glass. In the process, the human forms are reduced to blocks of abstract-like colours. In general, her colours were much more saturated than Fergusson's.

In 1913 Dismorr exhibited at the Salon d'Automne in Paris. That same year, her *Portrait of a Young Girl* was on display at the Allied Artists' Exhibition, where Clive Bell purchased it. This small oil, with its sombre palette of greys, browns and blues, demonstrates that the artist was moving away from Fauvism to engage with a psychological portrait of a frail, apprehensive woman. The sitter, absorbed in melancholic reverie, grips her arm to steady herself. The sense of sadness is reinforced not only by the restricted colour scheme but by the spatial flatness in which the girl and the chair are enclosed. This canvas can be read as a statement about how women were closeted in the patriarchy.

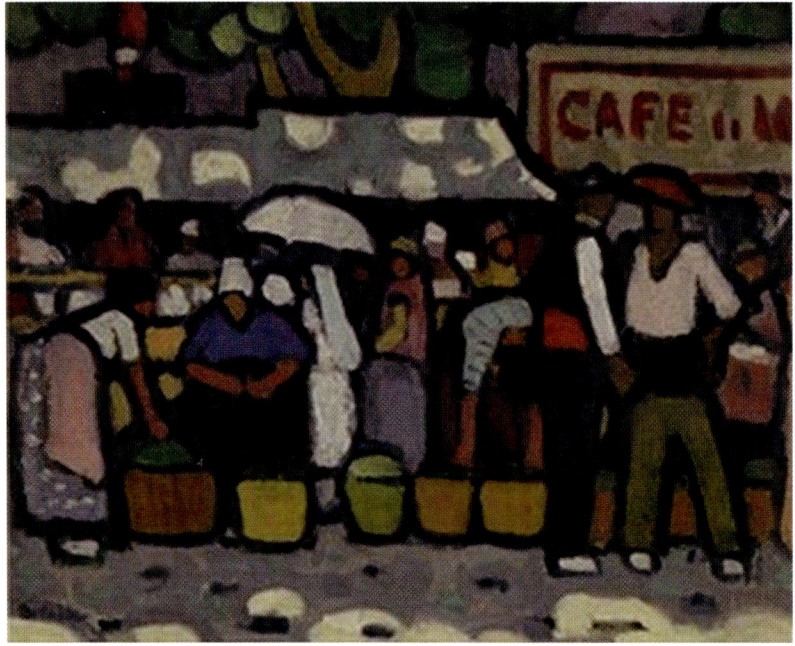

Jessica Dismorr, *Sunlight, Martigues*, 1911, oil on canvas.

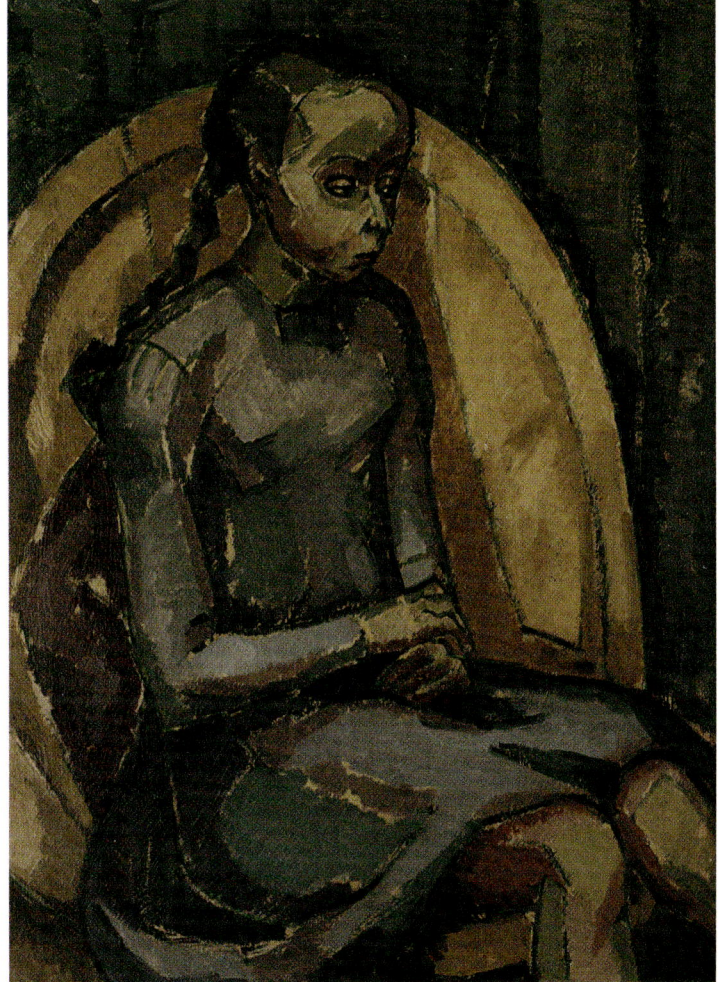

Jessica Dismorr, *Portrait of a Young Girl*, 1913, oil on canvas.

Very soon, Dismorr would make further advances in exploiting form. At that time, she and Saunders had studios near each other in Chelsea and became friends. Both women had allowances from well-to-do families that allowed them to explore the contemporary art world and to decide where they wished to situate themselves in it. Both had established contacts in the art world, although they had taken different routes to similar destinations. Intrigued by modernism, they had explored ways in which they could transform their work. To go further, they sought alliances with like-minded artists.

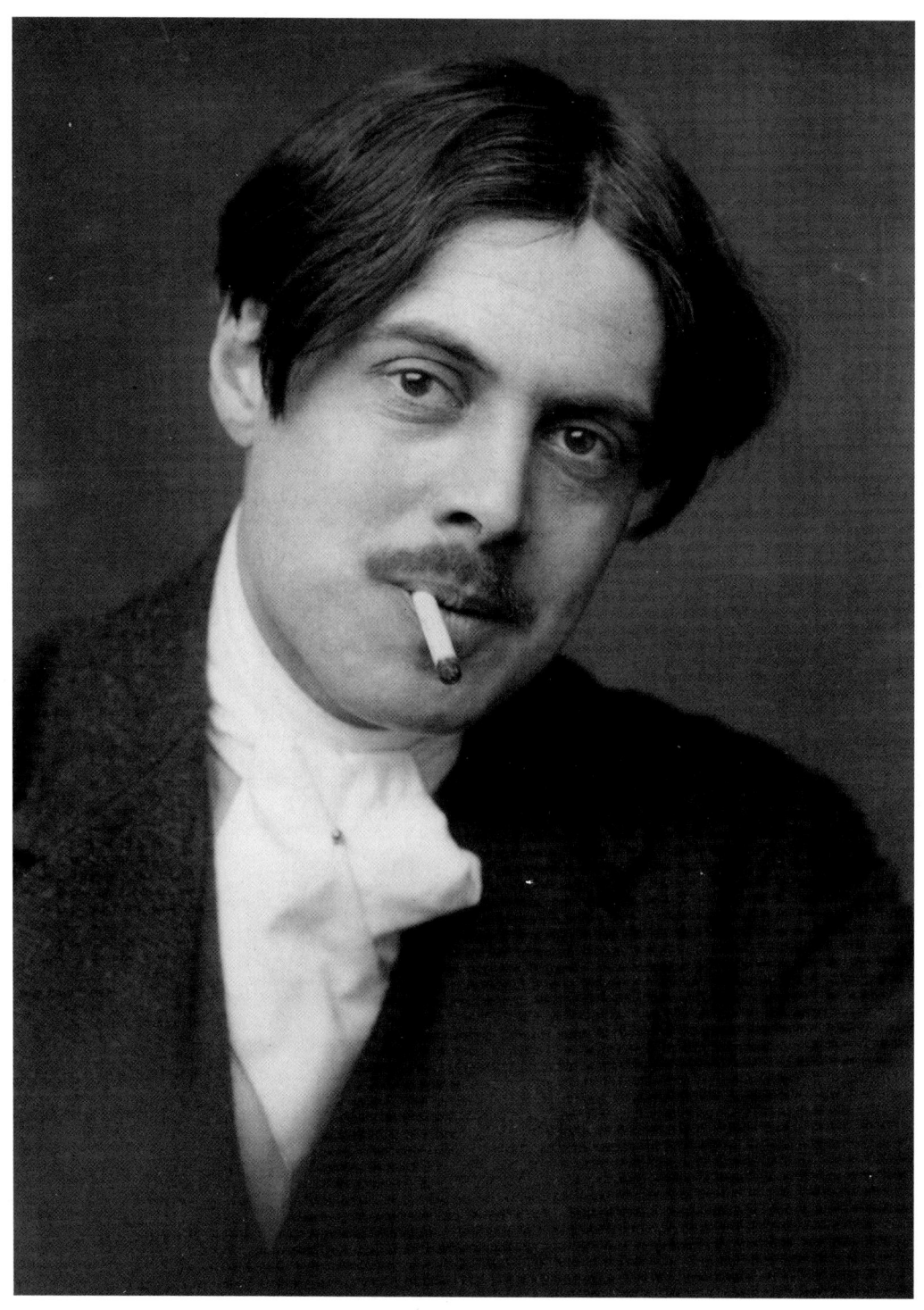

Wyndham Lewis, *c.* 1913.

6

THE PROVOCATEUR:
WYNDHAM LEWIS

Percy Wyndham Lewis was born on his wealthy father's yacht off the coast of Amherst, Nova Scotia, Canada, on 18 November 1882. Charles Edward Lewis was a graduate of West Point who served on the Union side during the Civil War. Wyndham's mother, Anne Stuart Prickett, had been living with her mother, who ran a boarding house in Upper Norwood, South London, at the time she married.

When in about 1893 the couple separated, mother and child moved to England. Their existence in London was peripatetic – they lived in a varied assortment of London neighbourhoods: Highgate, Hampstead, Beckenham and Ealing. From 1894 to 1896, the boy attended the Country School in Bedford, where he was an above-average student whose principal accomplishment was to write and illustrate 'Good Times', a thirty-page story about shipwrecks and other perilous adventures.

The child idolized his absent father but formed a close but enveloping alliance with his mother. Together, according to the son, they established a 'long foundation of delicate trustfulness and irresponsibility' in which his 'selfish, vigorous little mother' held him in thrall.[1]

Although his financial support for his wife and child remained meagre, Charles did provide the funds for his son to attend Rugby. Lewis was enrolled there from January 1897 until December 1898. He summed up his time there with bitterness and a dash of self-mockery: 'I am unable to say I had a disagreeable time . . . Scarcely did I learn to spell, certainly. Masters noticing this, and pretending it was my fault, took advantage of the fact to beat me mercilessly. They gave me a note to hand to my Housemaster. When he read it, he beat me too. But I understand it was their fun, and being healthy didn't mind.'[2] He once told a friend that he was the first Rugby man to receive six beatings by a prefect in a single day. Lewis may have been a master at insouciance, but these revelations are laced with residual anger. Throughout his life, he simmered with a rage that he never hesitated to bring to a boil.

Lewis claimed that he spent most of his time at Rugby in his study painting. That may be true. What is doubtful is his allegation that he never heard of the Slade until he was admitted there, where he enrolled in 1898 and stayed until 1901. A fellow pupil recalled that Lewis was 'surprisingly ignorant about art when he first appeared ... his favourite painter was a Victorian Academician who specialized in highland landscapes full of sheep grazing in the heather.'[3] A friend recalled that the would-be artist 'shroud[ed] himself in mystery. After hiding for weeks, he would suddenly reappear, having been, he would declare, in Sweden, or in some remote country; and he would hint at a conquest.'[4] This person doubted Lewis was telling the truth.

Lewis, like many of his peers, had no problem mocking Tonks, although he recalled that his instructor had urged him, as he did others, to go to the British Museum to copy Michelangelo and Andrea del Sarto. During these visits, Lewis was drawn to exhibition cases displaying art from Easter Island, the South Pacific and Africa. Enthralled by both cinquecento and 'primitive' art, he began to think of conjoining them.

All his teachers at the Slade despised Lewis. The artist Spencer Gore told a friend: 'So bitterly do the authorities at the Slade dislike Lewis that anyone going in for a prize or scholarship is apparently first questioned and his former life examined as to "whether he is a friend of Lewis's" . . . They must have a very high opinion of him to consider him dangerous.'[5] Tonks and his colleagues were threatened by him because he was exceptionally talented and extraordinarily rebellious – they simply did not know how to react to this strange combination. They rewarded his talent although they loathed him. In 1899 Lewis earned a Certificate in Figure Drawing; the following year he was awarded a Slade Scholarship.

From 1894 to 1899, Augustus John had been Tonks's star student at the Slade. Like Lewis, he was an outstanding draughtsman. Although only four years older, he was well on his way to fame when Lewis met him in 1902. John's talents were plentiful, and he played the role of the artist to the hilt: 'One day the door of the life class opened and a tall-bearded figure, with an enormous black Paris hat, large gold ear-rings decorating his ears, with the carriage of the utmost arrogance, strode in.'[6] For Lewis, it was hate and love at first sight.

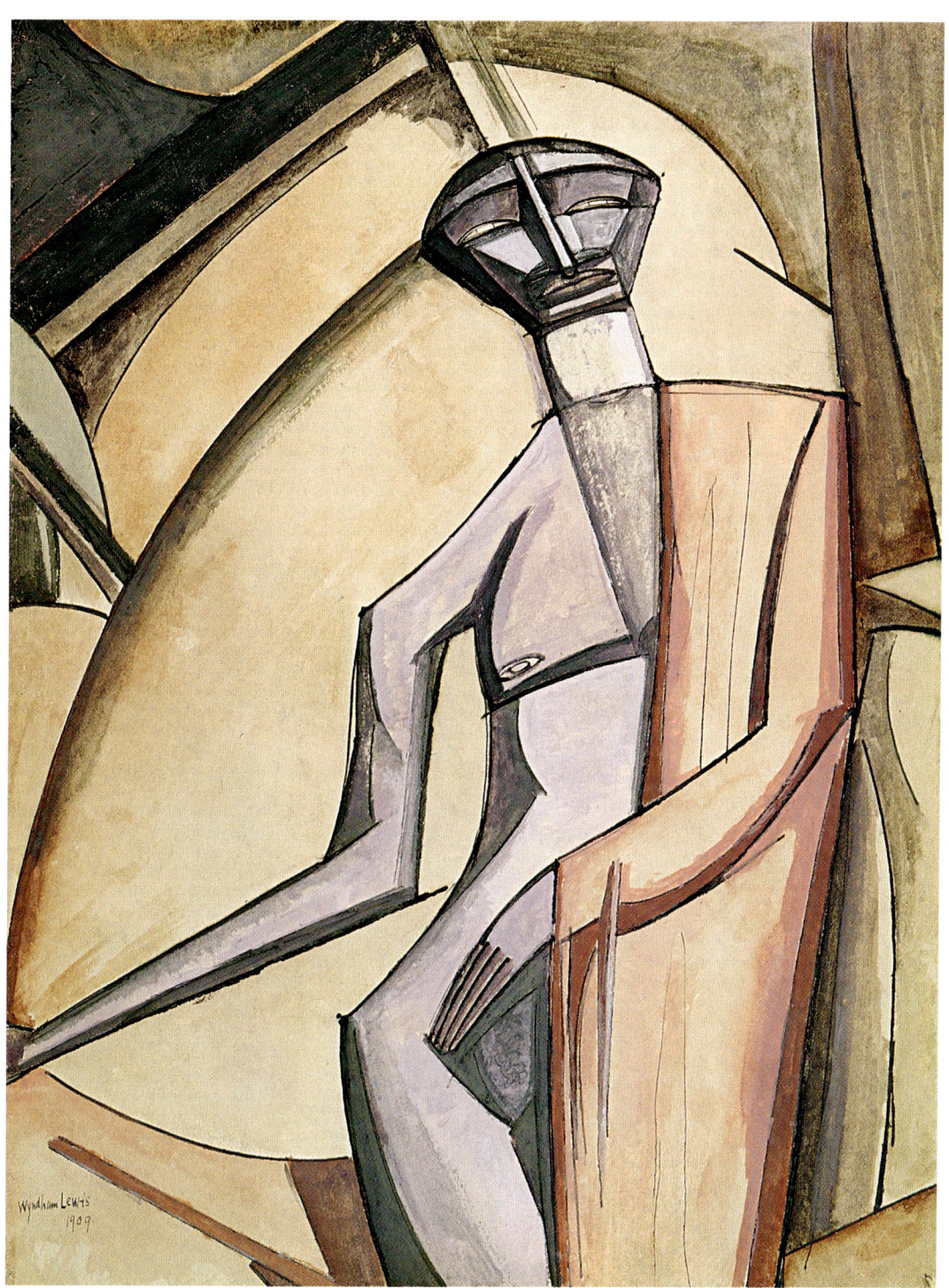

Wyndham Lewis, *The Celibate*, 1909, watercolour on paper.

The artist whose tutelage inspired Lewis was not a teacher at the Slade: it was the traditional William Rothenstein, whom he claimed 'was one of the last people in England able to distinguish between what is authentic, and what is not, in the field of art'. He was an 'inspiring teacher – smart and alert . . . [eager] to impart . . . his tremendous knowledge'.[7]

Despite his braggadocio, Lewis remained deeply insecure. He knew that he had to harness his volatile personality to become a good artist, but he never fully learned how to accomplish this. In 1902 he travelled to Spain accompanied by Gore and spent a great deal of the next seven years in various locales in France, Spain and the Netherlands. His friendship with the traditional John continued, although it was often interrupted by bickering. Still unsure of himself, he determined that he would have to emancipate himself from this father figure.

That rebellion from John's traditional approach to making art came to fruition in *The Celibate* (1909), in which the robot-like figure is an uneasy mix of representation and abstraction. The rigid, straight lines from which this creature is constructed stand in sharp contrast to the rounded shapes behind him. Here, Lewis, having taken in a number of modernisms he had seen in his time in Europe, incorporated them in this steely image. There are hints of Cubism and Expressionism, but the result is uniquely Lewis's. He may have been influenced by other artists, but, for him, to admit such was tantamount to weakness. He remained caustic about all other modernisms: 'The word, even, CUBISM, is a heavy, lugubrious word. The Cubist's paintings have a large tincture of the deadness . . . of Cézanne: they are static and representative, not swarming, exploding or burgeoning with life.'[8] The Expressionists were 'ethereal, lyrical and cloud-like'.[9] In order to elevate himself, Lewis habitually resorted to castigation. He was the supreme autodidact.

During the two years after he settled back in London, Lewis drew and painted intermittently and exhibited with the Camden Town Group in June and December 1911. *The Times* reported that December that he had shown 'three geometrical experiments which many people will take for bad practical jokes'.[10] About six months later, he submitted *Creation* to the London Salon of the Allied Artists' Association, which *The Times* labelled 'the one Cubist picture in the show': 'It is not intelligible, but we are persuaded the artist means something by it.'[11] Roger Fry was probably referring to this work in the *Nation* of 20 July 1912: 'one has the impression of some plastic reality brought about by deliberately intentional oppositions ... The rhythm is not merely agreeable and harmonious, but definitely evocative of a Dionysiac mood.' This canvas, like *The Celibate*, showed in protean form the work that was soon forthcoming.

Up to the time he left the Slade, Lewis had been exposed to teachers and artists of outstanding technical skills. He was especially well versed in draughtsmanship but wanted to harness his skills to create his own distinctive work. He remained intrigued by two different kinds of art – Renaissance and 'primitive'. One of his first opportunities to put theory into practice was in the spring of 1912 when he, Gore, Charles Ginner, Eric Gill and Jacob Epstein were commissioned by Frida Strindberg, the Viennese ex-wife of the playwright, to decorate her chic underground nightclub, the Cave of the Golden Calf, which opened on 26 June 1912.

Underneath her blazing eyes and pale white skin, Strindberg was a fierce, dedicated modernist. The journalist Ashley Gibson described her as 'an amazingly masterful, intelligent, and in her way fascinating Austrian ... She already gave proofs of a mesmeric faculty for getting people to do things for her and showed a rare discrimination in her choice of accomplices. Instinct led her without fail to select the young men who mattered, or were going to.'[12] When the occasion demanded it, she could be as ornery and tough-minded as Lewis. Augustus John recalled that she frequently 'committed suicide' but quickly recovered: 'for a woman of her constitution, no amount of veronal had any permanent effect – it merely upset her stomach for a week or two.'[13] In a more unguarded moment, he called her 'the walking hell-bitch of the Western World'.[14]

She conceived of the Golden Calf as a cultural oasis where the latest and most cutting-edge trends in amateur theatre and music would provide entertainment for well-heeled customers. The name she chose for her establishment signalled decadence – the Golden Calf was made by the Israelites when, in the absence of Moses, they succumbed to debauchery.

The reporter for *The Times* was suitably impressed:

The Cabaret has not sprung up naturally in the soil of London, and therefore it appears hazardous to transplant it thither. On the Continent it is traditional for men of letters and of art to have

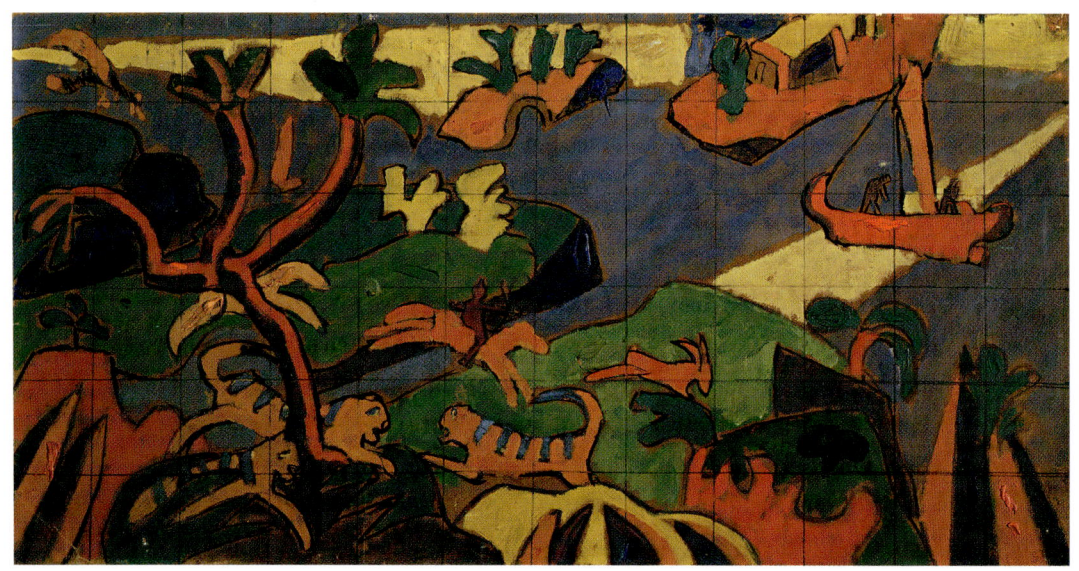

Spencer Gore, study for a mural decoration for the Cave of the Golden Calf,
1912, oil paint and graphite on paper mounted on board.

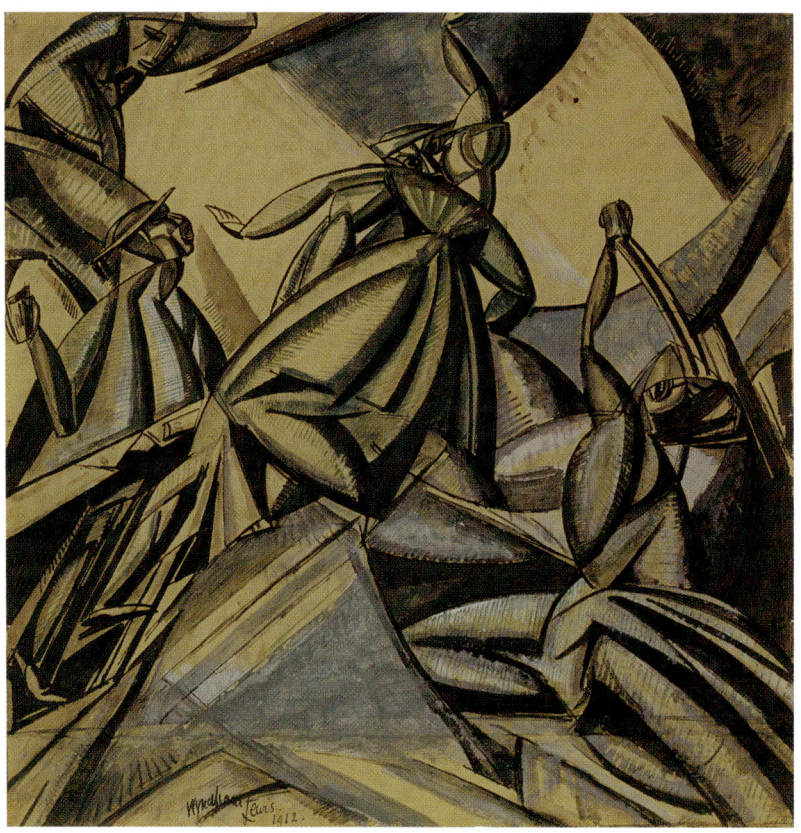

Wyndham Lewis, *Kermesse*, 1912, gouache and watercolour
with pen and ink over pencil on two joined sheets of paper.

their *café*, but in England one fancies it is the old-fashioned club or nothing . . . In London, too . . . there is the music-hall, perhaps nowhere else so dangerous a competitor to the cabaret.

For these reasons the prospect that the Cabaret Theatre Club will become a social centre remains for the present highly speculative; it seems on the whole more probable that its chief success will be found to lie in its dramatic activity, for it will have rare opportunities to produce works of theatrical and musical virtuosity. The club house is dubbed 'The Cave of the Golden Calf,' and it is certainly cavernous to the extent that it has to be entered by a sort of man-hole; within there is a small stage and mural decorations representing we should not care to say what precise stage beyond impressionism – they would easily, however, turn into appalling goblins after a little too much supper in the cave.[15]

To fulfil her agenda, Strindberg sought embellishments that mingled modernism with depravity. Gore, who oversaw the overall design, engaged his artist friends to assist him – his own work contained riotous Fauvist colours. His mural decoration was inspired by Gauguin's Tahitian work. Lewis's contributions – for which he was paid £60 – included a drop curtain showing raw meat. The legendary, now-lost, first version of *Kermesse* hung on the stairs down to the club.

Lewis might have viewed Peter Paul Rubens's *Kermesse* (1620–25) at the Louvre, in which peasants – much like the Israelites – give themselves over to debauchery; however, there are a substantial number of Flemish and Dutch Renaissance paintings of kermesses (outdoor gatherings). Lewis updated this tradition by combining elements of Cubism, Futurism and Expressionism. The figures and their distorted limbs are so flattened that perspective is abandoned. Their faces are exercises in monstrosity – these creatures are uneasy composites of the robotic with the representational. Another obvious source for Lewis was the combative, sadistic intertwining bodies of Apache dancers – the sexually aggressive, intrusive movements of male dancers towards their female partners in this form of Parisian street culture obviously appealed to him.[16]

Fry was sufficiently impressed by the work that he saw by Lewis that he wrote on 21 February 1912 to ask if he would attend a meeting to discuss the formation of a group that would include artists such as Duncan Grant and Frederick Etchells.

Later that year, Lewis was among the English artists whose works were included in Fry's 'Second Post-Impressionist Exhibition'. One of Lewis's canvases was the startling *Smiling Woman Ascending a Stair* (*c.* 1911–12).[17] The woman – grimacing rather than smiling – is constructed mainly of straight lines in browns and oranges. She is formed in deliberately abstract aligned fragments, almost as if she was a sculpture made of wood. The facial contortions and the resulting sardonic expression in *Smiling Woman* may be indebted to German Expressionism, especially as seen in the work of Ernst Ludwig Kirchner and his circle. *Mother and Child* in the same exhibition was beholden in part to Picasso, although the faces of mother and child are, as in *Smiling Woman*, grotesque. Once again, Lewis was skilfully aligning the representational with the abstract.

Lewis's other entries – one drawing and six designs (process engravings) – depict scenes from Shakespeare's *Timon of Athens*. Some of these drawings mingle representation with abstraction. In others, Lewis moved for the first time in the direction of complete abstraction.

At the beginning of Shakespeare's play (1623), Timon, a wealthy resident of Athens, is so generous that he recklessly gives away all his possessions. When he becomes aware of the dire situation he has landed himself in, he sends his servants to the home of his friends to plead for help. When they return empty-handed, Timon plots revenge by holding a gathering for those who have betrayed him. Servants bring in serving trays containing rocks and lukewarm water. Timon sprays his guests with the water, throws dishes at them and flees his own home.

He retreats to the wilderness, lives in a cave and feeds on roots. Then he discovers an underground trove of gold. When knowledge of that discovery spreads, individuals show up at his door begging for financial assistance, including the rebel leader Alcibiades, who wants to annihilate Athens. Timon gives most of the gold to Alcibiades so that he can revenge himself on those who forsook him. Then, Flavius, Timon's faithful servant, arrives. He asks for money but urges his master to rejoin society. Timon acknowledges that he has had one true friend in Flavius but laments that he is a mere servant. When envoys from Athens arrive, hoping Timon might placate Alcibiades, he tells them to hang themselves. Having done his best to revenge himself, he dies.

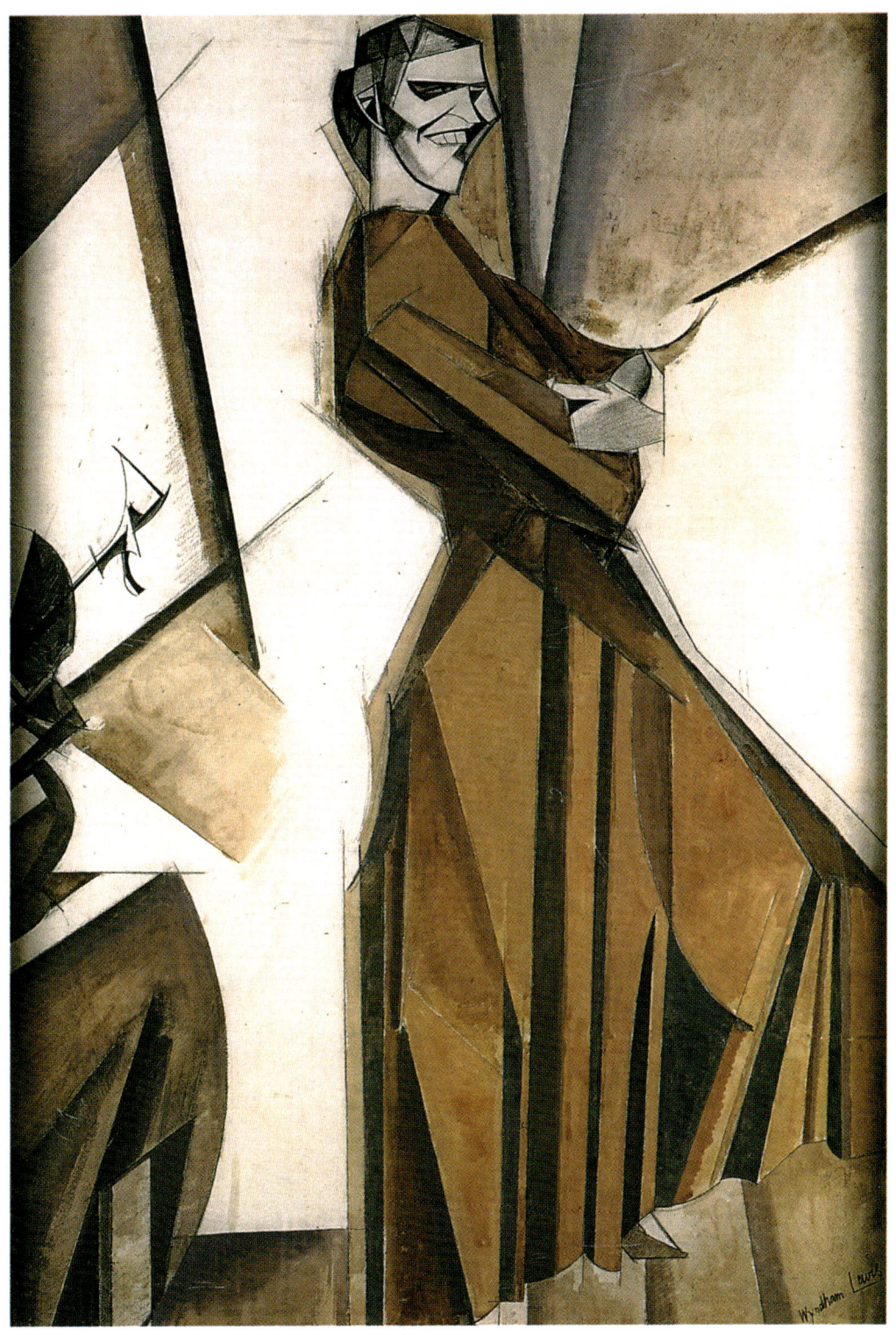

Wyndham Lewis, *Smiling Woman Ascending a Stair*, c. 1911–12, charcoal and gouache.

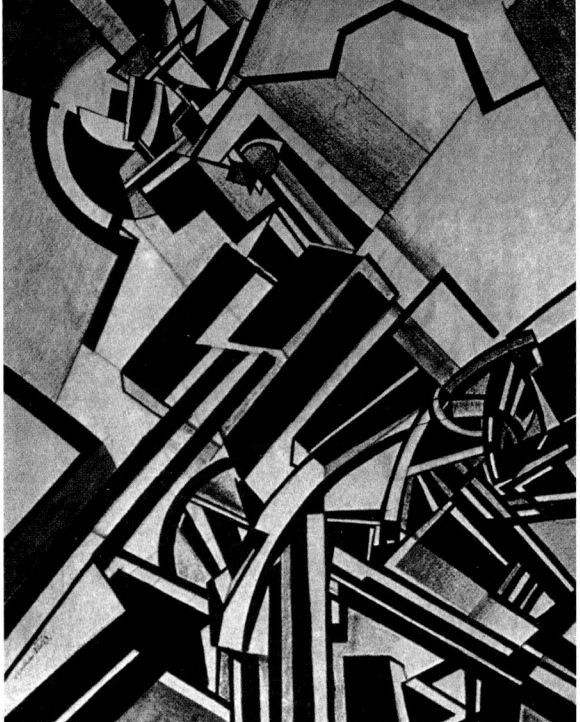

Wyndham Lewis, *Timon of Athens*, 1914, linecut. *Blast 1*, p. vi.

The paranoid side of Lewis's identification with Timon is fully encapsulated in the abstract versions of the Timon images where all traces of representation have vanished. These abstract designs are more powerful than the representational ones because they resort to a new visual language. The various shapes spar with each other, although the chaos is a contained one. In abandoning traditional ways of showing conflict, the anger captured is more universal – and perhaps more visceral – because it is less tied to previous ways of representing such clashes. The conflict between two forms of representation in these illustrations may reflect Lewis's indecisiveness as to whether abstraction or representation would best suit his art.[18]

The artist, who obviously viewed himself as more sinned against than sinning, felt forsaken by society. He never saw himself as having created any conditions under which he deserved to be badly treated. His sense of entitlement was punctured. Living from hand to mouth fuelled his sense that life had treated him unfairly.

Lewis also identified with Nietzsche's Superman. Although he declared that the German philosopher had influenced him strongly in his youth, he defiantly asserted: 'I was reasonably immune from Superman' and claimed, 'the impulse to titanism and supernatural afflatus pervading German romanticism [has] never had any interest for me.'[19] His aggressive personality and his belief in his power to reform the world of art belie this statement.

When Lewis paid Ford Madox Ford an unexpected visit, the novelist recalled he wore an 'immense steeple crowned hat. Long black locks fell from it.' He also had an 'ample cape of the type that villains in ... melodrama throw over their shoulders when they when they say "Ha-ha!" He said not a word ... I have never known anyone whose silence was a positive rather than a negative quality.'[20]

Although not in the least objective, Ezra Pound provided a portrait of the artist whom he judged the equal of Picasso. According to him, Lewis possessed 'not merely knowledge of technique, or skill [but] intelligence and knowledge of life, of the whole of it, beauty, heaven, hell, sarcasm, every kind of whirlwind of force and emotion'.[21] Pound and Lewis were kindred spirits. Douglas Goldring recalled: 'Pound contrived to look "every inch a poet", while I have never seen anyone so obviously a "genius" as Wyndham Lewis.'[22]

Just as cantankerous as Lewis, the 22-year-old Pound, after he arrived in London in 1908, quickly edged himself into the modernist movement there. A poet of considerable range, he was fixated on revolutionizing poetry. Specifically, he felt that the language of verse had become outdated: it had to become more direct, it should aim at brevity and precision, and it should concentrate on establishing imagery that was precise, focused and unadorned. Like Lewis, he wanted disciples for his 'ism' – Imagism. By forming an uneasy alliance with Lewis, he hoped that his notions of conciseness could be brought into alignment with what became Vorticism.

Clive Bell would not have been in accord with Pound's evaluation of Lewis as a genius, but he had been very receptive to the experimental daring of Lewis when Fry included him in the 'Second Post-Impressionist Exhibition'. Lewis's kind of art might not have been that preferred by Bell and Fry, but they made a genuine attempt to understand and appreciate it. Given this history and Lewis's abject poverty, it was natural that Fry invited Lewis to join the Omega Workshops when it opened in July 1913.

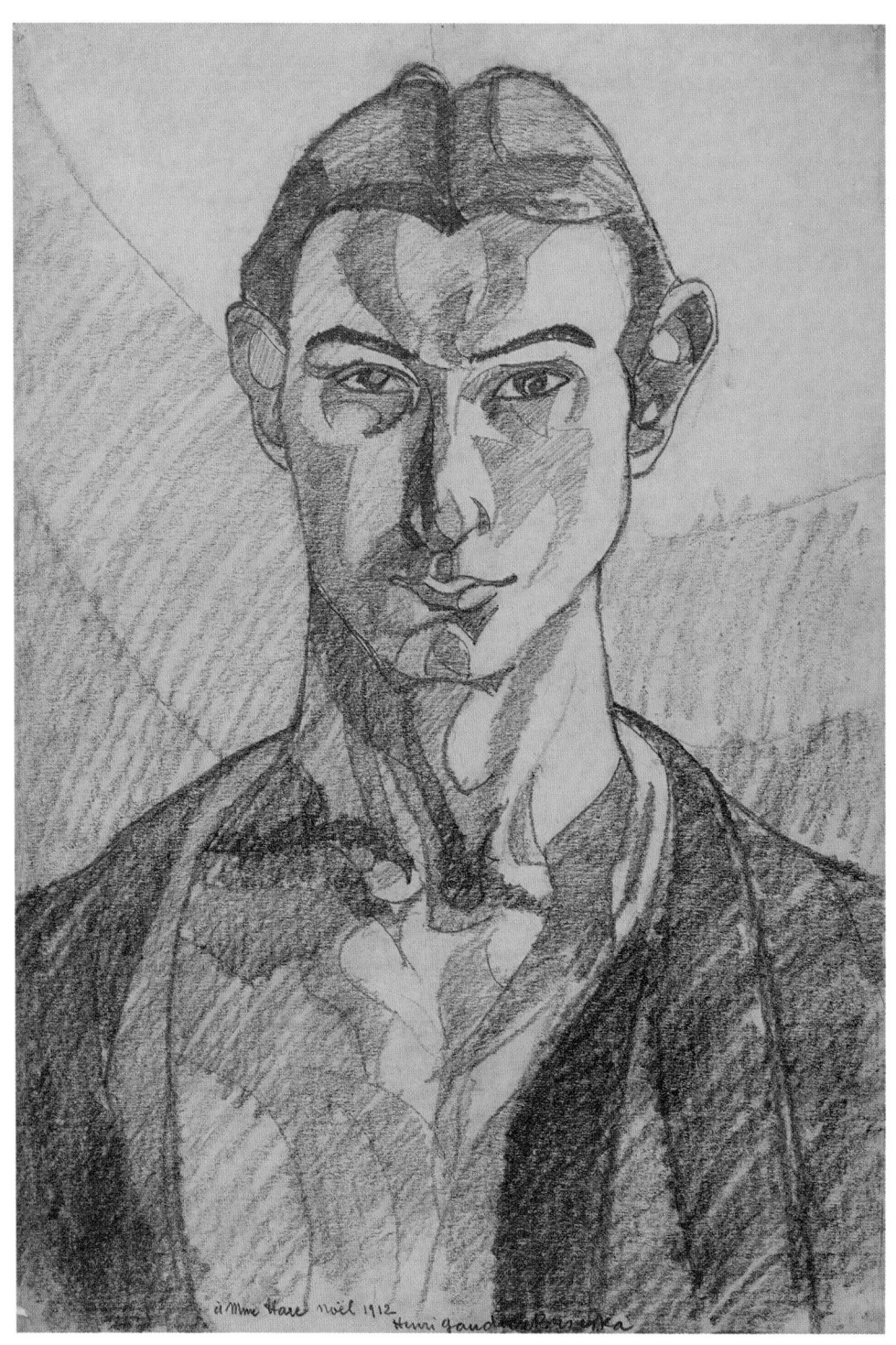

Henri Gaudier-Brzeska, *Self-Portrait*, 1912, pencil.

7

THE IDEALIST:
HENRI GAUDIER-BRZESKA

Henri Gaudier was born on 4 October 1891, in the hamlet of Grasdoux in north-central France, to Henri Joseph Gaudier, a joiner, and his wife Marie Alexandrine, the daughter of a wheelwright. At the age of six, Gaudier began to make drawings of insects, tearing each one up as soon as it was completed. When asked why he destroyed his work, the child replied, 'I have done them, and that is sufficient. If I keep them, I should be tempted to do them again, and that would be worthless.'[1] As this anecdote reveals, he was not only a perfectionist but someone who relentlessly challenged himself to do better.

At the age of eleven, he was enrolled as a scholarship pupil at the École Primaire Supérieure in Orléans, where he prepared for a career in the business world. An exceptional student, he received a bursary that allowed him to travel abroad for two years studying business and gaining work experience. He was almost sixteen when he enrolled at the Merchant Venturers' Technical College in Bristol. Late in 1908, he worked for a firm in Cardiff and was then posted to Nuremberg and, later, Munich.

Gaudier and his host in Nuremberg spent hours conversing on a variety of subjects. The older man recalled that the young Frenchman

> took up my opinions greedily, without however making himself a slave to them, but on the contrary worked them around in his way and used them as elements in his own view of life. For as long as he was here, he wanted to be a painter, and he practiced indefatigably at it. More often he said when alone that he doubted he was destined to be a painter and thought that drawing would be his only art; at the same time, he said that he was a sculptor. So the genius in him struggled for clarity.[2]

Earlier, on seeing the Parthenon sculptures at the British Museum, Gaudier jotted down an observation: 'The fair Greek saw himself only. HE petrified his own semblance. HIS SCULPTURE WAS DERIVATIVE: his feeling for form secondary.'[3] As if in seeing into his own future, Gaudier roundly rejected what he considered derivative. He was obsessed with form.

Unsettled, depressed and unsure of himself, Gaudier drifted to Paris, where he obtained clerical work at the firm of Armand Colin, publishers. After four months, he left or was dismissed. He later found work at C. P. Goerz, a company specializing in photographic equipment. There, he was a bookkeeper and, much against his will, sold cameras. Gaudier spent as much time as he could squeezing in drawing at the reading room at the Bibliothéque Ste.-Geneviève across the street from the Panthéon. Sometimes, he drew those seated around him. One subject had 'a beauty à la Baudelaire and might have stepped out of *Fleurs du Mal*. She is lithe and simple, with a feline carriage and enigmatic face, the fine character of which reflects her most intimate thoughts.'[4] He was describing the Polish-born writer Sophie Brzeska, whose life would be irrevocably intertwined with his and whose surname he would affix to his own.

The exact nature of their relationship is difficult to decipher. She was twenty years older than him. There was a great deal of sexual frisson but little actual sex. She once told him: 'I believe it is only right to establish some ground rules for our relationship. Would you like me to be a *mother* to you – an adoptive mother – since your own mother does not understand you?'[5] He answered in the affirmative. He told a friend: 'I love her with a purely ideal love – it is a flow of sensation which you must feel, since words are too coarse a medium to convey it.'[6] When he drew his beloved, he employed intense Fauve-like colours to capture his strong emotional connection to her, but, despite the brilliant colours, the sitter looks motherly. After Sophie was accused of being a prostitute because of Gaudier's frequent visits to her, the couple decided to move to London, where they took lodgings together.

Gaudier became obsessed with two things: his inextricably complicated bond with Brzeska and his passionate determination to express himself in sculpture. His relationship with that medium was as complex as the one with Brzeska. He knew what he wanted to become, but he darted from one

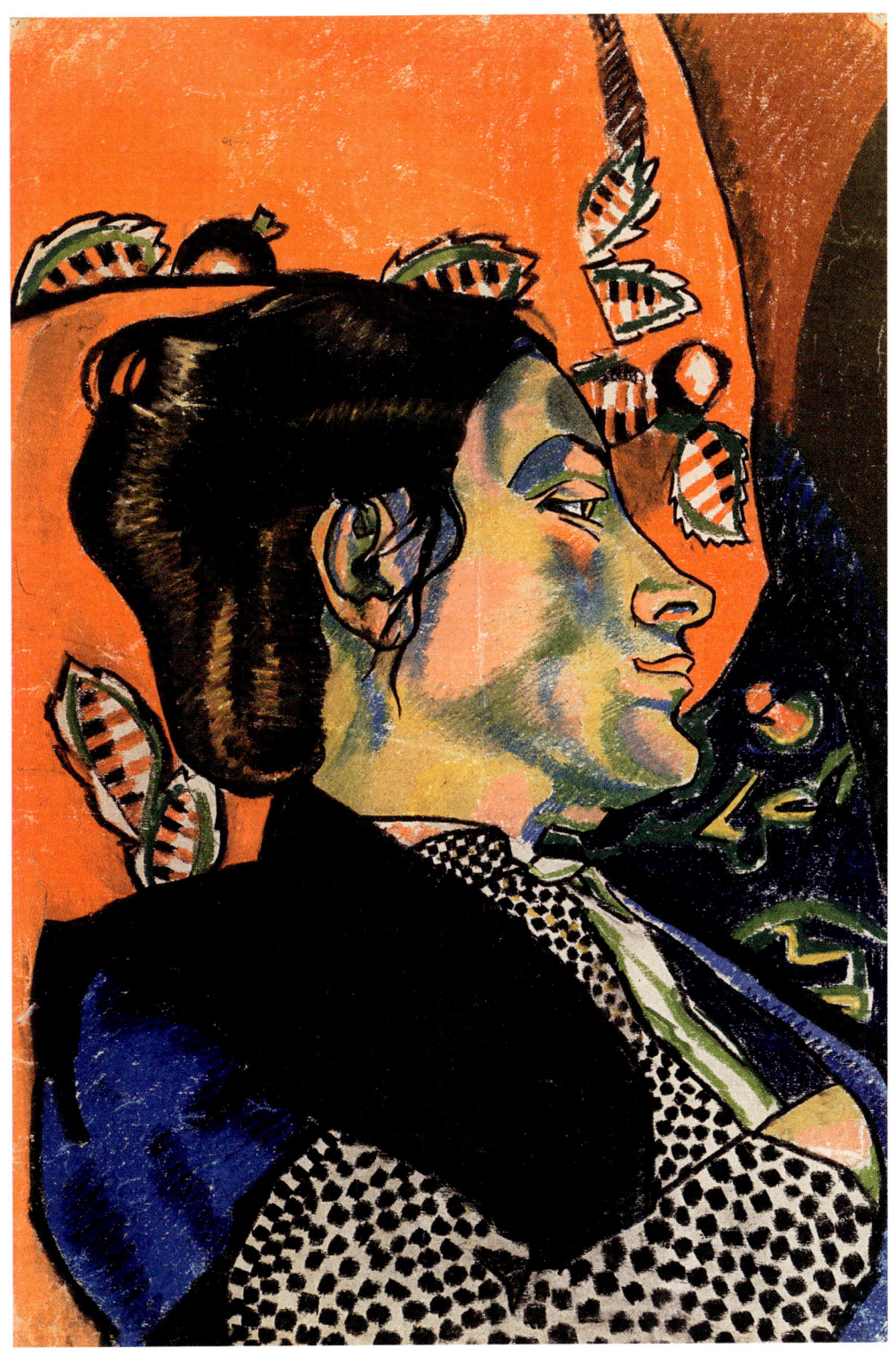

Henri Gaudier-Brzeska, *Sophie Brzeska*, 1913, pastel on paper.

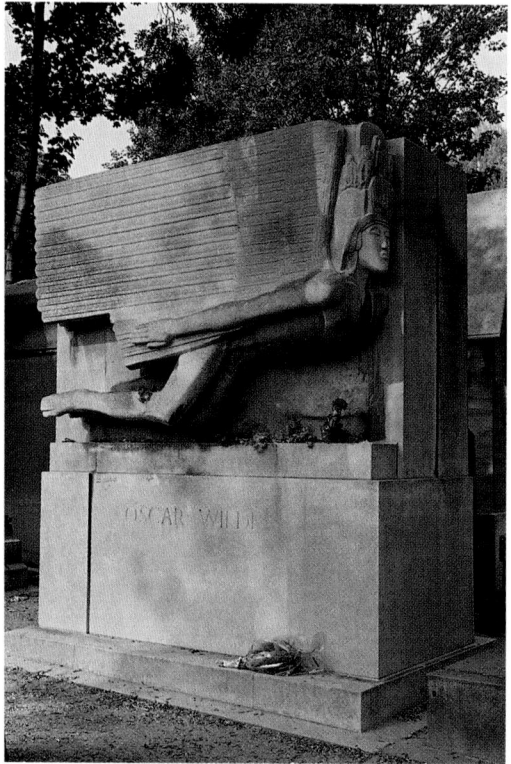

Jacob Epstein, *Tomb of Oscar Wilde*, 1912, Hopton
Wood stone. Père Lachaise cemetery, Paris.

approach to another. He told his companion in October 1912: 'I notice how
everything differs, mingles with and knocks up against everything else. I
am never sure that what I think is true, still less that what I have thought
or said is true; and I can't bring myself to sacrifice new ideas, quite different from those I had yesterday, just because the old ones happened to have
the honour of passing through my head and I advanced them ferociously.'[7]
The writer Enid Bagnold remembered he 'had a hungry face ... and a mind
made of metal. He talked like a chisel and argued like a hammer. Too many
things tore at him.'[8]

His early work was an uneasy mixture of styles. His moment of epiphany
came when he was invited in 1911 to Jacob Epstein's Cheyne Walk studio to
see the sculptor's monumental Oscar Wilde tomb prior to it being shipped
to France for installation at Père Lachaise. The already celebrated American-
born sculptor – then 32 – asked the scrubby Gaudier if he carved direct.

Realizing he had never considered that option, he rushed home to begin a carving. An enraptured Gaudier told a friend: 'I saw [the Oscar Wilde sculpture] in the studio. [He] is flying slowly into space, his eyes shut. The whole work is treated strongly – filled with insuperable movement and delicate feeling, in the expression and the medium – a piece of sculpture which will live forever.'[9]

The Frenchman's commitment to sculpture was further enlivened, if that was possible, by this encounter. Before, like many before him, Gaudier had modelled himself on Rodin. Now, he searched even more fervently for the 'right' form. He experimented wildly, but by 1913 Picasso's influence can be seen in his bust of Horace Brodzky, although Gaudier shied away from the rough Cubist-derived approach Picasso had made in his *Head of a Woman* (1909–10).

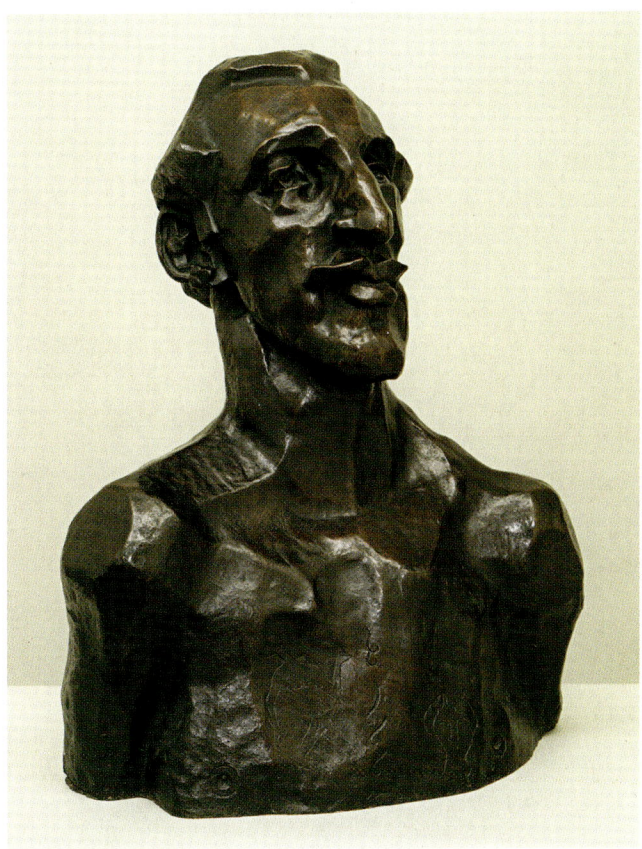

Henri Gaudier-Brzeska, *Howard Brodzky*, 1913 (cast 1956), bronze.

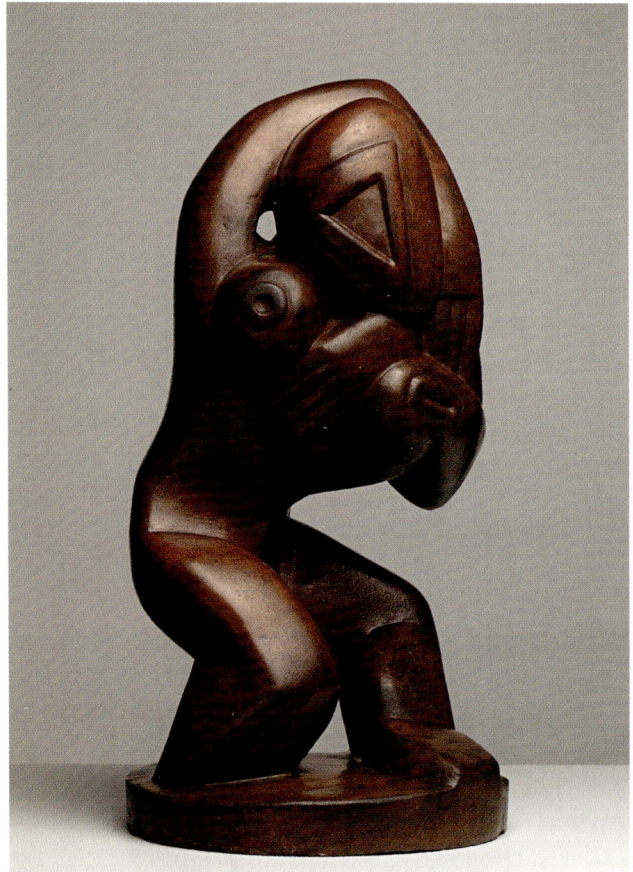

Henri Gaudier-Brzeska, *Red Stone Dancer*, *c.* 1913, red Mansfield stone.

One of the first sculptures to emerge was *Red Stone Dancer* (*c.* 1913), in which Gaudier blended abstraction and representation in the combination he had been seeking. He had finally put aside imitating the work of other sculptors and discovered himself. He could resolutely claim that he derived his 'EMOTIONS SOLELY FROM THE <u>ARRANGEMENT OF SURFACES</u>. I shall present my emotions by the ARRANGEMENT OF MY SURFACES, THE PLANES AND LINES BY WHICH THEY ARE DEFINED.'[10]

Gaudier was still in search of a style that he could make his own when Roger Fry offered him employment at the Omega Workshops. There, his design work gave him the opportunity to experiment with abstraction.

PART TWO:

IN THE VORTEX

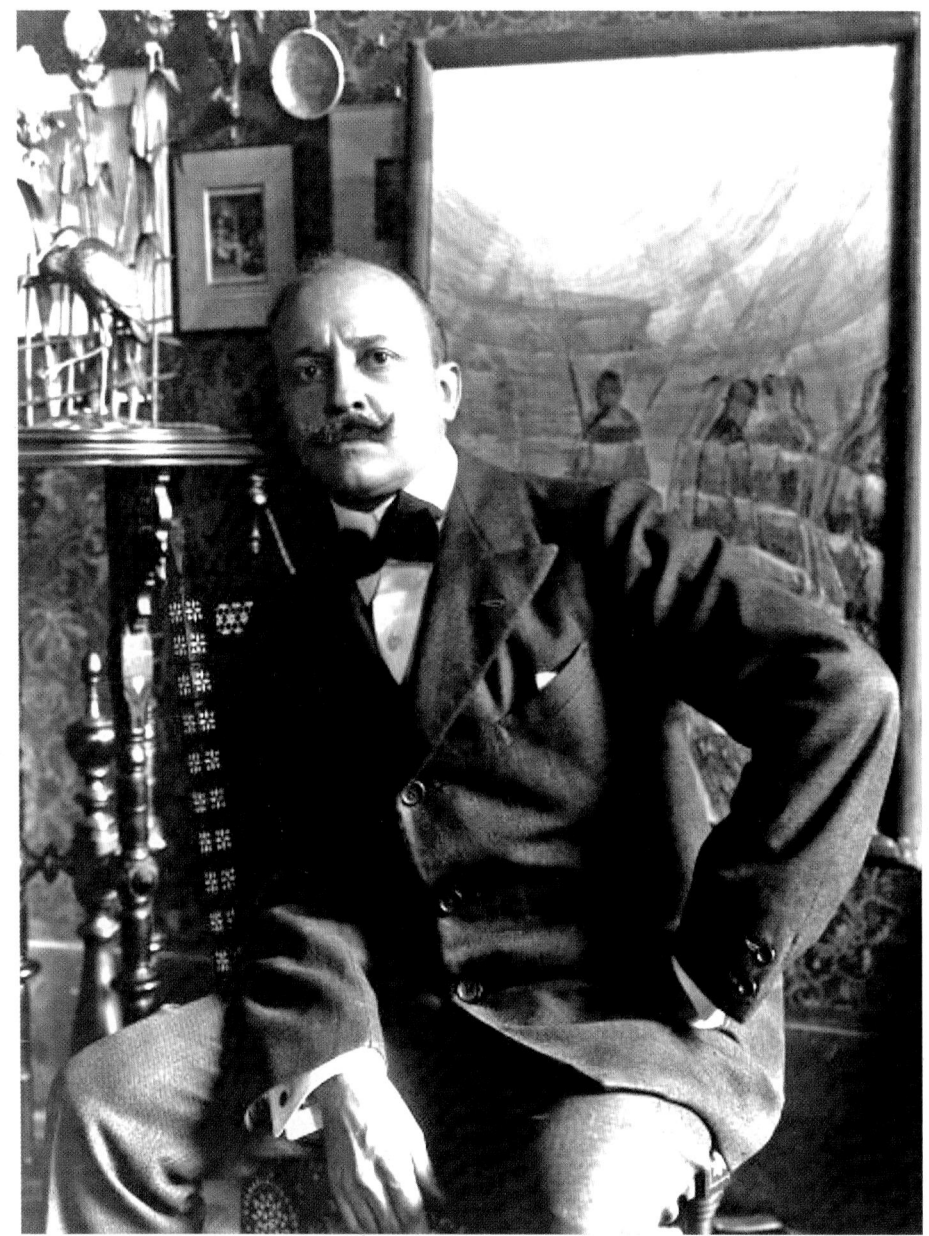

Filippo Marinetti.

8

THE ITALIAN CONNECTION

In 1912, in the wake of the 'Second Post-Impressionist Exhibition', English art remained at a crossroads. Did it allow the various modernisms rampant on the Continent to penetrate and irrevocably change its character or did it cling doggedly to the past? Those who wanted to create a distinctly English modernism were uncertain where to turn.

The seven about-to-become Vorticists were at different stages in their careers. Older than the others, Lewis was experimenting with several options. He wanted to exploit further his radical fusions of representation with abstraction. Roberts was fixated with Cubism whereas Bomberg was placing representations of the human body into abstract grids. In a manner not dissimilar to Bomberg, Wadsworth was conjoining landscape with abstraction. Gaudier was trying to introduce abstraction into sculpture. Saunders and Dismorr were searching for new ways to explore advanced art.

These artists were pushing themselves to create new modernisms. There were many options but one movement, Futurism, was gaining traction in England in large part because of the Messianic personality of its founder, the flamboyant Filippo Tommaso Marinetti. His Italian parents were living in Alexandria, Egypt, at the time of his birth in 1896. From his early years, he was rebellious: he was expelled from the Jesuit school he attended because he smuggled novels by Zola into the classroom. He later studied at the Sorbonne and obtained a degree in law from the University of Pavia in 1899. He rejected law in favour of poetry, in which he flirted with Symbolism. His overriding interest was in creating a new utopia and to further this ambition published his 'Futurist Manifesto' in 1909.

Marinetti's priority was to purge Italy of its oppressive past. In his 'Manifesto', he proclaimed, 'we will free Italy from her innumerable museums which cover her like countless cemeteries.' In place of antiquated institutions, he envisioned a world set free by advances in industry and technology. Existence, he asserted, was in a constant state of flux. In the past, he claimed, a false boundary had been established between objects, whereas 'Our bodies penetrate the sofas on which we sit, and the sofas penetrate our bodies. The motor-bus rushes into the house which it passes, and in their turn the houses throw themselves upon the motor-bus and are blended with it.'

Mankind had to be set free from that constricted past. In stirring prose, he envisioned a utopian future: 'We shall sing of the great crowds in the excitement of labour, pleasure and rebellion . . . of factories suspended from the clouds by their strings of smoke; of bridges leaping like gymnasts over the diabolical cutlery of sun-bathed rivers . . . of the gliding flight of aeroplanes, the sound of which is like the flapping of flags and the applause of an enthusiastic crowd.' For his new world order to come into being, remnants of the past had to be destroyed. He suggested, for example, filling the 'stinking canals' of Venice with rubble gathered from its 'old, collapsing leprous palaces'. When that city had been completely razed, it could be transformed into an industrial and military centre capable of dominating the Adriatic.

Such eradications necessitated violence: 'We wish to glorify War – the only health giver of the world.'[1] For Marinetti, only through armed conflict could society be cleansed. In his scheme, war became a necessary tonic.

Since the printed word alone, Marinetti felt, could have only a limited impact in spreading his doctrine, he presented his message in public gatherings where his charisma could give weight to his arguments. When the French writer André Gide attended one of those events, he characterized the Italian as a purveyor of 'artistic junk': 'He is a fool, very rich, and very self-satisfied, [someone] who has never learned to keep silent.' His lack of talent permitted him 'to indulge in every form of audacity'.[2]

The journalist Douglas Goldring reported that when Marinetti arrived in England in April 1910, he was 'adorned with diamond rings, gold chains and hundreds of flashing teeth'.[3] He lambasted the audience at the Lyceum Theatre: 'You adore the beautiful flying machines that skim over earth, sea and clouds, and yet you jealously preserve the least fragment of the past.'[4]

When Lewis heard him, he characterized him as a 'frenzied Jack-in-the-Box. He sprang about, a torrent of words pouring incessantly from his mouth . . . Banging and popping, rattling and whistling – the sweat pouring from him – he grimaced and shouted at you from the platform and really made you feel you had been at the heart of a barrage.'[5]

Marinetti was not an artist, but his philosophy quickly led a band of gifted artists, his countrymen, to strive to find visual equivalents to his doctrines. When Marinetti returned to England in 1912, it was to open the exhibition of works by the Italian Futurist painters at London's tiny Sackville Gallery. Thirty-five works by four artists, all of whom accompanied their leader, were on display (ten by Umberto Boccioni, eleven by Carlo Carrà, six by Luigi Russolo and eight by Gino Severini).

In practice, Futurist art, as William C. Wees has argued,

> express[es] 'universal dynamism' – a phrase intended to call up
> a violent sort of Bergsonian flux: 'All things move, all things run,
> all things are rapidly changing.' To catch this feverish flux, the
> Futurists tried to get beyond – in Bergson's words – 'sharply cut
> crystals' and 'frozen surfaces' of life, to find and express the 'con-
> tinuous flux' that is reality. 'The materiality of bodies,' said the
> technical manifesto, must be broken down and the boundaries
> between objects dissolved and their surroundings merged.[6]

This exhibition was just as successful in attracting attention as the Second Post-Impressionist one seven months later, although its aesthetics of 'feverish flux' attracted ridicule. The *Evening News* of 2 March gloated that the works on show proved that Futurism had 'fallen flat as a breathless pancake'; according to that reporter, the paintings looked like 'imaginative linoleum [or] the cut-out work' of kindergarteners.[7] P. G. Konody in *The Observer* was even more dismissive: 'the majority [are like] pictorial renderings of confused nightmares, in which all objects are not only in motion, but in dissolution under the impulse of violent forces.'[8] Contrary to others, Sickert was impressed by the sheer power on display: 'Austere, bracing, patriotic, nationalist, positive, anti-archaistic, anti-sentimental, anti-feminist . . . the movement is one from which we in England have a good deal to learn.'[9]

The pundit of Futurism also maintained 'that all objects previously used must be swept aside in order to express our whirling life of steel, of pride, of

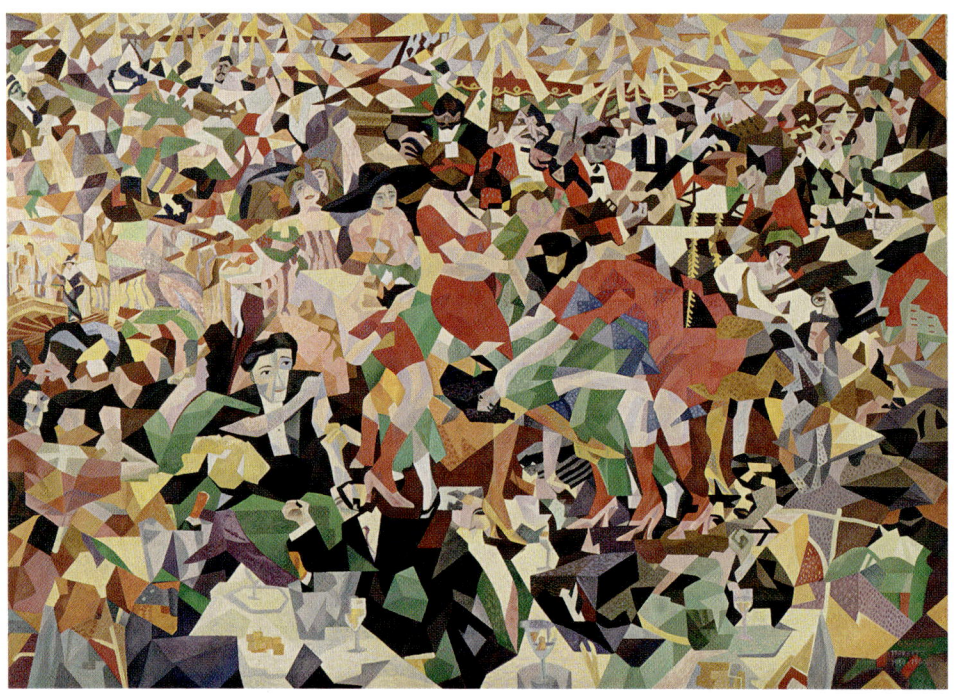

Gino Severini, *The Dance of the Pan Pan at the Monico*, 1959 version, oil on canvas.

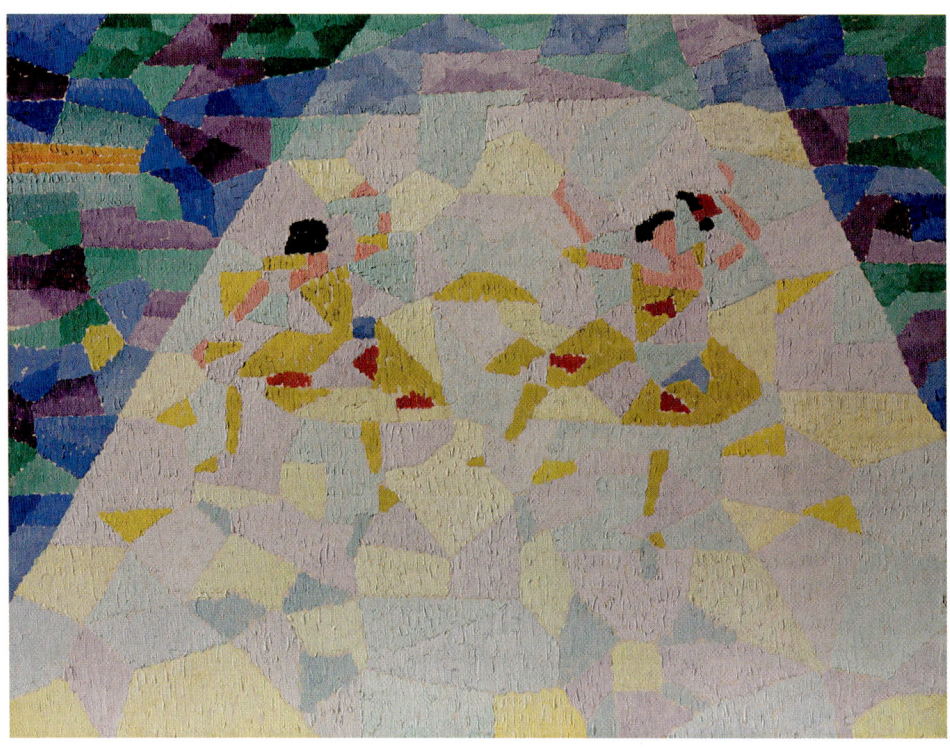

Gino Severini, *The Yellow Dancers*, c. 1911–12, oil on canvas.

fever and of speed'.[10] In response, Futurist art often portrayed speed with an emphasis on whirling – as in Severini's enormous *The Dance of the Pan Pan at the Monico*, which Lewis Hind in the *Daily Chronicle* accurately described as showing 'the bustle and hub bub created by the Tsiganes [gypsies], the champagne-sodden crowd, the perverse dance of the professionals, the clashing of colours and laughter'.[11] Rutter did not feel that the 'spasmodic, artificial oscillation of cinematography' was an appropriate way of depicting dance, whereas Fry admired the painting because its 'curious movements' conveyed 'the mental exasperation' of a dance hall.[12] He also praised Severini's *The Yellow Dancers* (*c*. 1911–12), but he was not prepared to take Futurism seriously – no examples of this movement were included in the 'Second Post-Impressionist Exhibition'. According to Fry, 'the Italian Futurists have succeeded in developing a whole system of aesthetic out of a misapprehension of some of Picasso's recondite and difficult works.'[13]

One reason for excluding Futurism was its link to Italian militarism – and actual, physical violence. The Irish-born war journalist Francis McCullagh, as Jonathan Black has observed, 'connect[ed] Italy's Libyan campaign with Marinetti and the Futurists and, particularly, with Marinetti's [poem] *La Bataille de Tripoli*'.[14] For him, art could assist in unleashing the savagery of war.

All the Slade graduates who were to become associated with Vorticism likely attended this exhibition, although no record of their visits exist. However, the fragmentation of space in *The Yellow Dancers* may have influenced Bomberg's *Ju-Jitsu* (*c*. 1913) and *In the Hold* (*c*. 1913–14).

Bomberg, fascinated with depicting dancers, may have been attracted to the Severini. But he was drawn to the Italian's form, not his content. Bomberg's brother, Mo, was a boxer and trained at a gymnasium called the Judaeans, where ritualized, carefully regulated ju-jitsu was practised. The artist's prefatory study shows half-human, half-abstract figures interacting with each other. The painting provides grids where semblances of combatants are arrayed on what looks like a chessboard. Each grid of the 64 squares is divided into triangles. The mosaic-like result reduces the wrestlers to abstract shapes; moreover, any sense of representation fades because of the kinetic-like interaction between the centre grids and the outer ones. As Richard Cork has argued, 'Figures and room alike are shattered by the intervention of the grid.' He also argues that the viewer is prevented 'from identifying either the

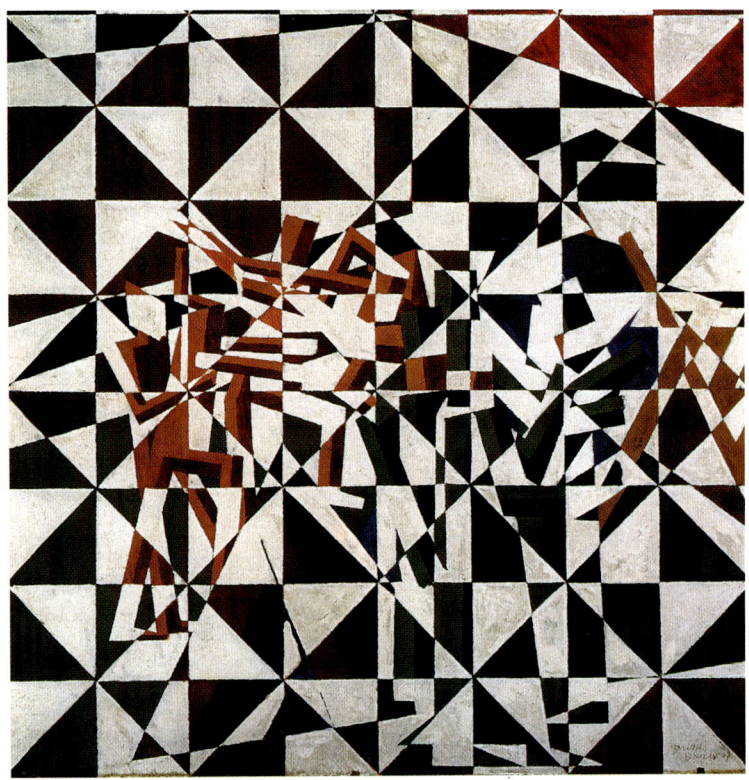

David Bomberg, *Ju-Jitsu*, *c.* 1913, oil on canvas.

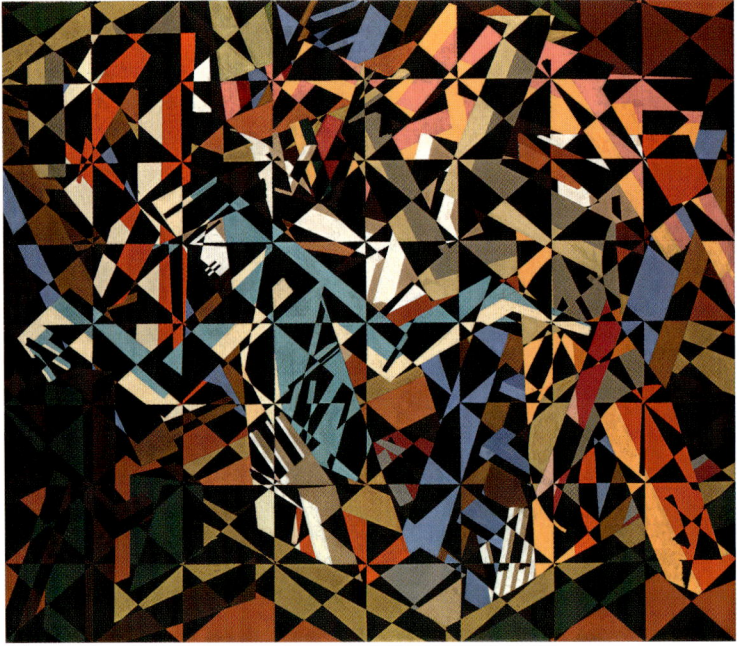

David Bomberg, *In the Hold*, *c.* 1913–14, oil on canvas.

performers' actions or the setting they inhabit'.[15] The result is that the canvas elicits a visceral reaction that one might experience witnessing the wrestlers in action. The radical flattening of perspective and the conversion of figures into abstract shapes preoccupied Bomberg in his early work.

In the Hold, which is just as challenging as *Ju-Jitsu*, may have a familial connection, as Richard Cork has pointed out. 'The possibility grows that the people in the hold of the ship have been enduring considerable discomfort, and that the journey is terminating in an atmosphere of bewilderment, harshness and apprehension.'[16] As such, this canvas is about the hazards of immigration and incorporates the legend of the Wandering Jew. The grids in *Ju-Jitsu* may be difficult to comprehend, but its surface is relatively tranquil compared to the shards of black insinuating themselves in *Into the Hold*.

What these artists would have noticed was how Futurism's emphasis on rapid movement was in marked contrast to the relatively quieter surfaces of the Cubist canvases of the School of Paris. Except for Bomberg, none of the future Vorticists were overly attracted to Futurism, although another Slade graduate, Christopher Nevinson, flirted with Vorticism before embracing Futurism.

Fry did not entirely dismiss Futurism, although he was wary of it. Marinetti's antics may have amused him – he apparently did not find him threatening. What Fry did not envision was that the advent of Futurism in England would revolutionize the future of English art. He had hoped that English artists – having been exposed to advanced art emanating from France through his two monumental exhibitions – would be transformed. He did not realize that Futurism would alter the playing field because it offered new options – to be accepted or rejected.

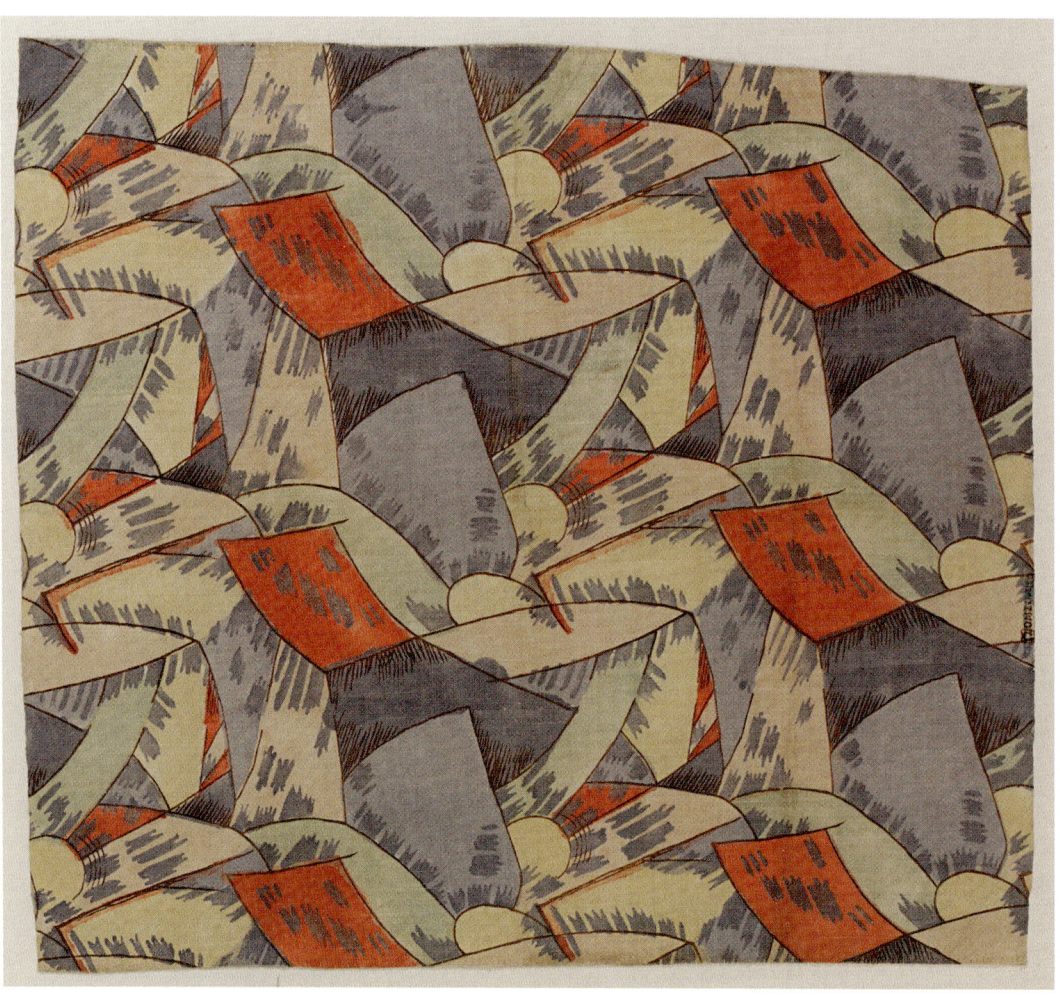

Roger Fry, *Amenophis*, 1913, printed linen.

9

AN IDEAL HOME?
THE OMEGA WORKSHOPS

In emphasizing the decorative arts at the Omega Workshops, Roger Fry wanted to fuse contemporary art with design. Many of the resulting decorations were supposed to demonstrate that the experimental nature of modernist art could be applied to chairs, tables, textiles and other household objects and thus create an environment in which modernism could make its presence more widely known.

The writer for *The Times* visiting the Omega recognized how

> Post-Impressionist principles [recognize] that the representation of real objects . . . is used as a motive of design, and not to the realities represented. This is, of course, the principle of all good design, but in these works it is carried much further than usual and in most cases with good results. Only an artist with very great ability can combine the amount of representation common in most patterns with a fine abstract design.[1]

Fry was obviously aware that decorative objects lent themselves to abstract patterning. His friends Vanessa Bell and Duncan Grant had incorporated Post-Impressionism into their art, as can be seen in their contributions to the 'Second Post-Impressionist Exhibition'. Their later work for the Workshops clearly demonstrated their eagerness to experiment with abstraction, but, as Richard Cork has pointed out, Fry himself 'could only allow his own art to broach abstraction when he executed fabric designs'.[2]

On the surface, it seemed that most artists working at the Omega had adjusted to the tasks assigned them. However, as the artists talked and gossiped with each other, trouble brewed. Born to wealth, Fry had a strong sense of noblesse oblige. He also relished the role of impresario. For him, the Workshops were a way of providing employment to those in need – as long as they followed his dictates.

Earlier, he had led the restoration of damaged works of art, such as the Mantegna frescoes at Hampton Court; such projects – before the Workshops opened – allowed him to provide work for the young. Among those was Paul Nash, who felt Fry was a dictator.[3] At the Omega, the disparity between Fry and some of his protégés became even more glaring. He could be generous to a fault while at the same time condescending.

Wadsworth's designs for the Omega moved in the direction of linear abstraction. There he became friends with Lewis and, in the process, intrigued by Lewis's experimentation. Wadsworth may have been quiet and reserved, but he was a sharp, careful observer of others. He forged a bond with Lewis and seemingly became the older man's disciple. The surviving Omega designs by Wadsworth are straightforwardly geometrical. He kept to such proclivities, but he began in his art to add much more complexity to them.

Two other fledgling artists were in the process of switching allegiances from Post-Impressionism to abstraction. One was Frederick Etchells, who had attended the Royal College of Art, contributed to the first Camden Town exhibition and was subsequently hired by Fry as one of the decorators for the *London on Holiday* murals for the students' dining room at the Borough Polytechnic. Up to 1912 his work was imitative of Duncan Grant's. His painting *The Dead Mole* (1912) – shown at the 'Second Post-Impressionist Exhibition' – has a similar fusion of Fauvist colour with pointillism; the elongated figures of the man and the boy are also reminiscent of Grant's approach. While at the Omega, Etchells began experimenting with abstraction in his rug designs. Those designs were influenced by Cubism. Another artist fascinated with abstraction was Cuthbert Hamilton, a classmate of Lewis's at the Slade, who had assisted with the decorations to the Cave of the Golden Calf and exhibited at the 'Second Post-Impressionist Exhibition'.

As a result of their decorative work at the Omega Workshops, Wadsworth, Etchells and Hamilton became more and more acquainted with abstraction and its benefits to themselves as artists. Like Bell's and Grant's, the designs they made for the Omega are mainly abstract. They were being provided with

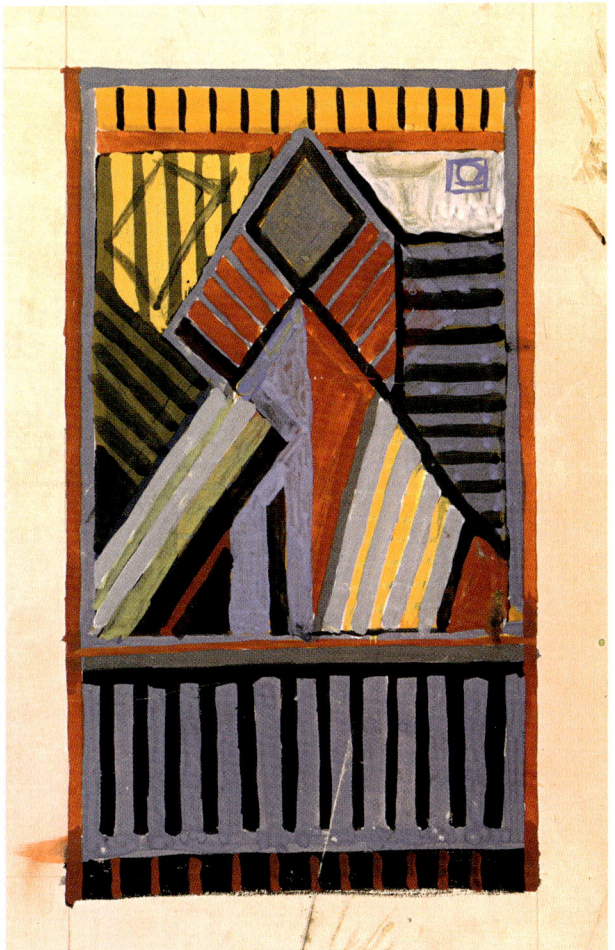

Frederick Etchells, design for a carpet, 1913, pencil,
watercolour and bodycolour on paper.

the training they would later employ as Vorticists. At the very same time, they forged strong links with Lewis.

Lewis's work had been actively promoted by Fry in 1912. The two clashed violently a year later when working together. Ill feelings surfaced almost immediately after the 'Second Post-Impressionist Exhibition' when Fry insisted, as Leonard Woolf recalled, 'upon deducting a higher commission without any explanation or apology to the painters. Most of them meekly accepted what they were given, but Wyndham Lewis . . . protested violently. Roger was adamant in ignoring him.'[4] There was another contretemps in August 1913 when Lewis protested that his work had been excluded from an exhibition of works from the 'Second Post-Impressionist Exhibition' at the Sandon Society in Liverpool. He told Fry: 'I am animated by most cordial sentiments as regards yourself . . . But to continue in an atmosphere of special criticism and ill-will, if such exist, would have manifest disadvantages . . . to me.'[5]

Fry did not heed this warning. Two months later, in October 1913, Lewis learned that Fry had usurped a commission given to Spencer Gore, Fry and himself by the *Daily Mail* to design a 'Post-Impressionist Room' (an installation) at the Ideal Home Exhibition. When Gore learned of the invitation, he went immediately to the Omega to break the good news. Since neither Lewis nor Fry was there, he asked Duncan Grant to inform his collaborators. Nothing more was heard about this project by Lewis until he was invited to design a mantelpiece for the room. Only then did a full version of what had transpired surface. At that point, Lewis – with good reason – became convinced that Fry, in his high-handed way, had once again excluded him.

An accurate account of what happened cannot be ascertained. Grant could have been at fault in forgetting to inform Lewis. Fry could have determined that the Omega Workshops – and not three of its artists – had been commissioned. This interpretation does not seem entirely plausible because

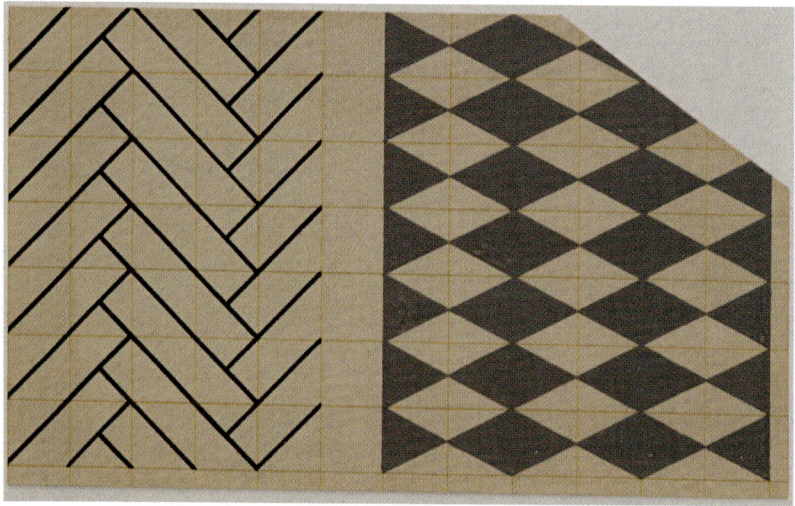

Edward Wadsworth, design for the Omega Workshops,
1913, gouache and pencil on squared paper.

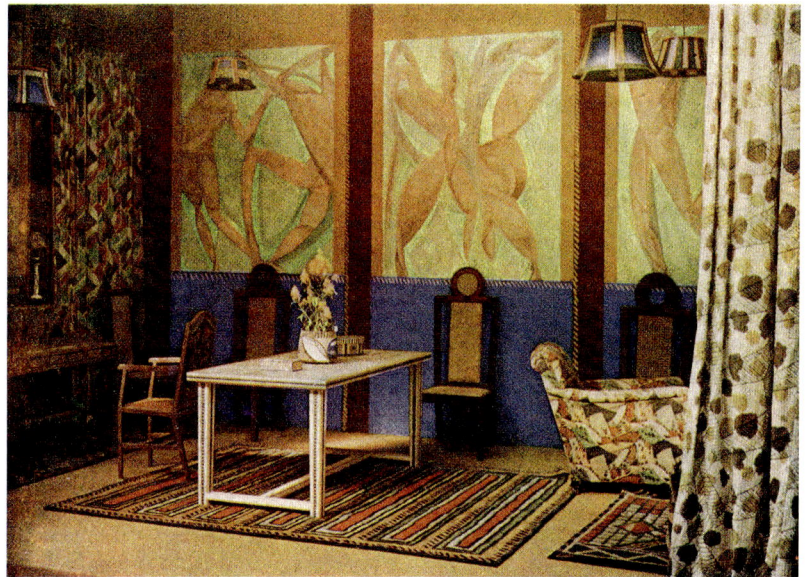

Omega Workshops, Post-Impressionist Room at the Ideal Home Exhibition, 1913.

of the publicity Gore and Lewis had received from their work at the Cave of the Golden Calf.

Despite their differences in taste, Fry and Lewis shared some common ground, although they obviously disagreed as to the direction in which contemporary art should venture. Fry's own drift to modernism was simply to introduce elements of Post-Impressionism into his art; Lewis wanted a complete overhaul in defining what a modern artist was capable of.

The other glaring reality was that Fry and Lewis saw themselves as trailblazers and, as such, leaders who could be ruthless in imposing their wills. In a sense, the conflict became Miltonian. Lewis became a proud Lucifer who rebelled against a remote God. In retrospect, a break was inevitable. Although he had not intended to do so, Fry inadvertently helped Lewis attract disciples because his attitude to those under his command was so off-putting.

The Ideal Home fiasco led an irate Lewis on 5 October 1913 to confront Fry on the staircase at the Omega and then march out of the building, accompanied by Wadsworth, Etchells and Hamilton. Although Bomberg quit the Omega Workshops at about this time, he did not storm out with the other four. He had likely found Fry intolerable on grounds similar to Lewis's.

In a round robin letter to Omega shareholders and the press, Lewis asserted: 'it was the idea of those who recommended these artists to the *Daily Mail* authorities that a room should be decorated on the lines of their joint decorations in the Cabaret Theatre Club.'[6] This claim might be essentially correct. He was on even more solid ground when he claimed that his rebellion stemmed from ideological differences: 'As to [the Omega's] tendencies in Art, they alone would be sufficient to make it very difficult for any vigorous art-instinct to long remain under that roof.' For Fry – and presumably his Bloomsbury associates Duncan Grant and Vanessa Bell – worshipped the mid-Victorian idol of 'Prettiness . . . despite the Post-What-Not fashionableness of its draperies'.[7]

Fry and his cohorts, Lewis claimed, were unable to abandon the past, whereas he welcomed the future. For Lewis, the Omega had been a doomed proposition from the get-go. Forgotten in Lewis's attacks on Fry and his circle was that Vanessa Bell constructed images that bear a strong resemblance to *Kermesse* (p. 50). The divide between the two factions on aesthetic grounds was not as deep as he maintained.

Hoping to remedy a difficult situation, Bell confronted Etchells, the signatory she felt would most likely listen to reason. She informed Fry that she had wanted 'to get [Etchells] to see that whether they were right or not, they had behaved monstrously in writing this letter without accusing you to your face'. Etchells would not budge. 'Evidently,' Bell told Fry, he had been storing up 'a long tale of grievances of how he had gradually become convinced of your meanness'.[8]

Etchells was perhaps not as obdurate as Bell feared. He later recalled: 'I don't think I helped write the "Round Robin". I simply thought it great fun signing it to give one in the eye to Fry.'[9] Wadsworth was enraged when a story appeared in a Yorkshire newspaper claiming that the rebels were disciples of Fry and referred to them as the Omega group. His anger abated when he gleefully told a friend that a prominent critic had informed him that he was 'very delighted with the round-robin – thoroughly sympathetic'.[10]

On personal grounds, Lewis despised Fry. According to him, his former mentor had 'some nasty, mean crookedness in his life, that has left a trail of particular unsavouriness in his life'.[11] For his part, Fry remained silent, although he told Gore, 'I fear nothing I can do comes up to his ideal of what

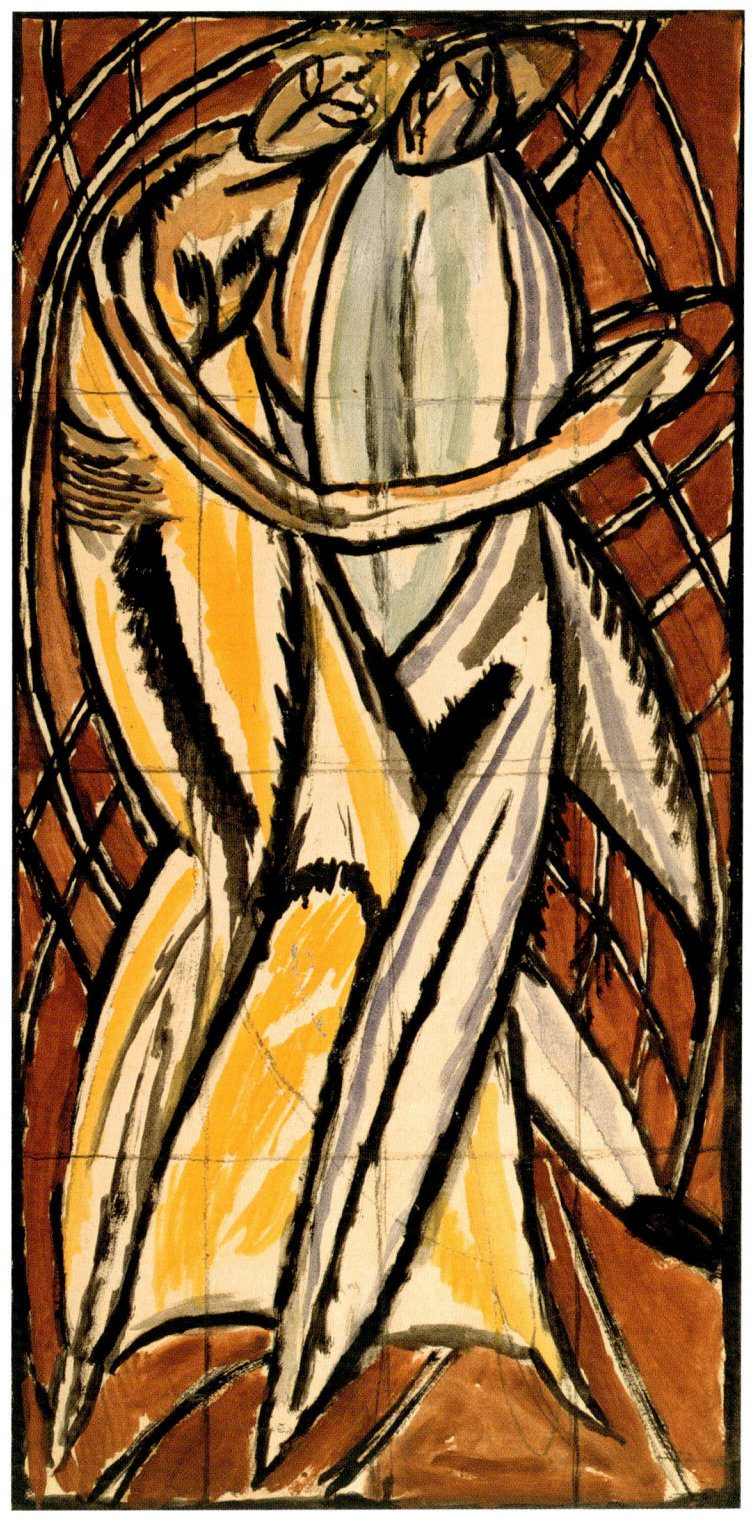

Vanessa Bell, *Couple Dancing*, 1913, design for panel.

is due to him.'[12] Fry was correct. He could have done nothing to alleviate the situation because he could never measure up to Lewis's exacting standards. Lewis imagined the worst about the Ideal Home Exhibition, and no evidence would have altered his sense of having been unjustly treated. Fry lamented: 'I think Lewis's vanity touches on insanity, and it is he who has led the others, who are not bad but only ignorant and romantic, astray.'[13]

There was another agenda in play. Lewis wanted to replace Fry as *the* apostle of modernism. One of Lewis's colleagues at the Omega, Winifred Gill, remembered him 'wearing a large black sombrero and his great coat and jacket were open showing the very first royal blue shirt I had seen'. He was bragging about all the letters he received, many of them from obviously admiring women. He was, she realized, carefully cultivating a public image. Once, she beheld him secretly preening himself in a mirror and rehearsing a possible encounter. He 'approached the mirror with an ingratiating smile. He backed again and tried the effect of a sudden recognition with a look of surprised pleasure.'[14]

Lewis was a brilliant actor who, chameleon-like, adjusted himself to his surroundings. If charm were required, he could display it in abundance. He had fine-tuned his display of outrage. Politically astute, he knew what pieces on the chessboard to manipulate.

Marinetti, another would-be apostle of modernism, helped fuel the divide between Lewis and Fry. Lewis may have considered the Italian a charlatan, but he had put on offer a modernism vastly different from Fry's. He was also a brilliant showman, a gift he shared with Lewis. He soon became another loathed rival.

What if apprentice artists like himself banded together to offer a modernism not dependent on Post-Impressionism or Futurism? Lewis began to envision himself as the leader of a group of brigands who could shake the London art world to its foundations. He and his castaways could create a new 'ism' – one that would challenge all others.

10

THE OTHERS

One of the first opportunities for the Omega outcasts to display their work was provided by Frank Rutter's 'Post-Impressionist and Futurist Exhibition' at the Doré Galleries in October 1913. Rutter, a curator at Leeds Art Gallery and the editor of *Art News*, made his intentions clear: 'this exhibition is an attempt to set forth in a coherent and as far as possible in a chronological order examples of various schools of painting which have made some noise in the world during the last quarter of a century.' He added that Cubism and Futurism 'have already stirred English artists [as] is shown by the contributions of Mr Wyndham Lewis, Mr Wadsworth ... and others'.[1] Earlier, in *Revolution in Art* (1910), he had argued that 'men like Picasso, Matisse, Derain and others are smashing the fallacy that imitation ... is art.'[2] What Rutter failed to mention was that he had excluded Fry, Vanessa Bell and Grant from his exhibition and was thus inadvertently advancing modernism as practised by Lewis and his followers.

Lewis further scored against Fry when Clive Bell praised a version of *Kermesse* (p. 50) – one of Lewis's seven entries: 'I do not grumble at the reappearance of [a painting] which has been altered and greatly improved since its last appearance at the London Salon [the Allied Artists' Association, July 1912].' Bell claimed that Lewis 'promises to become that rare thing, a real academic artist. He is academic in the good sense of the word, that is to say, he uses a formula of which he is the master and not the slave.'[3]

Perhaps recalling the Omega Room fracas, Bell proffered a further reflection on Lewis's art based on his warped personality: 'The enemy that dogs him in all his works is an excessive taste for life. He is inclined to modify his forms in the interests of drama and psychology to the detriment of pure design.'[4]

At the same exhibition, Wadsworth showed the highly stylized *Landscape* (*c.* 1913) (p. 32). Not on display was the even more daring *Radiation* (1913), in which triangular formations intersect in a manner like that of Severini.[5] Wadsworth was flirting with Futurism by showing a variety of pictorial elements conjoined, as Cork has pointed out: 'the wheel cogs and the floodlights are both basically naturalistic elements included in a non-figurative design.'[6] Pound claimed that *Radiation* showed the pictorial equivalent of a foundry.[7]

But there is more at stake in such an image. In *Blast 1*, Wadsworth would write spiritedly about Kandinsky's *On the Spiritual in Art* and the influence of the Russian master, who claimed 'that the artist can employ any forms (natural, abstracted or abstract) to express himself, if his feelings demand it'.[8] Wadsworth's *Cape of Good Hope* (1914) is an aerial view of the ground below and this map-like composition incorporates elements of the natural, the abstracted and the abstract. As an artist, Wadsworth was, like Lewis, partial to geometric abstraction, but he was also more open to including a diverse range of elements. He was in addition prone to arranging his work in the decentred manner of Kandinsky's abstracts.

In contrast, Etchells's *Woman at a Mirror* demonstrates how effectively he had imbibed Lewis's *Smiling Woman Ascending a Stair* (p. 53). Very unsure of himself, he exhibited two Cubist-style drawings entitled *Head* that are clearly indebted to Picasso; he also showed two landscapes that demonstrate he was also exploring Futurism. Years later, he reflected: 'I liked Lewis entirely, but he was an uncomfortable man to be with. He was a tremendous bully who wanted to be top dog all the time, and I used to get ratty with him.'[9]

When Lewis and his colleagues exhibited in the 'Cubist Room' at Brighton at the end of 1913, they scored another triumph, one achieved with astute behind-the-scenes manoeuvring. This exhibition was labelled 'The Camden Town Group and Others'. At that time, the Camden Town Group existed in name only. None of its three exhibitions had been a success. At that point, it merged with the so-called Fitzroy Street Group. Later, Sickert oversaw a meeting on 15 November 1913 that led to the formation of the London Group (which also comprised the Cumberland Market Group). Lewis had skilfully managed to obtain a place for his band of artists in this amalgamation. They became 'the Others'.

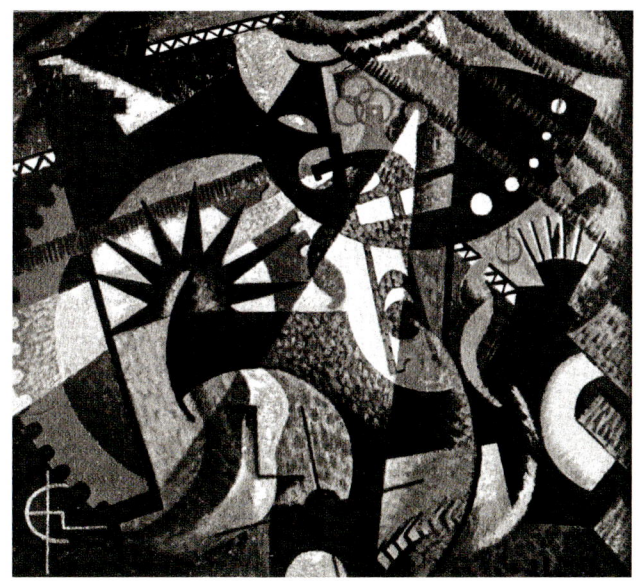

Edward Wadsworth, *Radiation*, 1914, reproduction in *Blast 1*, p. iv.

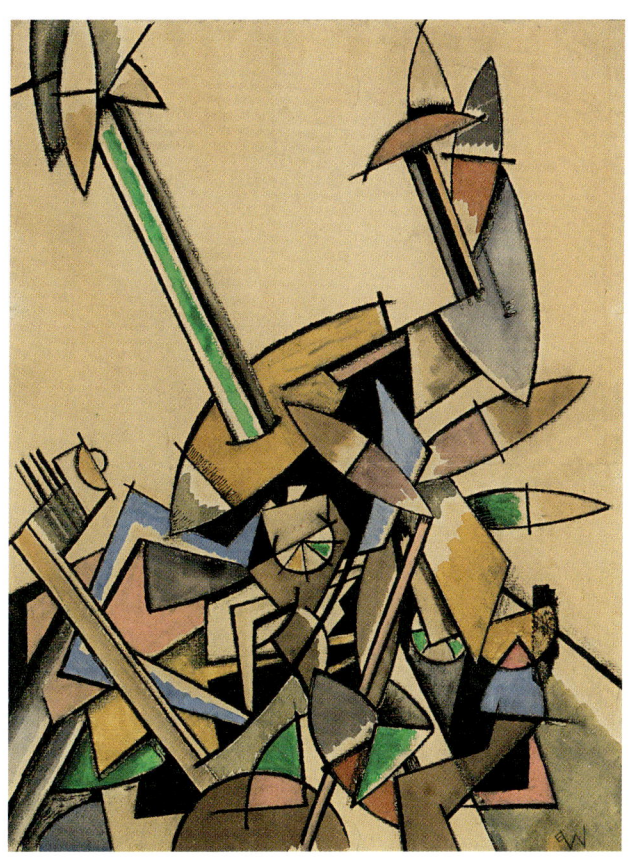

Edward Wadsworth, study for *Cape of Good Hope*, 1914,
ink, crayon, watercolour and gouache on paper.

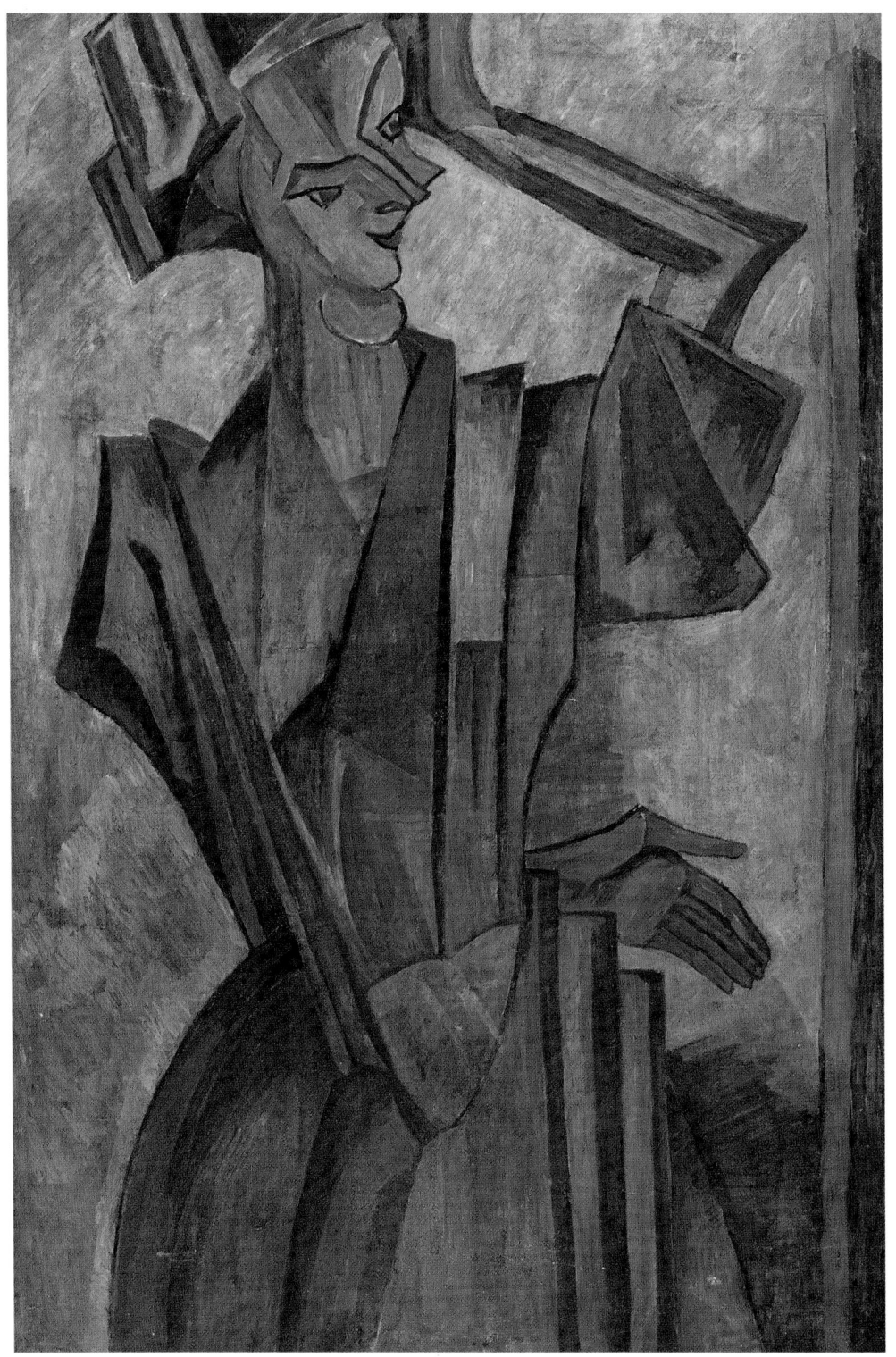

Frederick Etchells, *Woman at a Mirror*, 1914, oil on canvas.

In his introduction to the catalogue, J. B. Manson celebrated the fact that a wide variety of artists had taken refuge under the same umbrella. 'Cubism meets Impressionism, Futurism and Sickertism join hands and are not ashamed, the motto of the Group being that sincerity of conviction has a right expression.' The triumph was that 'the vital qualities in modern art should be concentrated in one group.'[10]

Manson's attempt to broker peace was very different from Lewis's pronouncements in his foreword to Gallery Three, the so-called Cubist Room. 'These painters are not accidentally associated here, but form a vertiginous, but not exotic, island in the placid respectable archipelago of English art.' In referring to his breakaway group, he notched up his metaphors: 'This formation is undeniably of volcanic matter and even origin; for it appeared suddenly above the waves following certain seismic shakings beneath the surface.' He insisted that his group was 'closely knit and admirably adapted . . . against all sides'. He also pronounced that all 'revolutionary painting today has in common the rigid reflections of steel and stone in the spirit if the artist.'[11] As usual, there was no hint of compromise in Lewis's rhetoric. He could justifiably celebrate the Cubist Room as the first occasion in which examples of his brand of English 'revolutionary art' were shown. Those whose work was on exhibit included Nevinson, Wadsworth, Epstein, Hamilton, Bomberg, Etchells and himself. For his purposes, Lewis saw Galleries 1 and 2 as devoted to artists whose time had come and gone; Gallery 3 was of the present and the future. He employed the adjective 'Cubist' as the equivalent of 'modernist' – even though he understood the works in Gallery 3 were not really Cubist.

The Vorticists were not as 'tightly knit' as Lewis suggested. What he did not refer to in his foreword was his attempt to exclude David Bomberg from the Others. Like Lewis, Bomberg had severed his connection with the Omega Workshops, but Bomberg bitterly recalled:

Not only did [Lewis] insult me in public but went so far . . . as to cause my character to be cleaved by an imputation wrapped up in buffoonery – that I was not a fit person to be elected a Foundation Member of the London Group – the onus was [placed] upon Harold Gilman, the first President, who insisted . . . that I had been elected – Harold Gilman obtained the evidence that Lewis's information was groundless.[12]

Lewis secreted away a canvas by Bomberg in hope that it would not be on the van travelling to Brighton. As Bomberg recalled, 'Spencer Gore . . . a painter and person holding the reputation for uncovering truth rescued my painting from Oblivion & himself ran it down to the van already moving off to Brighton.'[13] Undeterred that his ruse had been discovered, Lewis placed the canvas behind a door where it could not be seen. Outraged, Bomberg removed the painting and placed it on the roof of the taxi in which he headed back to London.

In his foreword, Lewis glossed over his jealousy by damning Bomberg with faint praise. According to him, his rival's work possessed a 'colourist's temperament', even though 'his form and subject matter are academic.' He then blandly described one canvas that had 'the structure of the criss-cross pattern [as] new and extremely interesting'.[14] The painting with the 'criss-cross' pattern was likely *Vision of Ezekiel*, for which there is no entry in the catalogue.

What Lewis recognized was that his form of abstraction and Bomberg's were profoundly different and difficult to place under the same label. Rather than emphasizing a single figure or subject to translate into abstraction, Bomberg concentrated on groups of monumental figures interacting with each other. His use of the vortex focused on the moment in which his figures reach an equilibrium between representation and abstraction.

Lewis, who obviously felt he could browbeat Wadsworth, Hamilton and Etchells, learned that such an approach would get him nowhere with Bomberg, who also possessed a volatile temper. Lewis did not want *Vision* to be shown because its style differed so completely from his own – and might outshine him.

A year earlier, on a night when the East End of London was under snow, Bomberg remembered that past midnight he heard a 'peremptory knock'. When he answered the door, Bomberg told Lewis that it was 'an inconvenient hour to tramp through the snow and mount three flights of stairs . . . anyhow how did you know I live here?' Nonplussed, Lewis rejoined: 'Nothing is impossible for Wyndham Lewis, Bomberg, I have come to see what you are doing.' After this abrupt start, Bomberg recalled: 'we had talked ourselves silly. When he left – at dawn, the next morning. I recognized in the conversation a Slade man honouring the same pledge to which I was staking my life – namely, a Partizan [*sic*].'[15] Bomberg soon learned that comradeship with Lewis was a dubious proposition.

By inclination, Bomberg was not a joiner. He was resistant to the idea of being part of any group. Lewis's attempt to circumvent him reinforced his decision to remain an outsider to the Vorticist circle. He was sympathetic to their aims, but his own work did not look like the work of the other confederates. He remained a Vorticist in spirit – an artist determined to infuse English art with a vigour and passion that it sorely lacked. From a carefully imposed distance, he lived on the fringes of Lewis and his circle.

11

A NEW ROOM

Among the words of both praise and condemnation he bestowed upon Lewis when he visited the Doré Galleries in October 1913, Clive Bell foretold that Lewis had the ability to create 'vast organizations of form, designed, I would imagine to have something of the austere and impressive unity of great architecture'.[1]

Since the 'Ideal Home' commission was a missed opportunity to display such talents, Lewis welcomed a letter from Lady Drogheda. She had been blown away when she beheld *Kermesse* (p. 50): 'it moved before me – and I am gradually having my stupid old brain taught to appreciate the great cleverness of futurism.' Lewis might not have been eager to see his painting linked to that 'ism' but was intrigued by the words that followed: '*Do* please come and see me. I should so love you to do a frieze for me.'[2]

The flirtatious edge in this missive may indicate that she was contemplating a liaison with Lewis. A friend of his recalled that Lady Drogheda was attracted to the artist and that Lewis, in an unusual turn for him, spruced himself up by purchasing a new shirt and putting it on before arriving at her home on Wilton Crescent in Belgravia.

Even before her marriage to Henry Charles Ponsonby Moore, the 10th Earl of Drogheda, in 1909, Kathleen Pelham Burn had been born to great wealth: her father owned a castle in Linlithgowshire and a home in Edinburgh; her mother had inherited a fortune from ironstone and coal deposits. The earl was a short, slight man who worked at the Foreign Office, in contrast to his wife, who was tall, shapely and commanding in both her attire and her manner of speaking. Her son once described her as larger than life. He also recalled that she actively pursued both men and women as sexual partners.

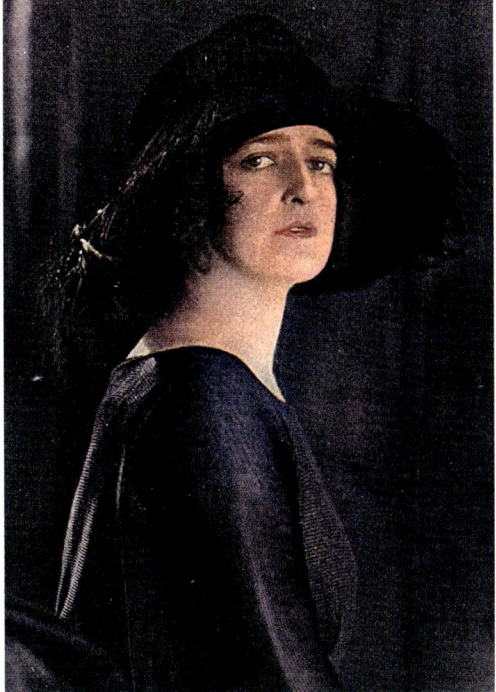

Lady Drogheda.

Lady Drogheda was also obsessed with speed. She was one of the first women to fly in an aeroplane and 'could often be seen in a very elegant electric car, black outside with grey upholstery, which glided silently through the streets of Belgravia'.[3] The earl and countess did not share a taste for the same works of art. He may not have objected to her commissioning Sargent to paint her portrait, but he was outraged by her purchase of a sculpture by Epstein exhibiting copulating doves. Seeing that object, the earl exclaimed: 'I won't have those fucking doves in here – I'll throw them out the window!'[4]

Possessed of an exceptionally unorthodox approach to interior decoration, the commission for Lewis that Lady Drogheda had in mind for her home was, not surprisingly, bizarre. Her son recalled: 'The walls of the drawing room were covered with a sort of silver foil paper and dotted about the room were several blue glass balls resting on columns the colour of lapis lazuli which were reflected in the mirror-like surfaces of the walls. There were masses of cushions lying about everywhere and there was a generally exotic feeling.'[5]

Lewis's decorations were for the dining room, where the walls were covered in black matt velvet. The ceiling and floor were painted black. The curtains were kept shut for dinner parties and, as a result, yellow translucent alabaster lights seemed to float from the ceiling. Lady Drogheda – what appears to be a perverse renunciation of her previous decorating scheme – wanted Lewis to introduce some colour into this eerie cave-like enclosure. His first task was to construct a frieze underneath the cornice running around the interior of the room. Although there are some representational elements, the frieze contained a wide variety of abstract forms. One magazine reviewer responded to the 'rioting mass of colours each vying with the other in brilliance, quite irrespective of form, meaning or design – colour for colour's sake, so to speak'.[6]

The designer's second task was to create a mantelpiece. On each side panel, totemic figures stood guard, as if protecting the mirror in the centre. In the creation of these two, Lewis may have been inspired by his

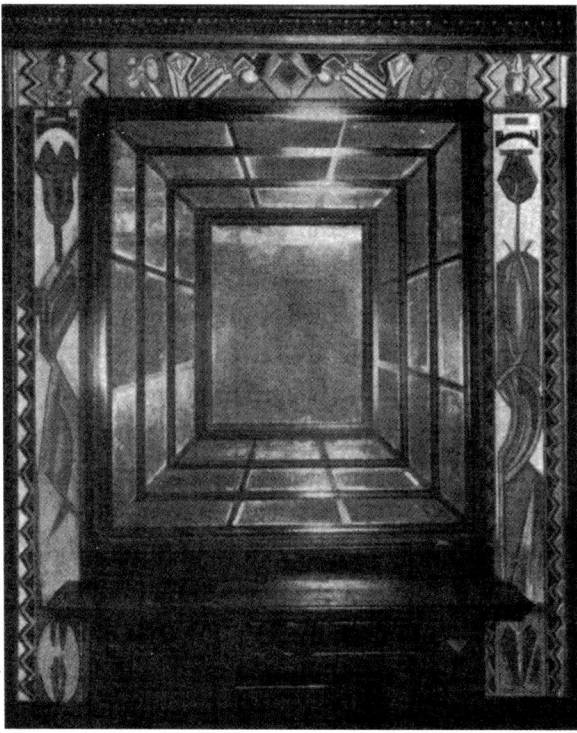

Wyndham Lewis, decoration for the Countess
of Drogheda's house. *Blast 1*, p. vii.

earlier interest in Pacific islands and other 'primitive' works he saw at the British Museum when he was at the Slade. Above the figures, the top panel contained an assortment of abstract shapes.

His third – and perhaps most important – job was to construct the large painting (86.5 × 145 cm) placed above the door that faced the mantelpiece. This lost work, which may have been titled *The Dancing Ladies*, was meant to interact with the mirror that captured its image. The dance was a trope that fascinated Lewis. For example, riotous dancing is the subject of the earlier *Kermesse*. From surviving photographs Lewis had moved into a more abstract handling of this theme – the 'ladies' were evidently difficult to discern.

Accustomed to controversy, Lewis was not disappointed. The writer in the *Athenaeum* saw some things to praise but much to dislike: this design project seemed to have been created more for 'the purposes of immediate sensationalism than in a serious monumental spirit'. He did not admire the 'scarcely legible hieroglyphics, and this hardly gives full scope to the power of sustained draughtsmanship which makes Mr. Lewis, in our opinion, the leader of the English Cubists'.[7]

The Drogheda commission provided Lewis with a welcome opportunity, especially financially. He had demonstrated that he was quite capable of carrying out the requirements of a demanding, if eccentric, patron. He had bested Fry in a very public forum.

12

ROOMS OF ONE'S OWN

If Fry had not founded the Omega Workshops in 1913, and become a father figure to be spurned, the Rebel Art Centre might never have come into being in March 1914. The proposal for the Centre was not Lewis's idea – it originated with his friend, the artist Kate Lechmere – although he relished the idea of taking on Fry by opening a competitive design space.

Always strapped for cash, Lewis could not have afforded the rent for two floors at the four-storey building at 38 Great Ormond Street – not far from the Omega. Lechmere, after attending school in Bristol, had been an art student in Paris and then a pupil of Walter Sickert at the Westminster School of Art. She met Lewis at a party in 1912, and two days later he invited her to dine. Attracted to this 'striking-looking' person, she was a bit surprised when not a word was exchanged during the meal. When they arrived a bit later at the Café Royal, Lewis spoke of two things: Dostoevsky and himself – unsubtly suggesting he was on the same level of accomplishment as the Russian novelist. Undaunted by his oafish behaviour, she found him 'a man of genius, a powerful but complex character'.[1]

They became friends. While in France, she heard of the Omega Workshops imbroglio and wrote Lewis to suggest they open a studio in London. Back in London, she and Lewis 'found a charming old house [on Great Ormond Street] and we took the first floor, and I had a flat on the top floor back. The rooms had to be enlarged and I paid for walls to be taken down and reinstalled. The studio walls were painted pale lemon yellow and the doors Chinese red. We had an office and an extra room for Lewis and prospective pupils to paint in.'[2] A grateful Lewis wrote her: 'I have as many kisses as the envelope will hold. The rest I keep in my mouth for you.'[3]

The Rebels distinguished themselves from the Omega by emphasizing that their products were more sober than their competitor's and thus more attuned to a Britain entering the machine age. Gaudier quit his job at the Omega to join the Rebels in their new home. The interior of the Rebel Centre became more like a museum than the Omega's. Among the paintings on display were William Roberts's *Dancers*, Edward Wadsworth's *A Short Flight* and *Caprice* and Lewis's *Smiling Woman* (p. 53).

The decorations differed markedly differ from its rival. Lewis painted a mural around the wall-frame leading from the main room to an adjoining one. Lechmere, coming upon a divan with what she called a 'stupid floral covering left by a previous inhabitant, painted the frame red and covered it with more acceptable red, white and blue material from Liberty's'. On a white curtain hung across the room, 'points of purple and cubes of green and yellow, intermingling with splashes of deep rose-red, formed themselves ... into fantastic human figures.'[4]

In comparison to the Omega Workshop's penchant for Post-Impressionist colours, the Rebel Centre was a riotous environment devoted to what the press labelled Futurism and Cubism. Even Lechmere's flat was resolutely cutting-edge. The reporter for *Vanity Fair* reported that she 'decorated a whole flat – her own – in Futurism (the only one in London) to show the possibilities of the new decoration. It contains black doors in cream walls, and black

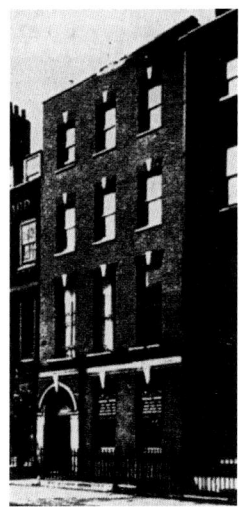

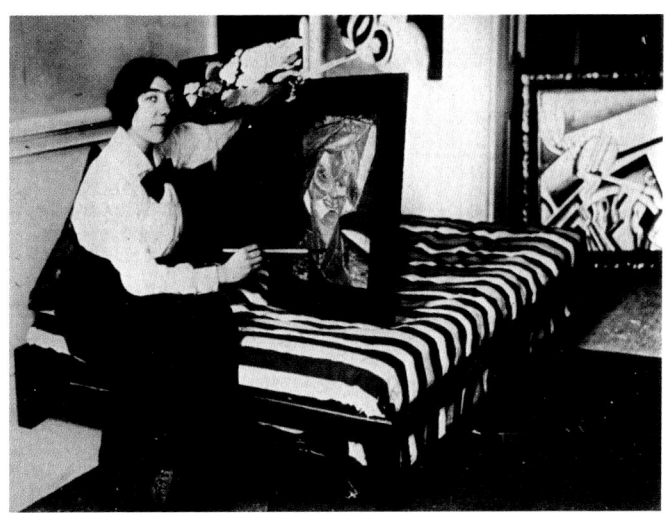

The Rebel Art Centre.　　　　　　　　Kate Lechmere, *c.* 1914.

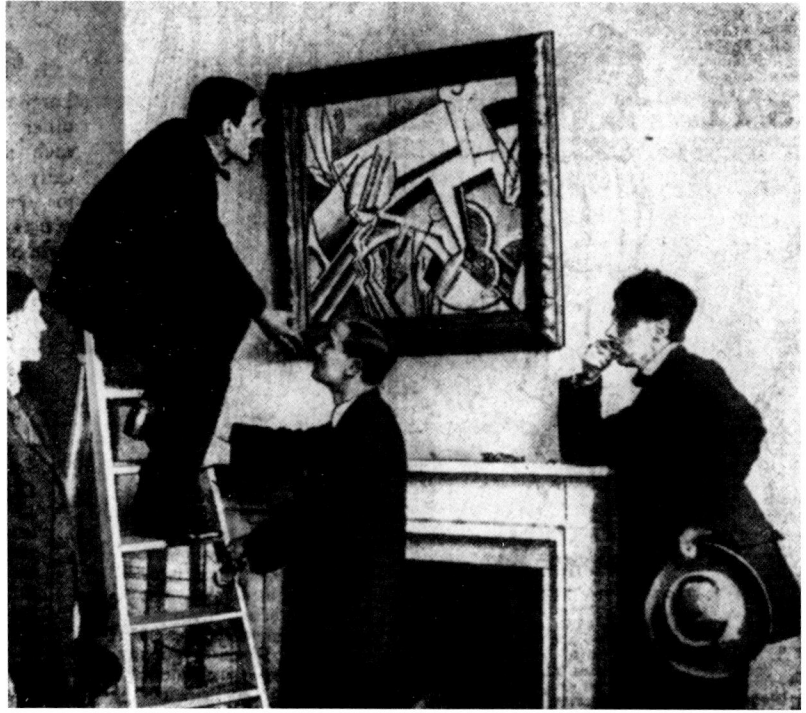

Hamilton, Wadsworth, Nevinson and Lewis hanging Wadsworth's
Caprice at the Rebel Art Centre. *Daily Mirror*, 30 March 1914.

curtains in addition to the usual orgies of colour. I am told she is engaged
in planning a Cubist rock garden, with strange stunted trees from Japan.'[5]

The Omega traded in banal examples of decorative arts, according to
Lewis. He wanted to sell items that avoided good taste and verged on the
primitive. One visitor found the Centre 'a Catholicism of Heresies, as it
were: orthodoxy alone is anathema, and there may be seen all the possibilities and, one might say, all the powers of the new movement. There you can
see curtains, carpets, tables, lampshades, fans, scarves, door panels, shawls,
dresses – all in Futurism. And you see examples of Futurism, Cubism, and
Expressionism . . . and an empty room for the next "ism" that comes along.'[6]
Helen Saunders and Jessica Dismorr – along with Lechmere – spent many
hours creating the various items on display. Their art did not grace the walls.

Although Lechmere paid the costs in establishing the Centre, she was
considered a second-class citizen. 'I had to do the honours', she recalled, 'of
organizing tea parties [because Lewis considered this] was a job for women,

not artists.' Lechmere characterized Saunders and Dismorr as 'little lap-dogs who wanted to be Lewis's slaves and do everything for him'.[7]

That claim is unmerited. Attracted by Lewis's charisma, the two knew that for women artists, fitting in with their male counterparts was a daunting task. Lechmere, who saw herself as an outsider, comforted herself with rendering the two other women as interlopers. By suggesting they wanted to be 'slaves', she downgraded them to make herself feel more secure.

In dealing with Saunders and Dismorr, Lewis's misogyny remained firmly in place. Saunders and Lewis knew each other from 1912 – he made eight portraits of her, and at least one, *Futurist Figure*, is from that year. At about this time, he suggested that she read Otto Weininger's *Sex and Character* (published in 1903 and translated into English in 1906), in which the author maintained that women were congenitally incapable of logical thought because their brains allowed them to construct only half-formed impulses that he called 'henids'. Saunders read this tract and in a letter to Lewis, she lamented: 'I had worked out most of his ideas for myself but persist in thinking that I have a soul.'[8]

There is no doubt Saunders was in love with Lewis, but she was also uncertain about the direction she was pursuing in her art and sought Lewis's approbation: 'I keep trying to tell you that I want you to help me out of the clouds – if you don't want me, please let me go and I will try and be something else, I can't live in this half-way country any more . . . I think you ought to help me because I am such satisfactorily unpromising material raw material . . . just what a good Vorticist ought to like.'[9] She persisted in her commitment to Vorticism in the face of external and inner pressures to think less of herself and her art.

Dismorr also had a conflicted relationship with Lewis. At the time of the Omega Workshops imbroglio, she reassured him: 'I am really with you in spite of my apparent want of sympathy.'[10] In 1914 he condescendingly informed her: 'I enjoy talking to you very much, and admire, as you know, your gifts as an artist. I should therefore be sorry if anything unpleasant occurred to disturb the even tenor of our intercourse. But I also value Helen Saunders very highly, & I would avoid at all costs giving her cause of mortification.'[11] Lewis wanted to keep both women under control.

The two were persistent because they felt a strong kinship with the art of the Centre. When Saunders had exhibited a now lost painting at the 1912

Allied Artists' Association Salon, Fry had observed it showed 'a real feeling for planning the structure of a design and is excellent as its unambitious presentment of form goes'.[12]

Three sketches from 1913 – *Female Figures Imprisoned*, *The Rock Driller* and *Bending Figure* – display a wide range of experimentation. The trapped women in *Female Figures* depict how women are crushed by society, whereas the similarly attenuated *Rock Driller* obliquely suggests that groups like the suffragettes must ruthlessly demand their rights.[13] *Bending Figure*, which resembles Blake's *Newton*, depicts the confined status of women. For her part, Dismorr was struggling to move from representation to abstraction. She was sufficiently unsure of herself to apologize to Lewis. Women, for him, did not really fit into his definition of a rebel – they could be at the most associates, not true revolutionaries. The two women realized this but persisted: they 'displayed . . . a Vorticist feminism – which involved enlisting the semiotics and imaginative strategies of Vorticist masculinity, both in their art and public affiliations, to pursue professional advancement as "New Women artists"'.[14]

Up to 1913 there is considerable evidence of the responses of Roberts, Bomberg, Wadsworth, Gaudier and Lewis to the various forms of modernism that had travelled to England from the Continent. Their experimentation with a new style that can be labelled Vorticist is not surprising. The willingness of Saunders and Dismorr to explore Vorticist expression is less documented and has led to them being downgraded to a lower tier of accomplishment.[15]

On 15 June 1914, in a review of the Allied Artists' Association exhibition at Holland Park Hall, Gaudier mentioned that the stand taken by the Rebel Art Centre there displayed the 'most rigorous forms of decoration . . . fans, scarves, boxes and a table . . . The Omega showed objects of subtlety . . . with too much prettiness' in contrast to those of its rivals that displayed 'great strength and manliness'.[16]

Although Lewis was supposed to attend the Centre five days a week, he had few callers: a man who wanted to improve the design of gas-brackets and a lady pornographer who would only show her drawings to Lewis behind closed doors. William Roberts claimed that small objects such as painted match-box holders were made by Saunders and Dismorr from Lewis's designs.

Richard Cork has argued that such designs 'were deliberately intended to fit the cubist form of the box, whereas Omega decorations often seem

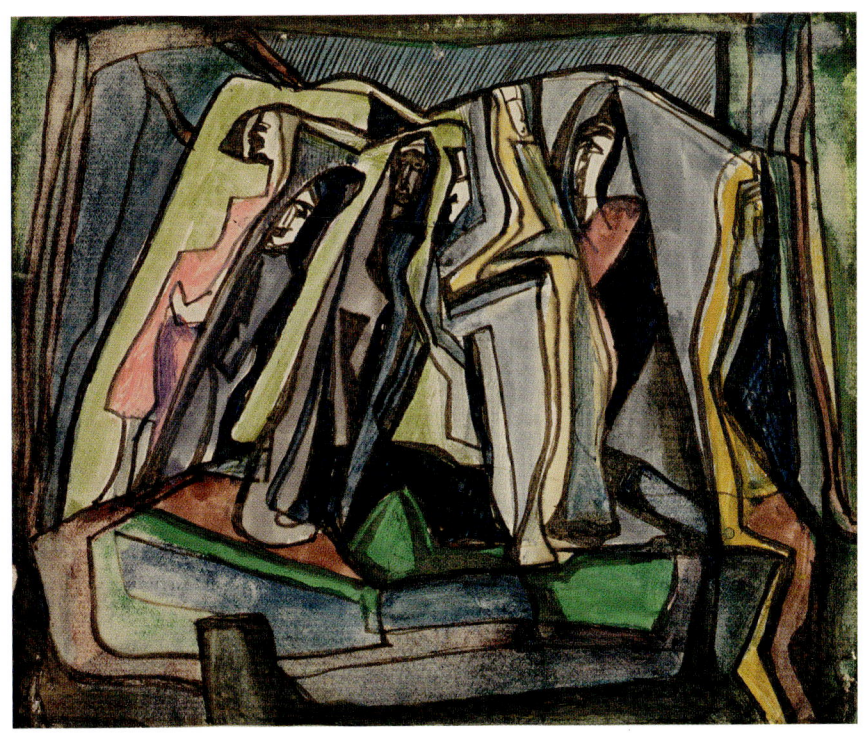

Helen Saunders, *Untitled ('Female Figures Imprisoned')*, c. 1913,
black ink, watercolour and bodycolour on paper.

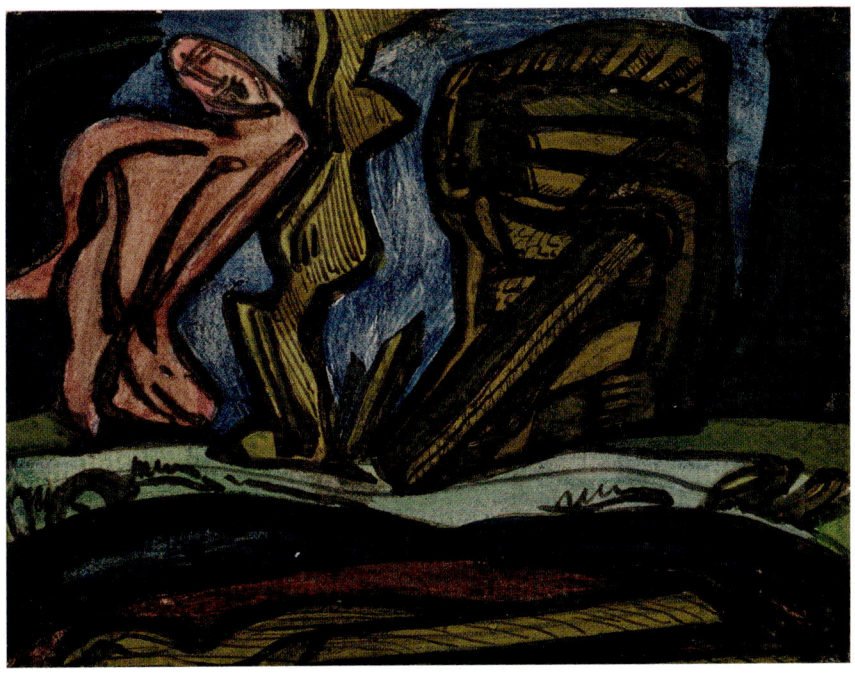

Helen Saunders, *Untitled ('The Rock Driller')*, c. 1913,
graphite, black ink and bodycolour on paper.

arbitrarily painted on surfaces without bearing the structure of the furniture in mind. The geometrical rigour displayed by Lewis therefore constitutes an implicit criticism of the work carried out in Fitzroy Square.'[17] This observation can be modified by keeping in mind the highly abstract designs for textiles carried out at the Omega by Bell, Grant, Etchells and Wadsworth. The Omega was never as out of touch with abstraction as Lewis boasted.

Lewis may have seen himself as the head of a group of like-minded artists, but his leadership skills were erratic at best. He did not think that an effective leader needed to establish strong bonds among his cohorts, although he once explained to Roberts that solidarity among artists was crucial: 'It is more difficult for an artist, working in isolation (a Painter of Abstracts, that is to say) to impress the public, than it would be if he were a member of a Group.'[18]

In this regard, in 1913 he had shown poor judgement when he attempted to exclude Bomberg from the Brighton City Art Gallery exhibition. In response, Bomberg, once bitten and twice shy, did not become a member of the Centre and (inaccurately) claimed that he never went near the place. Kate Lechmere recalled that Bomberg 'never came to our teas, and I can still see him, a timid, little thin man who looked starving, waiting for Lewis outside the Centre. He always refused to come in.'[19]

Since the nucleus of male artists at the Rebel Art Centre consisted only of Wadsworth, Hamilton, Gaudier and himself, Lewis attempted to recruit Roberts, who recalled: 'The fact that I was at the Omega . . . made him curious to meet me, for he too had worked there. One day he called on me . . . and borrowed a painting (*The Dancers*) and a drawing . . . to exhibit at the Rebel Art Centre . . . I visited the Rebel Art Centre only once and stayed about five minutes.'[20] Later in his career, Roberts resolutely insisted on labelling himself a Cubist and ingenuously disavowing his time as a Vorticist.

The look and atmosphere of the Omega Workshops and the Rebel Art Centre – in close proximity to each other – were worlds apart, but they possessed the same aims, as Lewis defined them in the 'Prospectus' for his Centre: both wanted to be places where 'metal-workers, craftsmen or painters can bring their work . . . and go on with it, if this atmosphere is congenial to them, without indifference or anything but the satisfaction of knowing that something is being done around them, and that an attempt is being made here to revive and sanify the art-instinct in this country'.[21]

Fry and Lewis were shadows of each other. Both were committed to energizing English art, but they possessed diametrically opposed definitions of what 'modern' was – and where it should head.

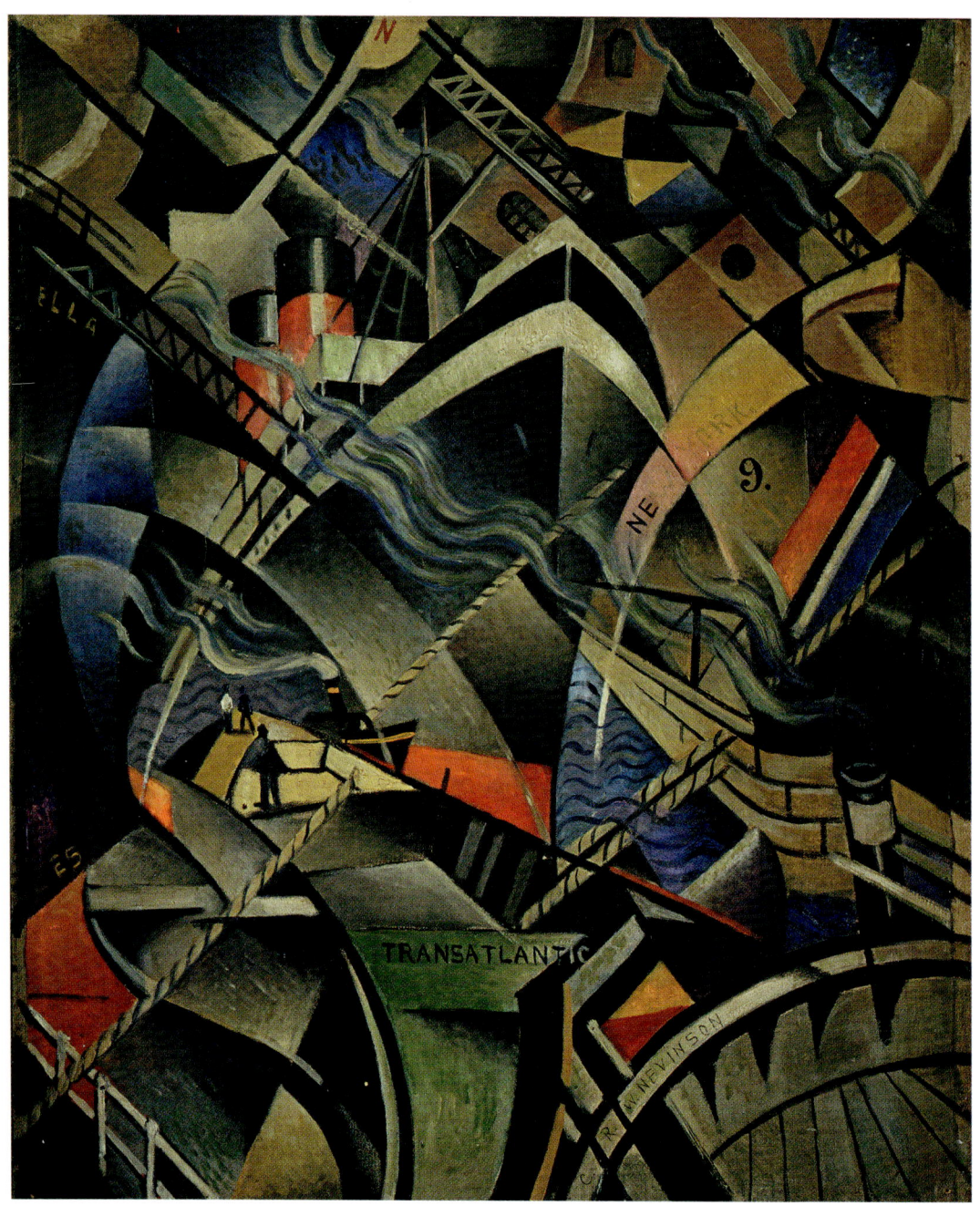

C.R.W. Nevinson, *The Arrival*, c. 1913, oil on canvas.

13

THE TURNCOAT

If the leader of a coterie wishes to retain control, he must be certain that he does not admit into his inner circle a person who might topple him. This was the mistake Lewis made with Christopher Nevinson. Outwardly, he was very much like Lewis – a profusely talented, self-assured braggart with a magnetic personality.[1] In his autobiography, Nevinson recollected: 'I found Lewis the most brilliant theorist I had ever met . . . He is essentially histrionic and enjoys playing a rôle.'[2] Those observations can easily be applied to the man who made them.

Nevinson was born on 31 August 1889 in Hampstead to a journalist father, Henry Nevinson, and his wife Margaret, a prominent suffragette. After he was expelled for bullying from Uppingham School, Rutland, in 1907, Nevinson returned to London, where he studied at St John's Wood School of Art for about a year before being admitted to the Slade. A natural rebel, he became an active member of the Coster Gang and keenly participated in its high jinks.

Impressed by Nevinson's precocity, Brown told him he could skip the antique and go straight to life class. Tonks was not unpleasant to Nevinson at their first encounter. When he asked Nevinson to define drawing, he seemed to agree with the answer. Nevertheless, Nevinson improbably claimed that this interaction shattered his self-confidence.

His academic path did not go well: he was crushed when Tonks advised him to abandon art. Unfazed, he did not follow this suggestion and exhibited with the Friday Club, the small exclusive society founded by Vanessa Bell that in 1911–12 was under the sway of Post-Impressionism.

Nevinson spent a frenetic winter in 1912–13 in Paris, where he attended the Atelier Julian and the Cercle Russe. He shared a studio with Modigliani and visited Gertrude Stein's salon and the studio of Pablo Picasso. During this heady time, he was confused: 'I was dissatisfied with representational painting, and already through Van Gogh I was using an outline simplifying form to accentuate my planes. Cubism was only one step farther, but it was long before Picasso began splitting up his forms into almost incomprehensible pieces. After all these years it is impossible to describe the worry, the doubts, which this form of technique gave rise to.'[3]

His troubles vanished when he became friends with Gino Severini, who, in turn, introduced him to Marinetti. Nevinson's early paintings had been quasi-Impressionistic but, inspired by the two Italians, he began injecting elements of Futurism into them. Quite soon, having become fully engaged with this style of painting, he realized he had discovered his métier. A canvas such as *The Arrival* (c. 1913), heavily influenced by Severini, demonstrates the remarkable adaptation Nevinson made to Futurism.

When he returned to England, he was somewhat at a loose end when Lewis, in the wake of the Omega brouhaha in October 1913, asked him to join his anti-Fry faction. Lewis told him Fry was a 'shark in aesthetic waters'.[4] Convinced that Marinetti and Lewis were of similar stripe, Nevinson quickly forged a bond with Lewis and, at the same time, took steps to invite Marinetti back to England. Nevinson was inspired by the notion that Futurism could effectively attack the 'malady of passé-ism . . . the intellectual curse'.[5]

Lewis was not a person who readily jumped on to the bandwagons of others, but, in this instance, he felt it prudent to welcome Marinetti to London that November, especially because Nevinson, his newest recruit, had become a rabid convert to Futurism. When he needed to be, Lewis could be a savvy politician.

On his return to London, Marinetti was invited to recite his verse at the Cave of the Golden Calf, Harold Munro's Poetry Bookshop, Clifford Inn Hall and Doré Galleries. Nevinson, Munro and Lewis were among those who organized a dinner in honour of the great man at the Florence Restaurant on 18 November. Marinetti 'recited a poem about the siege of Adrianople, with various kinds of onomatopoeic noises and crashes in free verse, while at the time a band downstairs played, "You made me love you. I didn't want to do it."' Marinetti then made a short speech in French followed by ones in French by Nevinson and Lewis. Nevinson saw that 'jealousy began to show its head' when the Italian, noticing that Nevinson was much more adept in French than Lewis, 'paid more attention to' him than to Lewis: Marinetti 'did not know, poor fellow, that he was wrecking a friendship that promised well'.[6]

In March 1914 Nevinson exhibited five works in the first London Group show. Among these was *The Arrival*. The reporter for *The Star* predicted that this ostentatious, riveting Futurist-inspired canvas would be the star turn of the entire exhibition. 'You detect funnels, smoke, gang-planks, distant hotels, numbers, posters, all thrown into the melting pot.' Nevinson told the reporter it showed 'a state of simultaneous mind'.[7] He had become an instant media star.

Nevinson – as well as Etchells, Gaudier, Roberts, Wadsworth and Saunders – was included at the Whitechapel Art Gallery's 'Twentieth Century Art: A Review of Modern Movements', which opened on 8 May 1914. This exhibition was unusual in several ways.

Whitechapel, where Bomberg had been born and which was home to predominantly Jewish immigrants, seemed to P. G. Konody in the *Daily Express* a strange location for an exhibition showing the 'progress of art', since although 'the new artists may differ from the older, they differ no less distinctly in aims and methods from one another.'[8] There were 465 entries divided into four groups, plus a Jewish section curated by Bomberg. The first group showed landscapes and metropolitan subjects influenced by Sickert and Lucien Pissarro, because they were 'a source of the new phase that are now prominent'; the second was dedicated to 'imposing decorative work' inspired by Puvis de Chavannes, Alphonse Legros and Augustus John; the work of the artists in the third group, which included Bell, Fry and Grant, had 'its origin [in] a feeling which had begun to appear . . . in the work of Cézanne, which did not develop in England until after 1910'. The fourth group, devoted to those who 'had abandoned representation almost entirely', included Wadsworth, Saunders and Lewis. In addition to the above groups, a large display from the Omega Workshops was included.[9]

The *Jewish Chronicle* characterized Bomberg's contribution as 'a Jewish section, which has been organized by Mr David Bomberg, a talented representative of the "Futurist" art that has aroused such fierce controversy among the critics'. Bomberg selected 54 works by, among others, Mark Gertler, Albert Rothenstein and Horace Brodsky. He also showed a drawing by Modigliani.

Bomberg gave pride of place to himself by devoting an entire wall to *Vision of Ezekiel* (p. 25), *Ju-Jitsu* (p. 70) and *In the Hold* (p. 70). In an interview published on 8 May in the *Chronicle*, Bomberg accepted the description of 'Futurist' with considerable reservation:

> It is easier for me to tell you what I think of Futurism than to explain for what it is that Futurist art stands, because the Futurist school is so largely destructive of its aims. Futurist art largely arose as a protest against the convention that all that is old, all that is antique, is the last word of art. It is a revolt against a worn-out tradition. The desire arose to create a new tradition. Where I part company from the leaders of the Futurist movement is in this wholesale condemnation of old art. Art must proceed from evolution. We must build our new art life of today upon the ruins of the dead art life of yesterday.[10]

Bomberg's own work was severely criticized by the *Chronicle* in a review signed 'L.K.' on 15 May: 'We certainly do not feel justified in praising work which . . . seems merely a waste of good pigment, canvas and wall space . . . we have no desire to be thought uncharitable, but if *In the Hold* is a work of art, we never wish to pen another criticism.'[11]

Lewis would have largely agreed with Bomberg's harsh evaluation of 'destructive' Futurism, especially when it gained even more traction at the time Marinetti returned to England for the third time in the spring of 1914, when the second Futurist exhibition was held from late April until May 1914. Nevinson even assisted Marinetti at one of his performances. Seated backstage, he replicated the sound of cannons – by pounding on a piece of wood with a hammer – while the master marched through the hall. Nevinson recollected: 'I made a great deal of noise and enjoyed myself.'[12]

Lewis was not pleased. Marinetti and Futurism were stealing *his* thunder. Moreover, he was alarmed by the increasing intimacy between Nevinson and Marinetti. One evening, he had an ugly confrontation with Marinetti, who asked him: 'Why don't you announce that you are a futurist?' 'Because I am not one,' was the reply. Lewis conceded that Futurism had 'its points. But you Wops insist too much on the Machine. You're always on those driving-belts, you are always exploding about internal combustion. We've had machines before in England for donkey's years. They're no novelty to *us*.' Marinetti pointed out that Lewis had no understanding of machines or the speed they could produce. Marinetti furthered his argument by suggesting that speed allowed one to see a thousand things rather than only one. Lewis rejoined that he did not wish to see a thousand things at once. 'I am not a futurist. I prefer *one* thing.' Marinetti insisted there was *never* one thing.[13]

This interaction prodded Marinetti and Nevinson to collaborate on *VITAL ENGLISH ART. A FUTURIST MANIFESTO*, which was published in *The Observer* on 7 June and later in *The Times* and the *Daily Mail*. It began: 'I am an Italian Futurist poet, and a passionate admirer of England. I wish to cure English Art of that most grave of all maladies – passé-ism. I have the right to speak plainly and without compromise, and together with my friend Nevinson, an English Futurist painter, to give the signal for battle.' The document, which did not reveal any passionate admiration for England, castigates a number of English institutions and traditions. It exclaims: 'FORWARD! HURRAH for motors! HURRAH for speed! . . . HURRAH for lightning!'

Although the tone of the manifesto is reminiscent of his round robin of the year before, Lewis would have been distraught by the entire document, but especially by its call 'To have an English art that is strong, virile and anti-sentimental'. Of course, that was exactly what Lewis was fighting for. He was in danger of being written out of the scenario by a showman he despised and a disciple he had nourished. To add to this bitter wound, the manifesto was signed – without their permission – by, among others, Bomberg, Hamilton, Roberts, Wadsworth and himself! Since Futurism was anti-woman, the names of Lechmere, Saunders and Dismorr were not listed as signatories.

On 12 June Lewis struck back. Realizing he could gain a strong tactical advantage, he mobilized his followers to disrupt a Futurist gathering that evening at the Doré Galleries. Gaudier, he gleefully recalled, 'went into action at once . . . He was sniping with him without intermission, standing up in his place all the while. The rest of our party maintained a confused uproar. The Italian was worsted.'[14] Nevinson fared even worse, as the *Evening News* reported: 'when Mr. Nevinson made a passionate outcry for motors, speed and lightning, a Vorticist set off some fireworks in the centre doorway.'[15] Well aware that Lewis or one of his crew was responsible for this intrusion, Nevinson took his seat.

Two days later, a letter from the Rebels appeared in *The Observer*: 'There are certain artists in England who do not belong to the Royal Academy nor to any of the passéist groups, and who do not on that account agree with the futurism of Signor Marinetti. An assumption of such agreement either by Signor Marinetti by his followers is an impertinence...We, the undersigned, whose ideals were mentioned or implied, beg to disassociate ourselves from' the Vital English Art declaration.[16] The letter, addressed from the Rebel Art Centre, was signed by Bomberg, Etchells, Hamilton, Roberts, Wadsworth and Lewis.[17]

Nevinson attempted to wiggle out of an unpleasant situation by telling Lewis he had not been aware of how much he loathed Futurism. But the die had been cast. On 13 June – the day before the Rebel Artists' condemnation of 'Vital English Art'– an ad appeared in *The Spectator* for a new periodical, *Blast*, 'the Manifesto of the Vorticists – The English Parallel Movement to Cubism and Expressionism [and] Death Blow to Impressionism and Futurism'. On the same day the advertisement appeared, the *Manchester Guardian* referred to 'the new Seceders from the Marinetti groups, Messrs. Wyndham Lewis, and Co., who now called themselves the Vorticists'.[18] Two days after the letter from the Rebel Art Centre castigating the Vital Art manifesto was published, Bomberg disassociated itself from that protest. He had not authorized Lewis to use his name. He was never a joiner but, stung by Lewis's behaviour, now kept himself as far away from him as possible.

Lewis and his followers had been indiscriminately labelled Cubists, or Futurists, or the Rebels. Previously, they had not minded. Now they had a name, but a major problem remained. What exactly did they stand for? How different were they from Cubists, Futurists or Expressionists? In what way exactly were they rebels?

14

'GREAT SILENT PLACE':
DEFINING VORTICISM

Cubism disrupts conventional notions of space and representation by employing multiple perspectives, introducing geometric shapes, and crowding and flattening elements in an image's foreground. Vorticism may be a form of Cubism, but Vorticism experimented even more boldly with colour, employed more angular shapes and distorted spatial perception more dramatically. In 1915, in the magazine *Drawing*, its writer made this observation: Vorticism 'is in reality our old and amusing friend Cubism, but Cubism heavily charged with electricity'.

For Lewis and his allies, Futurism was the real enemy. He could no longer permit his Rebel art to be confused with that movement. Vorticism did not exclude depicting 'speed' or 'simultaneity', but it never utilized them to the extent Futurism did. In addition, Futurist works of art are much more representational than their Vorticist counterparts. Whereas Vorticism moves easily into abstraction, Futurism does not.

Moreover, Vorticism was insistent on showing the 'one' – the still point of the vortex. The apparent paradox is that if the vortex is a mass of spiralling mixture of fluid and air caught in a whirlpool, it implies that movement should be depicted. Futurism attempted this. In contradistinction, it was Vorticism's agenda to *reveal the eye of the needle, the stationary moment amid chaos*. In Vorticist aesthetics, the 'one' is emphasized, although flux is often shown penetrating or attempting to penetrate 'stillness'. It stresses the opposing forces of flux and tranquillity. Although the vortex is often depicted as a sharply angled bolt of lightning, it is surrounded with forces that threaten its existence. Vorticist art may not accentuate movement, but it did focus on dramatic confrontations between opposing forces.

Futurist works in their renditions of speed almost always display their common ancestry – Vorticist ones frequently do not. Bomberg's *Vision of*

Ezekiel (1912) (p. 25) shares some affinities with Roberts's *The Return of Ulysses* (1913) (p. 17) in the ways in which abstract-like figures interact with each other. These paintings have little in common stylistically with Wadsworth's flirtation with Futurism in *Radiation* (p. 83) or Lewis's *Kermesse* (p. 50).

The spatial arrangements in Bomberg's *The Mud Bath* (1914) and Lewis's *Red Duet* (1914) may be similar, but Bomberg's blue and white forms reference bodies whereas in the Lewis – despite its title – the human presence is vaguely suggested by the interactions between two sets of geometrical forms: scarlet/mauve/crimson versus black/white/grey.

The two images may be abstract renditions of human forms, but they differ markedly in iconography. *The Mud Bath* originates in the 'Russian Vapour Baths' in Whitechapel, where there were no mud baths. Bomberg's title may derive from the notion that a mud bath could cleanse both body and spirit.[1] In *Red Duet*, there is a conflict between two forces – stolid reality in the darker passages versus creative vitality in the portions in the bright ones. In *Blast 2* in a piece titled 'BE THYSELF', Lewis proclaimed, 'You must be a duet in everything. For, the Individual, the single object, and the isolated is, you will admit, an absurdity. Why try and give the impression of a consistent and indivisible personality?'[2] Bomberg's image is concerned with reconciliation of body with soul whereas Lewis sees a permanent divide between them.

Ultimately, Bomberg's art stands apart from any attempt to label it. He was a Vorticist in the sense that he attempted to create his own unique approach to modernism at the same time as his colleagues. He never joined the group, and he remained deeply suspicious of its activities. In contrast, Lewis attempted to establish a visual paradigm for himself and his followers.

Compositions such as Lewis's *Workshop* (*c.* 1914–15) and Roberts's *Twostep II* (1915) display the closest to what could be called a Vorticist 'house' style. A contemporary critic offered this clue:

> They certainly fill their canvases with systems of interacting movement, the co-ordinations, and antagonisms of which are admirably stressed by a use of colour similar to that of any other capable designer. Their designs are now virtually rectilinear, the small sharp curve occasionally introduced as a kind of a knot being used not for purposes of transition, but rather to envenom the clash of opposing forces.[3]

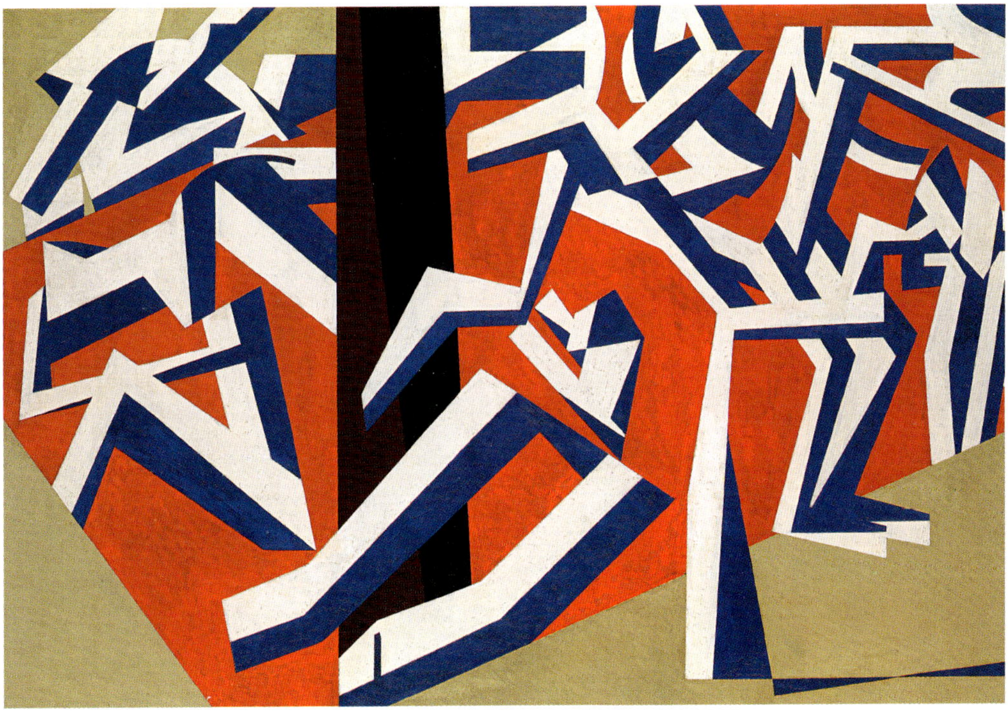

David Bomberg, *The Mud Bath*, 1914, oil on canvas.

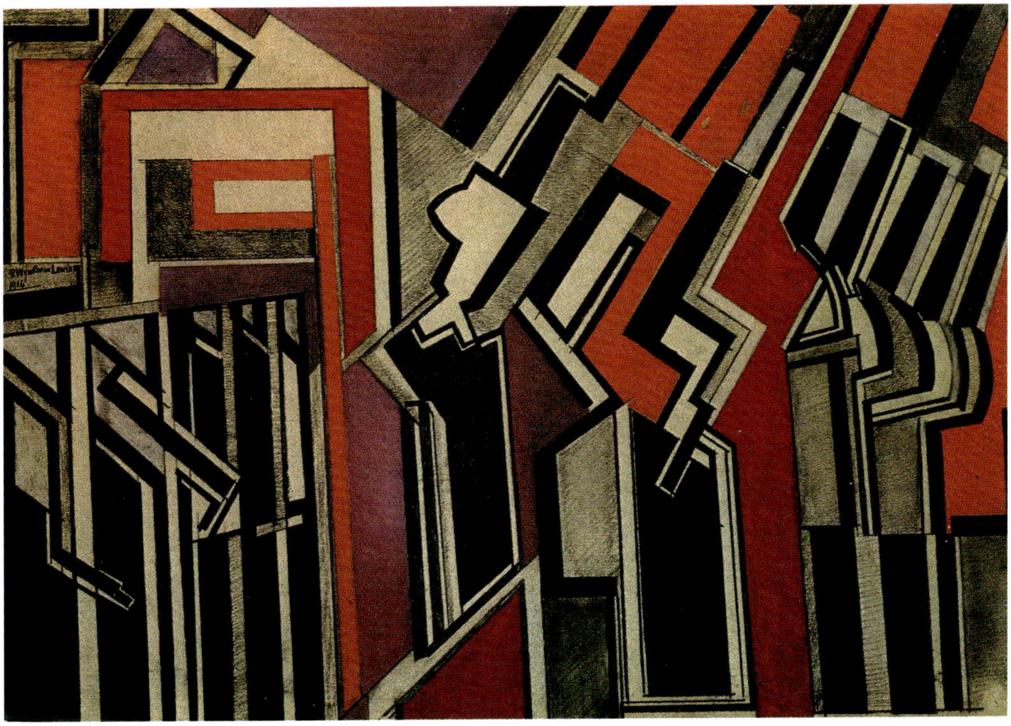

Wyndham Lewis, *Red Duet*, 1914, chalk and gouache on paper.

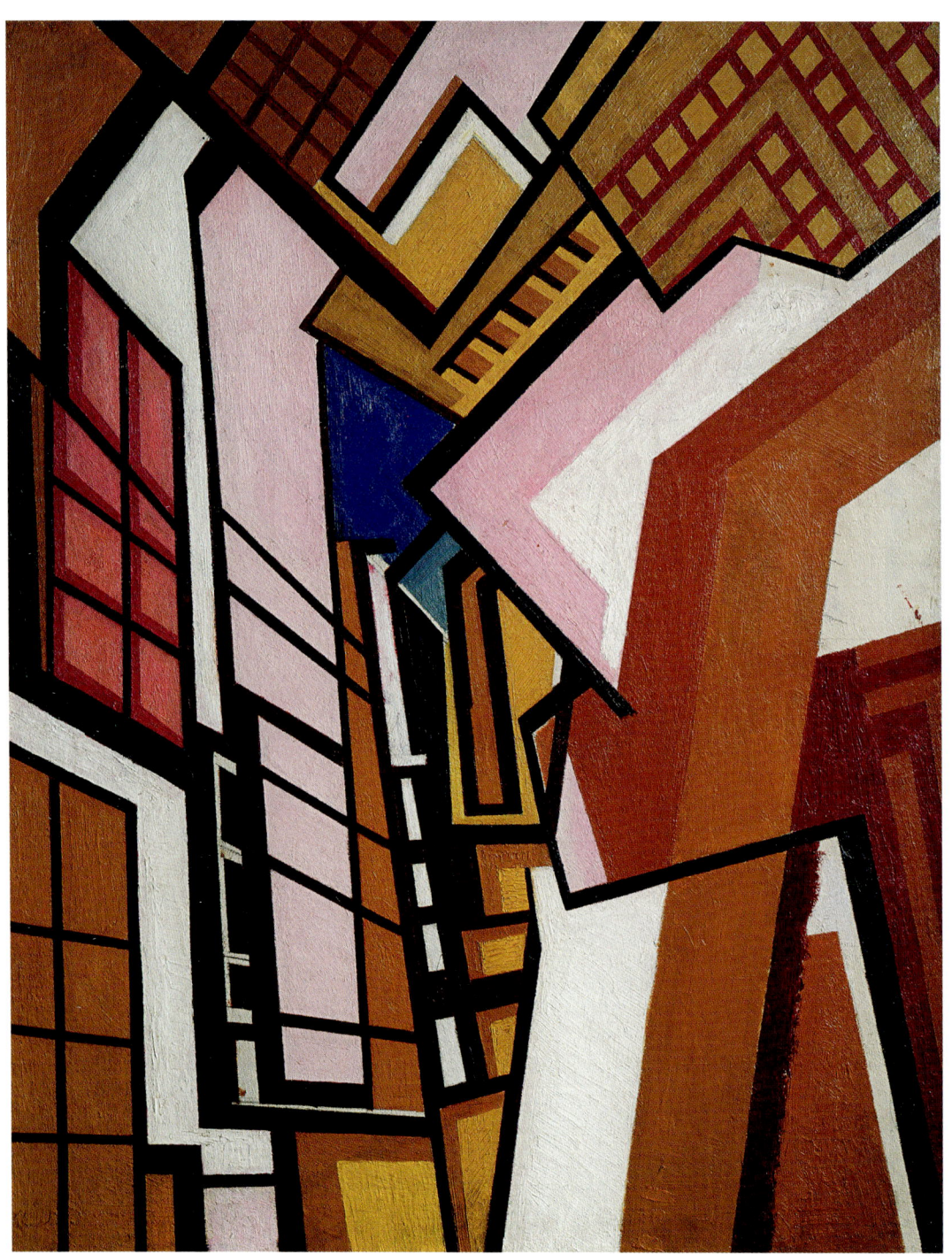

Wyndham Lewis, *Workshop*, *c.* 1914–15, oil on canvas.

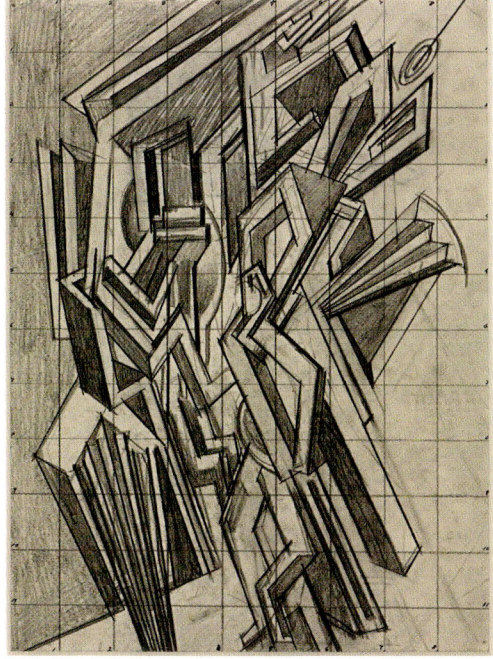

William Roberts, *Study for Twostep II*, 1915, graphite on paper.

In addition, the two images contain phallic shards.

Wadsworth's *Abstract Composition* (1915) and Helen Saunders's *Abstract Composition with Figure in Blue and Yellow* (*c*. 1915) are like those of Lewis and Roberts but their lines and colours are more delicate. The overall effect of both is not as aggressive as those by the other two. Wadsworth's Vorticist works were never as confrontational as those of his two male colleagues. Saunders skilfully introduced a softer, tranquil edge to her images and in the process subtly deconstructed the work of some of her male colleagues.

Dismorr also made images similar to her colleagues, as can be seen in *Design*, which she contributed to *Blast 2* (p. 146). However, this image emphasizes stillness and does not accentuate the conflict between the tranquil and the turbulent.

The sculptures of Gaudier do not look like the work of the other Rebels. But he followed Vorticist principles, as can be seen in his *Hieratic Head of Ezra Pound* (1914), in many ways a collaboration between subject and sculptor. Gaudier told the poet that it would not look like him: 'It will be the expression of certain emotions which I get from your character.'[4] In

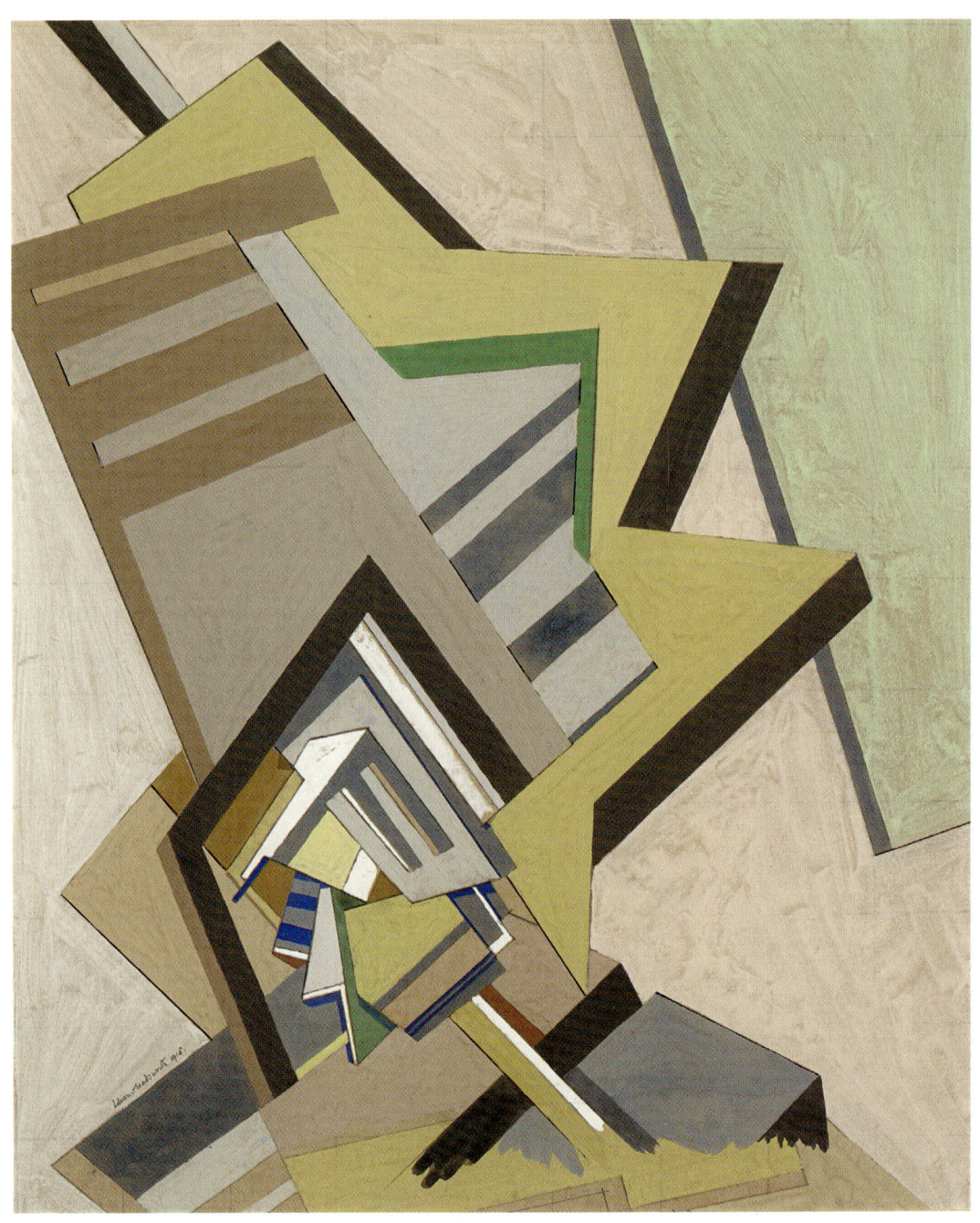

Edward Wadsworth, *Abstract Composition*, 1915, gouache, ink and graphite on paper.

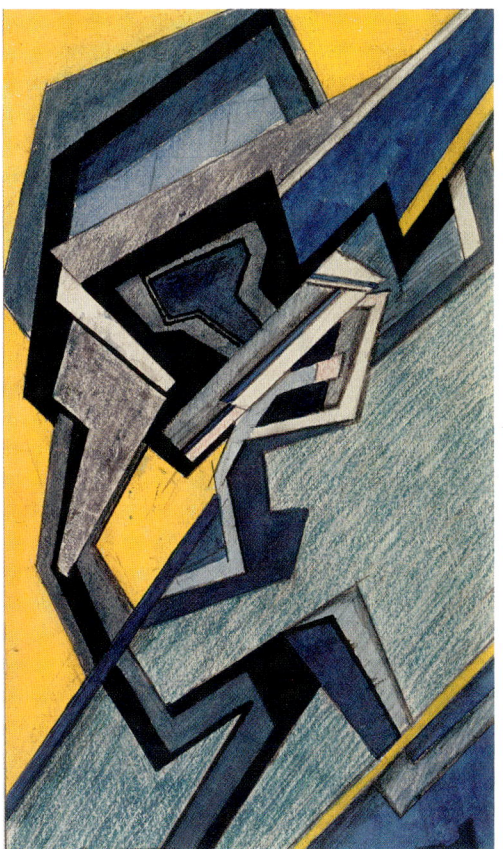

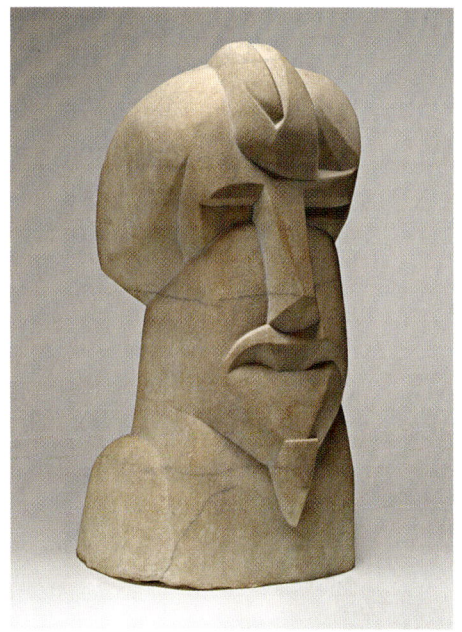

Henri Gaudier-Brzeska, *Hieratic Head
of Ezra Pound*, 1914, marble.

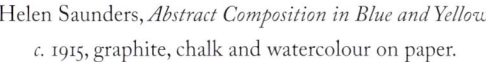

Helen Saunders, *Abstract Composition in Blue and Yellow*,
c. 1915, graphite, chalk and watercolour on paper.

that character, he discerned raw male sexual aggression. Gaudier also took inspiration from the Easter Island carved figure *Hoa-Haka-Nana-Ia* in the British Museum. Lewis approvingly and accurately described the result as 'Ezra in the form of a marble phallus'.[5] In that limited sense, the *Hieratic Head* can be labelled Vorticist.

Perhaps recognizing both the similarities and differences in Vorticist expression, Lewis searched for other ways to define the work of his circle. According to him, as argued above, Vorticism depicted moments in which tremendous forces of energy are channelled together in a single moment.

In this endeavour, he found an ally in Ezra Pound. When the two men met in 1909, Pound rubbed Lewis the wrong way: 'I was surprised to see an unmistakably "Nordic blond", with fierce blue eyes and a reddishly hirsute jaw, thrust out with a thoroughly Aryan determination . . . I took no further interest in this cowboy gangster.'[6]

Four years later, the two were drawn together by mutual self-interest. In the *Fortnightly Review* in September 1914, Pound stated: 'The image is not an idea. It is a radiant node or cluster; it is what I can . . . call a *Vortex*, from which . . . ideas are constantly rushing.' Pound also defined an image as 'that which presents an intellectual and emotional complex in an instant of time . . . It is the presentation of such a "complex" instantaneously which gives the sense of sudden liberation; that sense of freedom from time limits and space limits; that sense of sudden growth, which we experience in the presence of the greatest works of art.' He also emphasized that Imagism focused on direct treatment of the 'thing', and maintained that this type of poetry used 'absolutely no word that does not contribute to the presentation'.[7]

Pound, aware that Imagism could never easily venture into abstraction, provided a definition that he felt could be applied to both movements: 'FOR INDEED IT IS NOT ESSENTIAL THAT THE SUBJECT-MATTER SHOULD REPRESENT OR BE LIKE ANYTHING IN NATURE: ONLY IT MUST BE ALIVE WITH A RHYTHMIC VITALITY OF ITS OWN.'[8] Lewis's notion of 'silence' and 'concentration' are echoed in Pound's claim that instantaneity leads to 'sudden liberation'.

Pound's agenda was to link Vorticism to his literary movement, Imagism. His analogy was not a precise one. Imagist poetry uses word images to construct verse. Vorticism often has pictorial elements, but it moves away from images as such to the world of abstraction. Verse cannot easily move into abstraction, and so there is a divide between the two movements. What Pound admired about Vorticism was its insistence on capturing the silence and stillness in abstraction and he wanted to move verse as far as it could go in that direction.

When Lewis found some common ground with Pound, he was able to link Imagism with Vorticism and to gain a fuller understanding of why the image did not need to represent anything in nature. The connection between Imagism and Vorticism became an essential building block for Lewis in repudiating Futurism. This is exactly what he would do in *Blast 1*.

15

THE FIRST EXPLOSION:
BLAST 1

As the writer and journalist Douglas Goldring recalled: '*Blast* was designed to be totally unlike any previous publication and layout,' and Lewis 'required a printer humble enough blindly to carry out his instructions'.[1] Leveridge & Co. in Harlesden agreed to follow Lewis's directives closely. The other firms he had approached refused to have anything to do with his project. Ironically, despite Lewis's wish that *Blast 1* look markedly different from any other publication, it bears a close resemblance to Marinetti's *Zang Tumb Tuum*, which was also published in 1914. The puce cover is reminiscent of Ardongo Soffici's cover for *I Manifesti del Futurismo*, published the same year.

Blast 1 was dated 20 June 1914 but published on 2 July. As mentioned above, the first uses of the term 'Vorticist' in print were in *The Spectator* and *Manchester Guardian* on 13 June 1914. The term does not appear in *Blast 1*: on page 143 Lewis wrote: 'We may hope before long to find a new word.'[2]

Blast, calculated to startle its readers, employed a variety of ways to accomplish that objective: the cover with BLAST emblazoned on it, the mixing of text and reproductions, the use throughout of various sized typefaces – and, especially, the dramatic BLESS and BLAST proclamations arranged so that the resulting layout and typography replicate the emotional energy released to make those pronouncements.

Lewis's division of those two groups is based upon his demarcation between those who passively accept the status quo and are therefore blasted (socialists, mystics, pacifists, conservative politicians) and those who are blessed because they challenge society's norms (the valiant, the militant, progressive critics). Boxers, aviators, music-hall performers and suffragettes are also among the blessed.

Blast 1 assaulted its readers in other ways. 'The Great Preliminary Vortex', the 'Manifesto', the three narratives (two short stories and a closet drama) and all the other components repeat the same mantra in a variety of ways. In keeping with Lewis's showman personality, the reader is battered into submission. Put another way, a wide variety of methods are employed to raise the consciousness of the reader. The message is consistent. The 'WE' in 'Long Live the Vortex!' insists 'WE ONLY WANT THE WORLD TO LIVE, and to feel its crude energy flowing through us.' The document was signed by Richard Aldington, Malcolm Arbuthnot, Lawrence Atkinson, Gaudier, Dismorr, Cuthbert Hamilton, Pound, Roberts, Saunders (spelled Sanders), Wadsworth and Lewis.[3]

The text of *Blast 1* defined what Vorticist art was by appealing to the emotions. It did not contain a precise definition of what Vorticist art was but interleaved the text with reproductions that display it. Many of the works reproduced were selected to present a homogenous representation of Vorticist style: the works of Lewis and Cuthbert Hamilton are so similar that they could be by the same hand.[4] Gaudier's *The Stags* may not resemble the above works, but his 'Vortex' proclamation specifically applied Vorticism to sculpture. The only radical departure in the illustrations are the two reproducing the work of Spencer Gore, who died in 1914 at the age of 45. In a tender moment, Lewis laments an artist whose last work contained 'with the accentuation of spiritual qualities, a new and suave simplicity'.[5]

In the short play *Enemy of the Stars*, Arghol represents an artist – very much like Lewis – whose integrity is challenged by the villainous Hanp, his shadow twin. Argol's impulses are damaged beyond repair. 'Each time the instinct to merge overwhelms the instinct to give form, each time habit overtakes consciousness, each time empathy supplants intellect in the human psyche,' Arghol comes closer to death but, in the end, is murdered by Hanp.

In this text, 'merge', 'habit' and 'empathy' are part of the old dispensation whereas 'form', 'consciousness' and 'intellect' are symbolic of a new age. Arghol finds himself entangled in the past because his instincts are irrevocably 'damaged'. He is destroyed because his human predispositions do not allow him to reject the past. Lewis's 'Blessed' are those who connect with the future whereas the 'Damned' cannot or refuse to do so. *Enemy of the Stars*

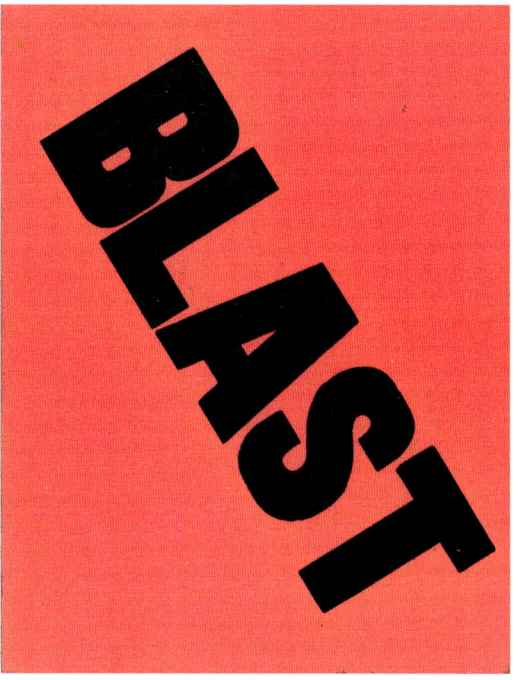

Blast 1, 1914, cover.

No. 1.   June 20th, 1914.

BLAST

Edited by WYNDHAM LEWIS.

REVIEW OF THE GREAT ENGLISH VORTEX.

2/6 Published Quarterly.

10/6 Yearly Subscription.

London :
JOHN LANE,
The Bodley Head.
New York : John Lane Company.
Toronto : Bell & Cockburn.

Blast 1, 1914, title page.

BLAST First (from politeness) ENGLAND

CURSE ITS CLIMATE FOR ITS SINS AND INFECTIONS

DISMAL SYMBOL, SET round our bodies,
of effeminate lout within.

VICTORIAN VAMPIRE, the LONDON cloud sucks
the TOWN'S heart.

A 1000 MILE LONG, 2 KILOMETER Deep

BODY OF WATER even, is pushed against us
from the Floridas, TO MAKE US MILD.

OFFICIOUS MOUNTAINS keep back DRASTIC WINDS

SO MUCH VAST MACHINERY TO PRODUCE

THE CURATE of "Eltham"
BRITANNIC ÆSTHETE
WILD NATURE CRANK
DOMESTICATED
POLICEMAN
LONDON COLISEUM
SOCIALIST-PLAYWRIGHT
DALY'S MUSICAL COMEDY
GAIETY CHORUS GIRL
TONKS

11

Blast 1, 1914, p. 11.

CURSE 3

WITH EXPLETIVE OF WHIRLWIND

THE BRITANNIC ÆSTHETE

CREAM OF THE SNOBBISH EARTH
ROSE OF SHARON OF GOD-PRIG
OF SIMIAN VANITY
SNEAK AND SWOT OF THE SCHOOL-ROOM

IMBERB (or Berbed when in Belsize)-PEDANT

PRACTICAL JOKER
DANDY
CURATE

BLAST all products of phlegmatic cold
Life of LOOKER-ON.

CURSE

SNOBBERY
(disease of femininity)
FEAR OF RIDICULE
(arch vice of inactive, sleepy)
PLAY
STYLISM
SINS AND PLAGUES
of this LYMPHATIC finished
(we admit in every sense
finished)
VEGETABLE HUMANITY.

15

Blast 1, 1914, p. 15.

presents its readers with a choice: do you remain immured in the past or do you seize the opportunity to be transformed?

The two pieces of fiction compliment Lewis's radical piece of theatre. In 'The Saddest Story' by Ford Madox Ford, John does not see unwholesome truths before his eyes. He is the quintessential unreliable narrator, a man who refuses to deal with reality. A similar claim can be made about George Silverton, the husband in 'Indissoluble Matrimony' by Rebecca West, a vociferous spokeswoman for feminist and socialist causes. West's description of Silverton's consciousness is chilling. In this passage, he fantasizes he has murdered his wife.

> Once more hatred marched through his soul like a king: compelling service by his godhead and, like all gods, a little hatred for his harsh lieu on his worshipper. He saw his wife as the curtain of flesh between him and celibacy, and solitude and all those delicate abstentions from life which his soul desired. He saw her as the invisible worm destroying the rose of the world with her dark secret love. Now he knelt on the lowest stone step watching her wet seal-smooth head bobbing nearer on the waters. As her strong arms, covered with dark little points where her thick hairs were clotted with moisture, stretched out towards safety he bent forward and laid his hands on her head. He held her face under water. Scornfully he noticed the bubbles that rose to the surface from her protesting mouth and nostrils, and the foam raised by her arms and her thick ankles. To the end the creature in turmoil, in movement, in action . . .
>
> She dropped like a stone.[6]

Lewis is often characterized correctly as misogynistic. However, *Blast 1* contained mitigating elements. West's story depicts how men despise and misunderstand women and how society has in the process become stagnated. In 'To the Suffragettes', Lewis suggested some agreement with that movement but warned its members: 'stick to what you understand . . . leave works of art alone.'

Kate Lechmere characterized Saunders and Dismorr, both of whom signed the *Blast* manifesto, as 'terribly proper women who both came up to me at the *Blast* tea party when my name was added to the "Bless" list and said, very huffily, that "some people need blessing".[7] Years later, Saunders recalled, 'Lewis *was* to all intents and purposes *Blast* and carried the rest of the team with him, some from conviction and some no doubt for their own purposes of advertisement.' In *The Egoist* of 15 June, Gaudier characterized the art of both women as displaying a 'revolutionary spirit' but couched his praise in a condescending manner: they 'are well worth encouraging in their endeavours towards the light'.[8]

Wadsworth, who had learned German as a student, in a 'Review' entitled 'Inner Necessity', translated extracts from Kandinsky's *Über das Geistige in der Kunst* (Concerning the Spiritual in Art). The translator offered some introductory remarks: 'European artists of the past have treated art almost entirely from a too obviously and externally human outlook. Europe to-day, which is laying the solid foundations of the Western Art of to-morrow, approaches this task from the deeper and more spiritual standpoint of the soul.[9] For Wadsworth, Kandinsky was the apostle of this new sensibility.

A passage by Kandinsky such as this strongly appealed to Wadsworth: 'the more the artist uses . . . abstract form or abstracted form, the more he becomes at home in their kingdom, and the deeper he enters this sphere. And in the same way the spectator, who gathers more and more of the abstract speech until he finally masters it, is guided in this by the artist.'[10]

Kandinsky suggested that abstract form can take two paths: 'Either the form serves as a shape, and by means of this shape, to cut out a material object on the surface . . . or 2. The form remains abstract: i.e., it represents no real object, but is a perfect abstract entity.'[11]

Wadsworth then proposed 'that the artist can employ any forms (natural, abstracted or abstract) to express himself, if his feelings demand it'. Based on 'his feelings, the only aesthetic impulse means logically that the artist is not only entitled to treat form and colour according to his inner dictates, but that it is his duty to do so.'[12]

Here Wadsworth emphasized a key point in Vorticist aesthetics about abstract form: it can display a 'material object on the surface' or 'it represents no real object'. His *Cape of Good Hope* (p. 83) follows the first option in depicting the ground from an aerial perspective – it shows material objects in a highly abstracted way.

In conclusion to his translation, Wadsworth offered a moving account that can be read as autobiographical: 'The insistence on the value of one's feelings is the only aesthetic impulse . . . [the life of the artist] becomes the raw material out of which he carves his creations.'[13] Wadsworth's distinction between two kinds of abstract form is an important contribution to Vorticist aesthetics. Moreover, his adherence to the Russian painter's conception of abstract art demonstrates how markedly he differed from Lewis's more volatile and angrier defence of abstraction.

The writer Edward Crankshaw once observed that Wadsworth, like Kandinsky, practised 'an art where form and emotional content are part and parcel of each other; the emotion . . . is pinned down in the form'.[14]

The mix of text and illustration in *Blast* is deliberately reminiscent of Blake's *The Marriage of Heaven and Hell*, and the *Blast/Blessed* dichotomy is based on the 'Proverbs of Hell' from that text. In those adages Blake created a series of paradoxical statements that go against orthodoxy. For instance, rather than seeing pride as a moral flaw, Blake praised the pride of the peacock. In a similar way, Lewis attempted to overthrow conformity by demonstrating its inherently misguided thinking. As a battle manual, *Blast 1* was a bravura performance.

Not unexpectedly, the publication was reviled. One of the unkindest cuts was in a letter Nevinson wrote to *The Observer:* 'it would be a pity to have the two movements confused, especially as it is so entertaining to watch ex-Futurist professors performing intellectual contortions "within the stationary centre of a whirlpool!" that the strong and swift-flowing stream of Futurism was bound to cause and has left behind.'[15] A writer in the *New York Times* issued this invective:

What is Vorticism? Well, like Futurism, and Imagism, and Cubism, essentially it is nonsense. But it is more important than these other fantastic, artistic, and literary movements because it is their sure conclusion. It is important not because it is the latest, but because it is the last phase of the ridiculous rebellion which has given the world Duchamp's 'Portrait of a Nude Descending the Stairs' and the writings of Gertrude Stein. It is the reductio ad absurdum of mad modernity.[16]

Lewis seized the moment to fete the successful publication of the magazine by holding a dinner at the Dieudonné Restaurant on Ryder Street in London on 15 July. Gaudier, who could not afford the ten-shilling admission ticket, gave a small carving of a fawn as his contribution. When one befuddled guest announced he could not make head or tail of *Blast 1*, Lewis declaimed: 'you have insulted Miss Lechmere, who paid for the magazine and is present here tonight with fifty copies piled up underneath her chair!'[17]

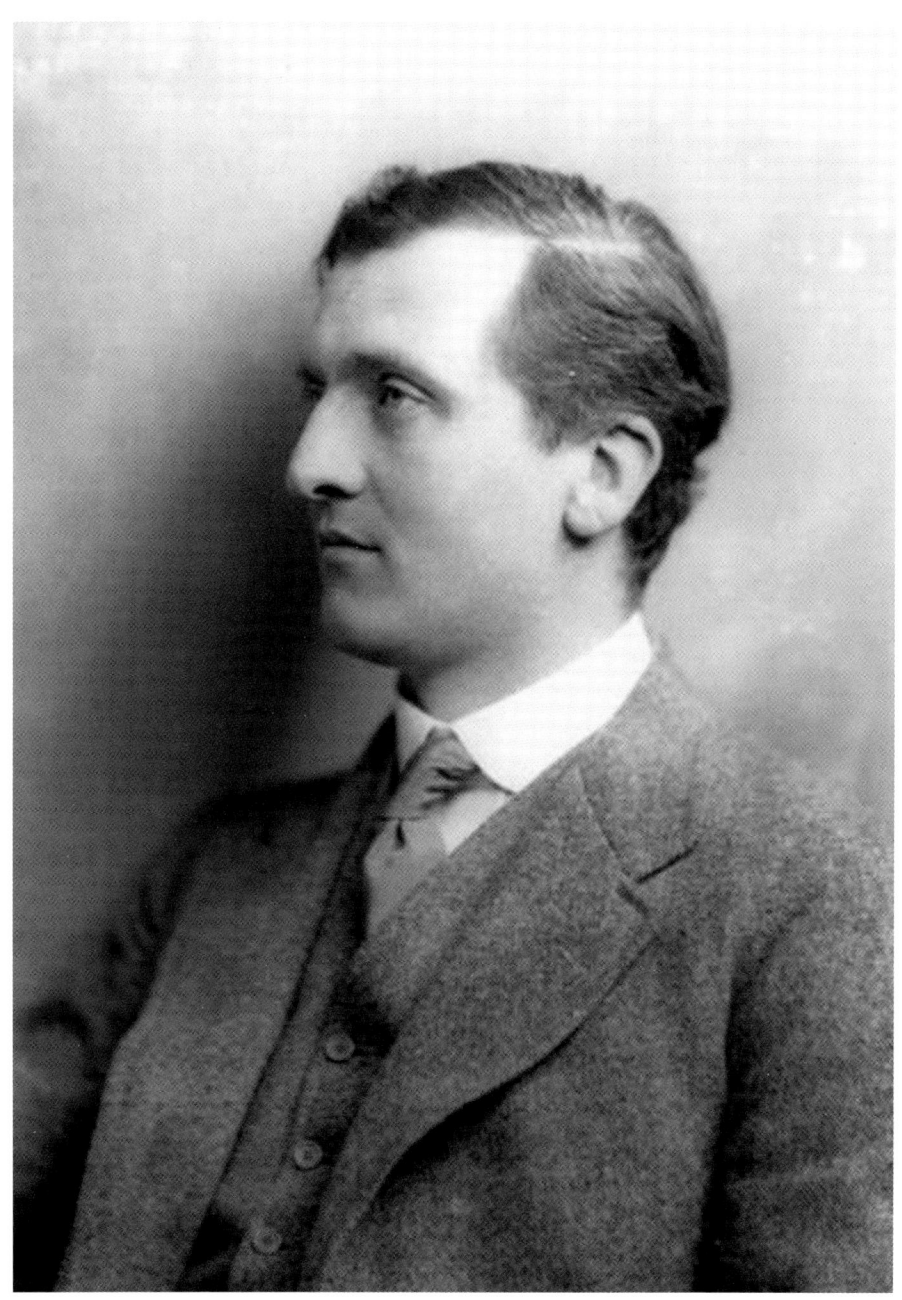

T. E. Hulme, *c.* 1915.

16

THE THEORIST:

T. E. HULME

In *Blast*, Lewis attacked romanticism, sentimentality and humanism. That position had emerged slowly. He had attended lectures by Henri Bergson at the Collège de France in which the French philosopher claimed that intuition – not logic – was the basis for understanding reality. He also maintained that all material objects were in a continuous state of flux. This hypothesis is one on which Marinetti based his creation of Futurism and to which Lewis fiercely objected. On these grounds, Bergson became one of the 'blasted'.

In defining a Vorticist aesthetic Lewis found assistance from a former admirer of Bergson, T. E. Hulme, who possessed, as everyone who met him agreed, a larger-than-life personality. He was born on 16 September 1883 in Endon, Staffordshire, to Thomas Hulme, a gentleman farmer, and his wife Mary. He attended Newcastle School for Boys and was admitted in 1902 to read mathematics at St John's College, Cambridge, where he became celebrated for rebellious behaviour that led to his being sent down in 1904. The mock funeral that his friends staged to commemorate his 'passing' got so out of hand that it was noted in *The Tatler*.

Hulme enrolled at University College, London, but left in 1906 without taking a degree. After spending several months in Canada, upon his return he joined a poet's group, where he advocated 'impressionistic' verse. That stylistic inclination was abandoned in 1909 when he took up with Ezra Pound and T. S. Flint, who were attempting to create a new, more precise kind of poetry – Imagism.

At about this time, Hulme became fascinated with Bergson but abandoned that interest when he became convinced that the French philosopher's belief system was nothing more than a disguised form of romanticism. In contrast, Hulme saw himself as someone who believed that man was by nature corrupt. T. S. Eliot, an admirer, described Hulme 'as classical, reactionary, and revolutionary; he is the antipodes of the eclectic, tolerant, and democratic mind.'[1]

Any flirtation on Hulme's part with romanticism was thoroughly dispelled when, in the winter of 1912–13, he heard Wilhelm Worringer lecture in Berlin. The German art historian's theories are contained in his 1906 doctoral dissertation, *Abstraktion und Einfühlung*, where he made a distinction between empathetic and abstract art. Empathetic art arose from an 'imitation impulse' and found expression in Greco-Roman sculpture and Renaissance art. In contrast, abstract art had no relation to everyday experience, used non-representational forms and was highly stylized and often geometrical.

In lectures and essays, Hulme applied Worringer's hypothesis to the work of the Vorticists. Since the Vortex exists in a liminal space, it cannot be rendered in representational art. When the 'imitation impulse' is put aside in abstract art, it allows – paradoxically, he felt – deeply personal statements to emerge.

Before, as Bomberg recalled, Fry and Bell 'had not the remotest idea what we were doing. Hulme had and wrote about it and in this way, he became the spokesman for the innovators.' But he remained a spokesman or interpreter, as Bomberg also pointed out: 'There is no evidence of [his] having any influence on visual art or artists.'[2]

This is a crucial point. Hulme offered a way of understanding Vorticism, but he did not shape Vorticism. Bomberg argued – correctly – that an artist such as himself worked from intuition and instinct. For instance, Hulme rejected the Futurist argument that art should create structures that are organized like that of machinery. And yet Hulme recognized that Vorticism's use of 'mechanical lines' reflected that a new order was coming into being. He envisioned an art 'where everything tends to be angular, where curves tend to be geometrical, where the presentation of the human body . . . is often non-vital and distorted to fit into stiff lines and cubical shapes'. The resulting art 'exhibits no delight in nature and no striving after vitality'.[3] The kind of sentiment voiced by Hulme is echoed in the belief systems of some of his contemporaries, such as John Middleton Murry, who, in the first issue of *Rhythm*, called for an art 'that strikes deeper, that touches a profounder reality . . . Before art can be human, it must learn to be brutal.'[4]

Machines had become a 'brutal' fact of life. Vorticism recognized this and populated its imagery accordingly. Their art had to be abstract and use strict demarcations, rigidity and precise outlines.

When he reviewed the first London Group exhibition, Hulme labelled the work of Fry and his circle as 'faked stuff'. He was very cautious in balancing praise and blame in considering Lewis's work: 'In Mr. Lewis's work there are always certain qualities of dash and decision . . . His imagination being quick and never fumbling, very interesting relations are generated . . . but the whole sometimes lacks cohesion and unity.'[5]

Although Hulme praised Wadsworth's and Etchells's submissions, he was lavish in extolling Bomberg's *In the Hold* (p. 70), which some critics considered to be no more than linoleum designs. Bomberg, Hulme argued, rejected the traditional approach to looking at a painting. In most canvases, 'one never sees it as a whole, one's eyes travel over it'; Bomberg, he argued, rejected such an approach as a 'non-aesthetic emotion'.[6]

There is a coda to the first London Group exhibition. At the hanging, Bomberg secured an excellent viewing position for *In the Hold* only to discover at the private view that Lewis had moved the picture to a less prominent position and substituted one of his own. When Bomberg confronted him about this second nasty trick, Lewis beat a hasty retreat.

There was another noteworthy twist. Fry, who had good reason to despise Lewis, attempted to be objective when he reviewed his rival's five entries: He 'is by nature highly gifted, and, by training, highly accomplished so that whatever he does has a certain facility and completeness . . . in front of his abstract designs one has to admit to their close consistency, the clear and definite organizing power that lies behind them.'[7]

Despite Hulme's criticisms, the relationship between Lewis and Hulme might have remained on an even keel if Hulme's strong sex drive had not intervened. The good-natured but truculent Hulme was an exhibitionist and a braggart. He was readmitted to Cambridge in the spring of 1912 – owing in part to a letter from Bergson – but he escaped to Germany that summer to avoid prosecution by an enraged don whose sixteen-year-old daughter had received sexually explicit letters from Hulme while she was at school at Roedean. It was during this sojourn that he heard Worringer speak.

David Garnett remembered Hulme pulling out his watch when he was with a group of friends. 'I have a pressing engagement in five minutes,' he said, and excused himself. 'Twenty minutes later he would return, wipe his brow, and complain that the steel staircase of the emergency exit at Piccadilly Circus Train Station was the most uncomfortable place in which he had ever copulated.'[8]

In 1911 Hulme had tried to settle down to a semblance of ordinary domestic life with Ethel Kibblewhite. She was ten years older than Hulme, had trained at the Slade, and when she encountered Hulme she had walked out of her marriage to a violent and abusive husband. After her separation, she worked as a designer at the Royal School of Needlework and lived at her parents' home at 67 Frith Street on the corner of Soho Square, where she held a salon on Tuesday evenings.

Frith Street became Hulme's base. Although he never lived there, a large room was set aside for him. He enjoyed playing the role of *pater familias* and took special delight in his adopted daughters. Hulme may have been devoted to his mistress, but he retained a roving eye. And that eye would be responsible for his break with Lewis.

17

JULY 1914

June 1914 had been a good month for Lewis. He and Wadsworth had defined Vorticism in *Blast 1*. Pound had linked Vorticism to Imagism. Hulme had established further guidelines. In contrast, July 1914 was disastrous. The Rebel Art Centre closed four months after it had opened, and his rival David Bomberg was given a major exhibition – over fifty works – at the Chenil Gallery.

Trouble began when Kate Lechmere was supposed to be away on a luncheon date when Lewis brought Hulme to the Centre. She had no idea who the stranger was but learned from a friend that he was a 'real philosopher' whom they might chance upon at his favourite restaurant. Hulme asked her to dine with him at a future date.

'What I did not realise', Lechmere recalled, 'was that Lewis had an actual fear that he might be supplanted by another at the Rebel Art Centre.'[1] He fantasized that Hulme was grooming the sculptor Jacob Epstein to stage a coup. To protect himself from such an eventuality, he insisted that the Centre be made into a limited company.

Lewis became so distraught by a possible liaison between Lechmere and Hulme that he swore he was going to kill him. When he encountered the philosopher in Piccadilly, he accosted him and cried out, 'What are you doing to me?' Nonchalantly, Hulme picked up Lewis and planted him down on some railings.

When 'Poor Lewis quite lost his head and … accused [her] of this Hulme attachment,' Lechmere replied that Hulme had recently shown little interest in her. During her friendship with the philosopher, Lewis continually 'made himself most unpleasant. Some mornings he would arrive in a very excitable state and rapidly pace up and down the Studio calling me a "bloody bitch."

This hurt and shocked me at first – [but] as the "bloody bitch" was so often repeated I took it quite calmly which only irritated Lewis the more.'

> By now my very small bit of capital was running out. No effort
> had been made by Lewis to get art students or members. After
> all the vitality and enthusiasm we had for the Rebel Art Centre it
> now seemed to go sour and to be arriving at nothing. I told Lewis
> he and his friends must carry on without me and that I could not
> pay the next quarter's rent. Some days later I went out in the after-
> noon and on returning found the Studio in confusion and denuded
> of most of its contents. So ended the Rebel Art Centre and the
> Vorticists retired to some garret.[2]

What Lechmere did not state was whether Lewis's behaviour influenced her resolve to discontinue her support for the Centre.[3]

That resolve would have been strengthened because, despite what she led Lewis to believe, her relationship with Hulme blossomed into a full-blown affair. For a while, Lechmere and Kibblewhite were Hulme's mistresses, but he eventually became engaged to Lechmere.

Lechmere had characterized Saunders and Dismorr as obsessed with Lewis, but her own conduct belies those observations. Hulme informed his new lover that a woman's place was in the home and in finding contentment in motherhood. Women, he informed her, 'cannot enter the pure realm of reason'. She felt that 'anyone, man or woman, would flounder badly on first acquaintance with him.'[4] When they had disagreements, he would thrust a knuckle-duster into her buttocks. Such devices are metal pieces designed to be worn at the back of a person's hand as a weapon. (The one Hulme used was designed for him by Gaudier.)[5] For Hulme, a knuckle-duster or K.D. was a substitute penis. In such instances, she would encourage him to kiss her. She once confessed to a writer: 'It is rather difficult for me to tell you much that can be published about Hulme. Our relationship was so completely as that of man and woman and I had his love.'[6] They called each other K.D. and signed their letters thus.

Lewis, the would-be leader of the Vorticists, obviously did not like it when the art of his comrades garnered more publicity than his. Such exclusion, for him, was anathema, especially when it was Bomberg who received much coveted media exposure – his show at Chenil being a case in point. That gallery employed an advertising stunt to gain attention: the enormous *Mud Bath* (p. 109) was 'hung', the catalogue proudly stated, 'outside the gallery so that it may have every advantage of lighting and space'. The *Daily Chronicle* lamented: 'art is love, we used to say, and art should be reticent . . . But some of the new spirits seem to be inspired by the idea that art is hate and must be aided by advertisement.'[7] The horses drawing the [Number] 29 buses, 'startled by the painting, shied away from it as they rounded the corner' approaching the canvas.[8]

Reviewing the exhibition in the *New Age*, Hulme, Lewis's new arch-enemy, praised Bomberg for eschewing the Rebel Art Centre. Specifically, Bomberg had a 'sense of form that seems to have been always excellent'.[9] Of all the Vorticists, Bomberg's art was the most different from Lewis's and, so by implication, his work was being put down.

Although Bomberg received acclamation by Hulme, the general critical consensus was not positive. The reviewer in the *Pall Mall Gazette* was scathing:

> his paintings suggest he has energy without patience; a great self-confidence without the power of expressing it . . . Had Mr Bomberg allowed his art to develop in close study of natural forms he might have been longer in attracting attention, but his artistry would have gained. One may remind Mr Bomberg that it is a pure artistry alone, and not any theoretical juggling with shapes, that is the constant element in a work of art.[10]

Not all exhibitions succeeded in elevating the status of an artist, but in this case, Hulme had, at least, understood what Bomberg was trying to accomplish.

Lewis would have been further displeased by Hulme's advocacy of Epstein, who had moved to London in 1905 and become notorious in 1908 for his carvings for the British Medical Association building in the Strand in London. Gaudier had been awestruck when he saw the Oscar Wilde tomb at Cheyne Walk. Epstein had become friendly with Lewis when they met at the Cave of the Golden Calf but the sculptor – despite his admiration for Gaudier – resisted affiliation with the Vorticists.

Epstein characterized Hulme as a man

of a candid and original nature like that of Samuel Johnson, and
only his intolerance of sham made him feared. Personally, I think
he was of a generous and singularly likeable character, and with
artists he was humble and always willing to learn. In his own
subjects of philosophy and religion he was a profound student . . .
Of this side of him I understood little, although I often listened
to his argumentative exegesis.[11]

The bullyish side of Hulme became annoyed when Epstein stuck to
realistic busts. He wanted the sculptor to provide work that supported his
theories. What attracted Hulme to Epstein was that his works brought back
to mind his reaction to the Byzantine mosaics he had seen in Ravenna in
1911. He had been taken with the angularity he saw in these mosaics and
later applied this concept to Epstein's work.

Like Hulme, Pound realized how effectively sculpture could connect
Imagism to Vorticism: he defined sculptural feeling as an 'appreciation of
masses in relation' and sculptural ability as 'the defining of masses by planes.'
For him, 'there comes a time when one is more deeply moved by that form of
intelligence which can present masses in relation than by that combination
of patience and trickery which can make marble chains with free links and
spin out bronze until it copies the feathers on a general's hat.'[12] For Pound,
Gaudier remained the sculptor of choice.

Lewis had further worries. Bomberg very determinedly did not sign the
manifesto attached to *Blast 1*. The idea of fastening himself to a label was
abhorrent to him, and he had good reason to distrust Lewis. Bomberg's wife,
Alice, recalled her husband telling her 'that Lewis wanted to take some photographs of his pictures at the first London Group show, and reproduce them
in *Blast*; but David was adamant. He not only told Lewis that he did not
want any of his work published in *Blast* – he also threatened to sue Lewis if
anything did appear in the magazine.'[13]

Although four drawings by Etchells appeared in *Blast 2*, he explained
why he did not sign the manifesto: 'I got out of signing . . . because I was
very cagey about the whole idea. I remember the terrific discussions we

used to have: Lewis would talk and talk . . . I was never a willing captive for Lewis, despite our strong friendship because I always thought Vorticism was a manufactured, faked movement.'[14] Roberts boasted: 'if anyone were to imagine we signed his Manifesto, pen in hand . . . they would be making a big mistake. I, in fact, signed nothing. The first knowledge of [its] existence was when Lewis . . . knocked at my door and placed in my hands this chubby, rosy, problem-child *Blast*.'[15]

There was another holdout. At some point, Hulme was supposed to contribute an essay to *Blast* on Epstein; his absence from the magazine was not because he and Lewis had any fundamental disagreement about aesthetics – Lewis's jealousy was the likely cause.

Lewis might have been eager for the spotlight, but he soon learned that not all publicity was necessarily good publicity. For him, the notoriety gained by *Blast* was distasteful, especially when it came from some of the blasted. Suddenly, his outsider art had become insider art. He lamented:

> So the luncheon and dinner-tables of Mayfair were turned
> into show-booths. For a few months I was on constant exhibition.
> I cannot . . . enumerate all the sightseers, of noble houses . . .
> They were legion. Coronetted envelopes showered into my
> letter-box. The editor of *Blast* must at all costs be viewed; and
> its immense puce cover was the standing joke in . . . fashionable
> drawing-room[s].[16]

July had been ghastly for Lewis, but in August, when the Great War commenced, he was thrown into an entirely new maelstrom.

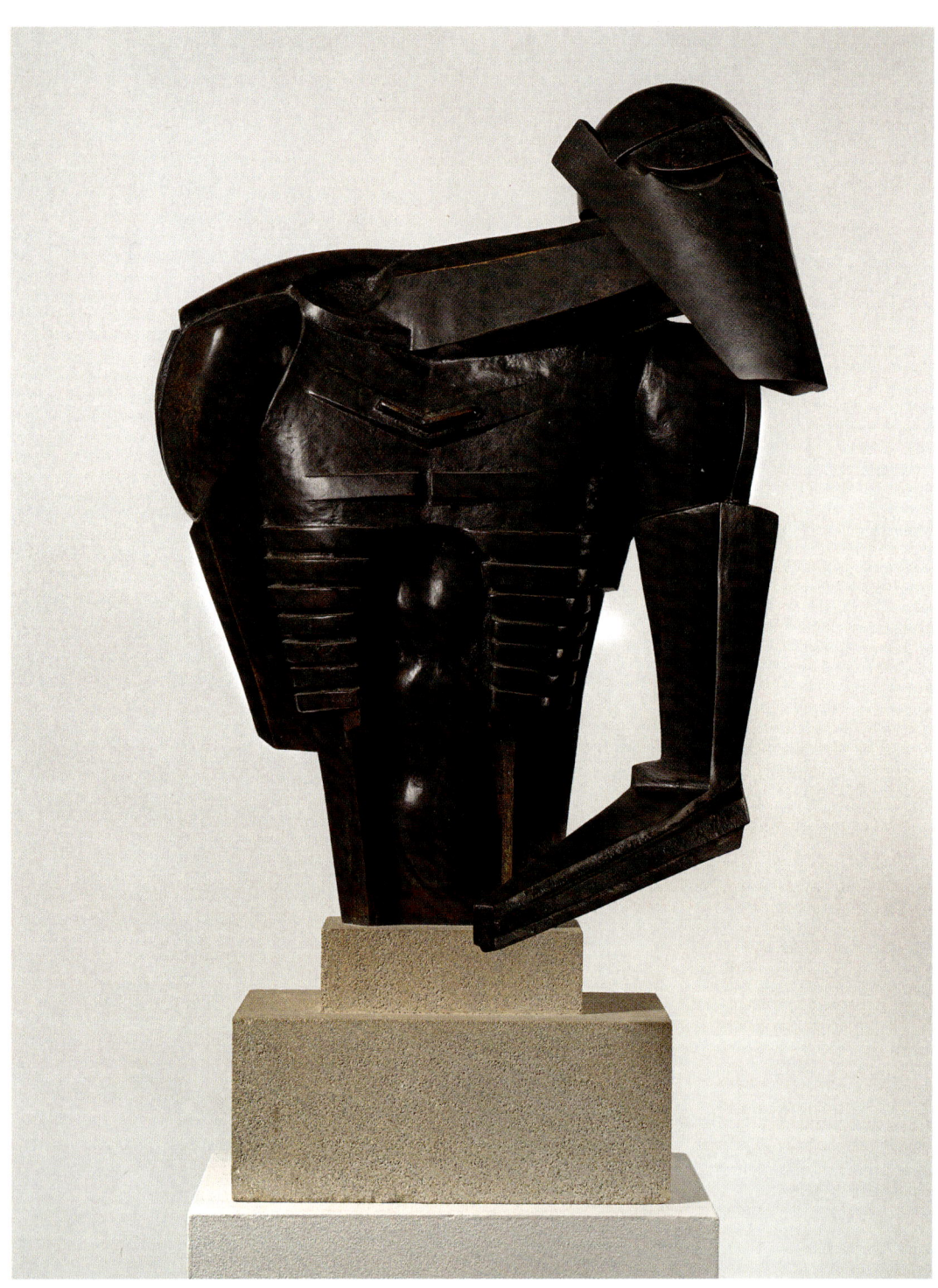

Jacob Epstein, torso in metal from *Rock Drill*, 1913–15, bronze.

18

THE WAR

Vorticism had been born under the shadow of war. The *concept* of the vortex originated in the idea of establishing a still point in a raging whirlwind. Vorticism could depict chaos brought under control in a decisive moment. But war brought genuine, uncontainable chaos.

The possibility of war became reality when on 28 June 1914, a few days before the publication of *Blast 1*, a Serbian terrorist assassinated Archduke Franz Ferdinand, the heir to the Austro-Hungarian Empire. That event had a ricochet effect, eventually leading Britain to declare war on Germany on 4 August. That night, Bomberg was at the Café Royal. A friend informed him: 'this is going to be bad for art.'[1]

Most of the Vorticists adopted a wait-and-see attitude towards volunteering for military service. The exception, paradoxically, was Gaudier. In 1912 he had refused to return to France for compulsory military service and was seriously considering becoming a British citizen. In August 1914 he changed course when he determined to enlist to 'kill Germans to avenge all the brutalities they have committed against my family'.[2] Epstein, Lewis and Hulme were among those who saw him off at Charing Cross. When he reached Boulogne, Gaudier was arrested as a draft dodger. He managed to return to London and, through the assistance of the French embassy, was allowed to return to France to join the 129th Infantry Regiment.

Although some of the other rebels wrote to Gaudier at the battle-front, the usually reticent Wadsworth also sent woodcuts and food parcels. He had been touched by the Frenchman's kindnesses to him, especially his review of his two submissions to the Allied Artists' Association where Wadsworth, according to Gaudier, was 'well represented by *A Short Flight*: a composition of cool tones marvellously embodied in revolving surfaces and masses. His bigger picture [*Cape of Good Hope*, p. 83] gives more pleasure on account of the warmer pigments used and the construction: growing in a corner and balanced at the other by a short mass.'³

In Gaudier's letters, his gruelling description of life at the front is preserved. In December 1914, he told Wadsworth: 'We suffered a little where we stood before but now it's the third circle of Dante's *Inferno*. We have to stand in ditches with a foot of fluid mud at the bottom for four days at a time.'⁴ In the middle of February 1915: 'The only thing I can prey on for my own work of sculpture are putrefying corpses of dead Germans which gives fine ideas to sculpt war demons in black stone once the war is over.'⁵ Later, he sent 'the two less worst drawings' that he made in the trenches to his friend so that they could be shown in the second London Group show in March 1915.⁶

Jacob Epstein's *Rock Drill* remains the finest Vorticist-inspired depiction of the horrors of the approaching Great War. Like Gaudier's, Epstein's sculpture seems at first glance not to resemble two-dimensional Vorticist work. This is true, but it is defiantly Vorticist in spirit – it fuses abstraction with representation and challenges preconceived notions of what a work of art should be. Like Bomberg, Epstein kept a measured distance from Lewis and the other Vorticists. He shared many of their convictions, but he saw no advantage in attaching any kind of label to his work.

Lewis said *Rock Drill* was 'one of the best things [Epstein] has done. The nerve-like figure perched on the machinery, with its straining to one purpose, is a vivid illustration of the greatest functions of life.' He also observed that 'its lack of logic has an effectiveness of its own. I feel that a logical co-ordination was not intended.'⁷ The almost 9-foot-high robotic figure was first shown at the second London Group show.

Epstein wrote: 'it was in the experimental pre-war days of 1913 that I was fired to do *The Rock Drill*, and my ardour for machinery (short-lived), expended itself on the purchase of the actual drill second-hand, and upon this I made and mounted a machine-like robot, visored, menacing and carrying within itself its progeny protectively ensconced.'⁸ He could have added that the fusion of sculpture with the drill is likely indebted to Duchamp's ready-mades. When he stated that his 'ardour for machinery' was short-lived, he provided a clue to how he saw the work as prophetic:

he was hinting that the world could be destroyed by machines, such as the artillery used in the war.

Pound and Gaudier saw *Rock Drill* in 1913 at Epstein's studio. Pound, as he often did, began to rant about the work, whereupon Gaudier told him to 'shut up. You understand nothing!'[9] Another visitor to the studio, David Bomberg, told Roberts that the 'tense figure [was] operating the Drill as if it were a Machine Gun'. For him, *Rock Drill* was a 'Prophetic Symbol' of the 'impending war'.[10]

The union of the plaster sculpture with metal suggests that the driller might have control over the drill. But does he? Haven't the two become one? In this version, the driller can be seen as an artist figure attempting to control what he has created. The question is whether the driller can do this indefinitely or whether he will reach a moment when he loses control. There is another dimension to the original driller: he is male with a long penis provided by the drill but carries within his body an embryo. When separated from the drill, the gender identity of the figure becomes less identifiable; the figure also looks confused and disheartened. Does this sculpture portend the birth of some sort of monster edging towards Jerusalem, as in Yeats's Imagistic 'The Second Coming'? Or, in its altered state, does it become a representation of a disheartened, incapacitated humanoid?

Unlike the Futurists, the Vorticists remained suspicious of machines, and *Rock Drill* expressed that anxiety. In the same exhibition, Epstein showed the more traditional *Mother and Child* and *Carving in Flenite.* As an artist, Epstein was torn between venturing in the direction of experimentation or retreating into more conventional work. Later, in March 1915, when he showed a penchant for mixing representation with abstraction, he came the closest he ever did to the Vorticist standard in making art.

Helen Saunders, aware of Epstein's sculpture, created her own version of a rock driller (or perhaps more accurately a gouger) in a small, intensely coloured drawing (p. 97). Her driller, rendered in browns and blacks, occupies the right-hand side of the composition; at the left, in vivid contrast, is the brightly coloured female. Her vivacity suggests that the feminine point of view may be extremely different from its male counterpart.

At the outbreak of the war, Nevinson, eager to enter the fray but unable to serve as a soldier because he suffered from severe rheumatism, joined the Friends' Ambulance Unit. From the middle of November, he spent nine weeks

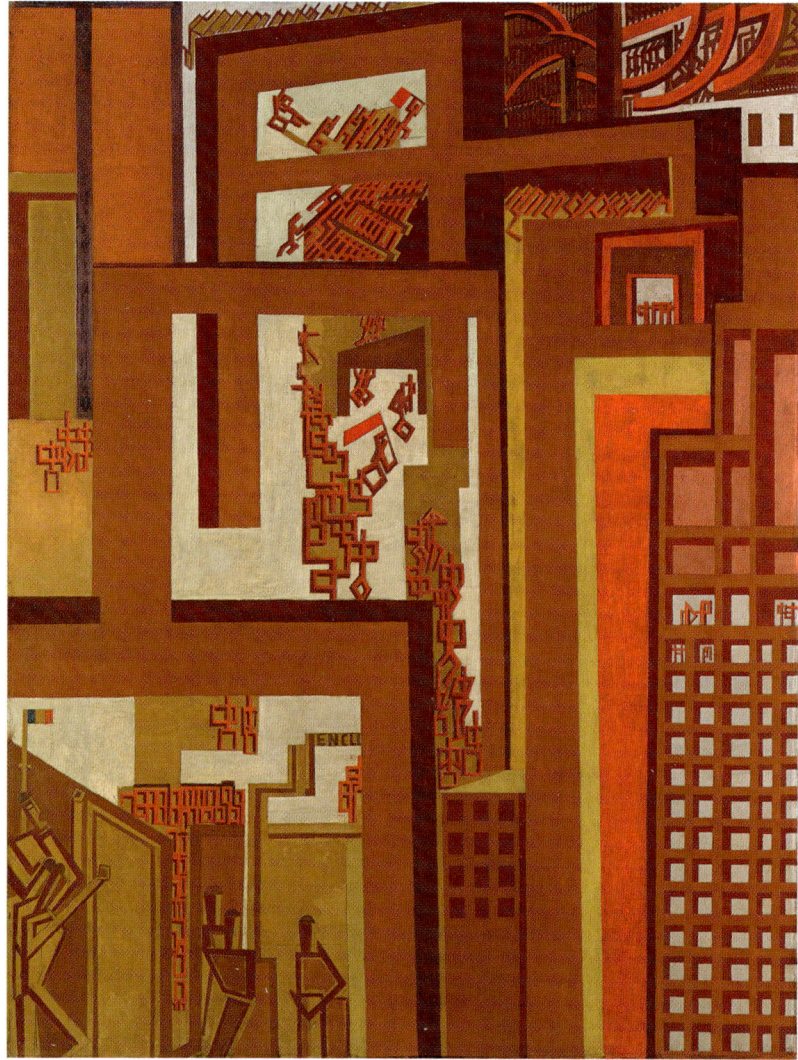

Wyndham Lewis, *The Crowd*, 1914–15, oil and pencil on canvas.

with that group and the British Red Cross Society at a disused goods shed near the Dunkirk rail station known as the Shambles. There, 3,000 badly wounded soldiers evacuated from the front were housed. Among other tasks, Nevinson dressed wounds. When the French assumed responsibility for the Shambles, Nevinson became an ambulance driver, but his bad health prevented him from steering the vehicles properly. On 15 January 1915, no longer fit for service, he returned to England. He later recalled: 'When a month had

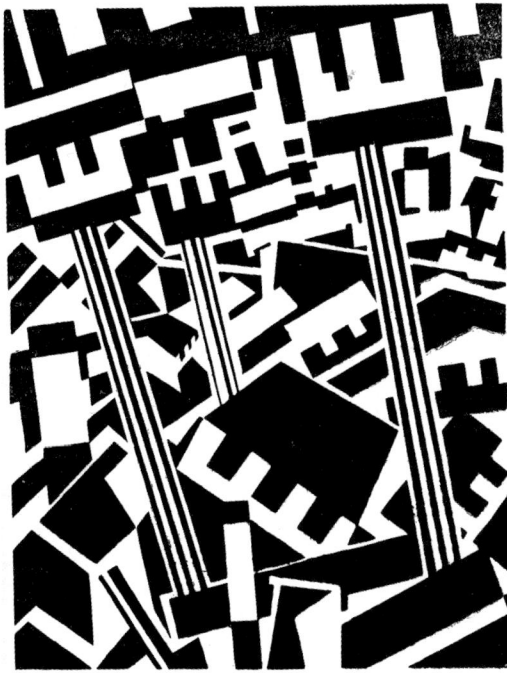

Edward Wadsworth, *Rotterdam*, linecut. *Blast 2*, p. 59.

passed, I felt I had been born in the nightmare. I had seen sights so revolting that man seldom conceives them in his mind . . . We could only help, and ignore shrieks, pus, gangrene and the disembowelled.'[11]

Many of his Futurist colleagues eagerly served in the Italian army. Like them, Nevinson portrayed the war, but unlike them he could not glorify it. At the second London Group exhibition in March 1915, he showed four works, including *Returning to the Trenches*. In that canvas, the forward movement of the soldiers may be captured by using Futurist techniques, but the overall effect is of a group of men marching towards their extinction. Here, Nevinson's growing dissatisfaction with Futurism can be seen.

Lewis remained deeply suspicious of a society dependent on machines. In the *Sunday Times*, Frank Rutter praised *The Crowd* (1914–15), a huge canvas of Lewis's over 2 metres in height (like *Returning to the Trenches* and Epstein's *Rock Drill*, it was shown at the second London Group exhibition): he called it 'a wondrous pattern of imaginative parquetry, formed apparently of brick forms of dull red, which combine very happily in juxtaposition to the gold

bands that form the principal lines of the composition'.[12] Looking through
the abstract patterning created by the bricks and bands, the viewer sees
human beings reduced to mechanized robots imprisoned within grids. In
its castigation of a mechanistic society intent on self-destruction, it bears
comparison to Epstein's driller.

Of Wadsworth's two oils in the show – *Rotterdam* and *Blackpool* – the
whereabouts are unknown. However, *Rotterdam,* as reproduced in *Blast 2*,
is like the works of Lewis and Roberts in the same exhibition in its use of
sharp diagonals. Wadsworth's speciality at this time – aerial views of urban
streets reduced to grid-like structures – can also be read as a critique of a
society about to be taken over by machines.

Gaudier told Wadsworth: 'I have some preference for *Rotterdam*. I do
not know why, as the same qualities persist through them all, at the same
degree. When you send me some more, as I am greedy to see much vorticism just now, print them on . . . thin paper. The reason is this, I have room
for them in my knapsack and the less weighty the individuals are, the more
I shall be able to stuff in.'[13]

From the trenches, he remained resolute despite the horrors he witnessed:

I HAVE BEEN FIGHTING FOR TWO MONTHS, and I can now gauge
the intensity of life.
HUMAN MASSES teem and move, are destroyed and crop up
again . . .
WITH ALL THE DESTRUCTION that works around us NOTHING IS
CHANGED, EVEN SUPERFICIALLY. LIFE IS THE SAME STRENGTH.
THE MOVING AGENT THAT PERMITS THE SMALL INDIVIDUAL TO
ASSERT HIMSELF . . .
THIS WAR IS A GREAT REMEDY.
IN THE INDIVIDUAL IT KILLS ARROGANCE, SELF-ESTEEM, PRIDE . . .
MY VIEWS ON SCULPTURE REMAIN ABSOLUTELY THE SAME.[14]

Passionate, obstinate, determined, he was slaughtered in a charge at
Neuville-Saint-Vaast on 5 June 1915.

19

THE SECOND EXPLOSION:
BLAST WAR NUMBER

For once, Lewis was hesitant. He could not make up his mind about a second *Blast* or its contents. After the war began, the sometimes reticent Wadsworth told him how to proceed.

> The only papers that will sell now are those that deal with war, either with news or some other way. Why not therefore have the next number of *Blast* a special War number? A smaller thing to cost 1/ – with line blocks – no half tones. I should think you could make it extremely interesting and it would sell like hot cakes and also would keep the name of the magazine before the public which, if it is not published again for a long time, may lose interest and it would have to fizzle out with its second number a big failure.[1]

Despite Wadsworth's encouragement, for once Lewis remained indecisive.[2]

Finally, Lewis decided to go ahead.[3] The significantly smaller *Blast War Number* (*Blast* 2) was published on 2 July 1915: it contained 102 pages versus the 160 of its predecessor. Despite Lewis's cover image of soldiers marching into battle, *Blast* 2 is not pro-war. In large part, Vorticism came into being because its artists were anxious about war. Their art may be filled with references to guns and engines of war, but this is because its artists were frightened by the magnitude and destructive power of the approaching devastation.

Lewis made his views on the war clear in his editorial when he asserted that Germany 'stands for Romance'. He did not clearly define what he meant by 'Romance', but he labelled England as a place of 'Genial and Realistic Barbarians' as opposed to Germans who are 'Champions of melodramatic philosophy'. In preferring realism to melodrama, he was suggesting that

Germany was lost in the past whereas England, despite all its failings, was moving in the direction of the future: 'Germany has stood for the old Poetry, for Romance, more steadfastly and profoundly than any other people in Europe. German nationalism is less realistic, is more saturated with the mechanical obsession of history, than the nationalism of England or France.'[4] This observation led to the declaration: 'Under these circumstances, apart from national partizanship, it appears to us humanly desirable that Germany should win no war against France or England.'[5]

In another contribution, 'The European War and Great Communities', Lewis expressed his fear that 'War won't go [away]. It will be the large communities that make war so unmanageable, unreal and unsatisfactory, that will go. Or at least they will be modified for these ends. Everything will be arranged for the best convenience of War. Murder and destruction is man's fundamental occupation.'[6] This negative prophecy could only be avoided, he felt, if the Great Communities were eradicated.

Although Lewis supported Britain's involvement in the war, it was nevertheless one of the Great Communities that had to be destroyed. These views are intimately connected to his belief that art – especially Vorticism – could provide a way of toppling complacent English society.

In another contribution to *Blast War Number*, Lewis claimed: 'VORTICISM is the only word that has been used in this country and nowhere else for a certain new impulse in art.' He then proposed to define 'the way in which English VORTICISTS differ from the French, German or Italian painters of kindred groups'.[7] Cubists 'are static and representative, not warming, exploding or burgeoning with life, as is the ideal of the Futurists'.[8] There was also a third category, Expressionism, that was embodied in the work of Kandinsky.

As was to be expected, Lewis castigated Cubism as having 'pulled Nature about with her cubes', and Futurism was concerned with the 'hurly-burly and exuberance of actual life'. As he had argued before, both these approaches were inherently flawed. Moreover, Lewis targeted the Russian-born Kandinsky as 'the only PURELY abstract painter in Europe. But he is so careful to be passive . . . and is committed, by his theory, to avoid all powerful and definite forms, that he is, at the best wandering and slack.'[9] By definition, Lewis was arguing, Kandinsky's form of abstraction failed because it did not consider human reality in its attempt to depict spiritual reality. Lewis's point

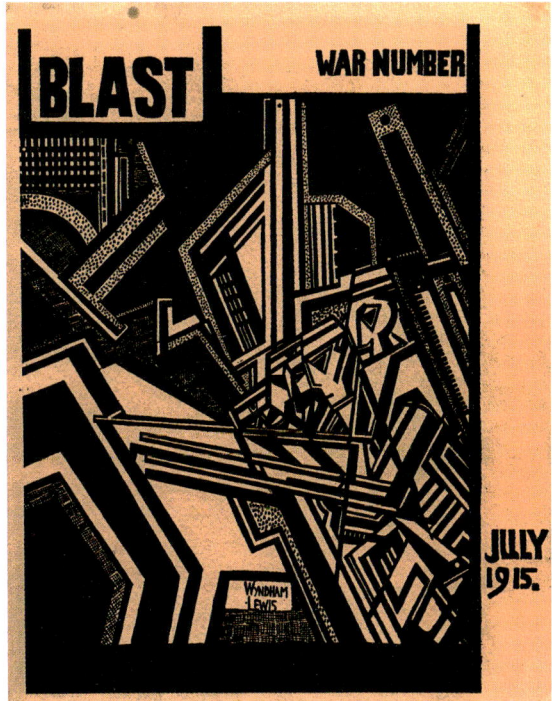

Wyndham Lewis, *Blast 2*, 1915, linecut, cover.

was that abstraction – as could readily be seen in the illustrations in *Blast 2* – must contain representational elements. In making such a claim, he was attempting to pinpoint the element that segregated Vorticism from other forms of abstraction.

His statement – 'The first reason for not imitating Nature is that you cannot convey the emotion you receive at the contact of Nature by imitating her, but only by becoming her' – had a corollary that defined Vorticism: 'the literal rendering in the fundamental matter of arrangement and logic will never hit the emotion intended by unintelligent imitation.' For him, the 'essence of an object is beyond and often in contradiction to the simple truth'.[10]

To get to this simple truth, the representation of the quintessence of an object could only be achieved by displaying its 'essence' – not by 'literal rendering' – in the blend of representation and abstraction in Vorticism. Wadsworth had praised Kandinsky warmly in *Blast 1* – this essay can be seen as a subtle warning by Lewis to one of his staunchest supporters not to deviate into pure abstraction.

Lewis was also aware that the invention of various kinds of machines was a hallmark in the advancement of twentieth-century existence. In particular, he realized that the war had introduced new forms of machinery – what he sometimes labelled 'war machines'. Moreover, he discerned that the shapes of various machines had an abstract look to them. Despite these observations, Lewis remained deeply suspicious of machine culture.

Machines could kill. This fact haunted Lewis when Gaudier sent him a sketch of bursting shells. 'Here is one, a great artist, who makes drawings of those shells as they come towards him, and which, thank God, have not killed him or changed him yet.'[11]

With the surprising exceptions of a drawing by Jacob Kramer called *Types of the Russian Army*, one by Nevinson, and a photograph of Gaudier's *Ezra Pound*, the remaining illustrations by Dismorr, Etchells, Roberts, Saunders, Wadsworth and Lewis are remarkably uniform.[12] Etchells's *Progression* shows a movement from left to right where all the elements, consisting of various geometric forms, advance to the black passage on the right. This movement to blackness might be a depiction of Europe's slow march to the Great War.

Roberts's *Combat* depicts a confrontation of two opposing sets of abstract forms; in *Drawing* he is even more explicit about the apparatus of war by

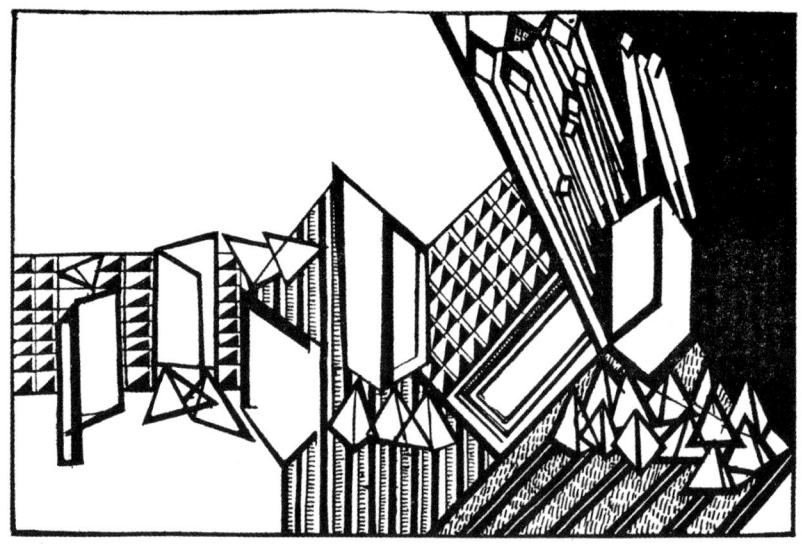

Frederick Etchells, *Progression*, linecut. *Blast 2*, p. 53.

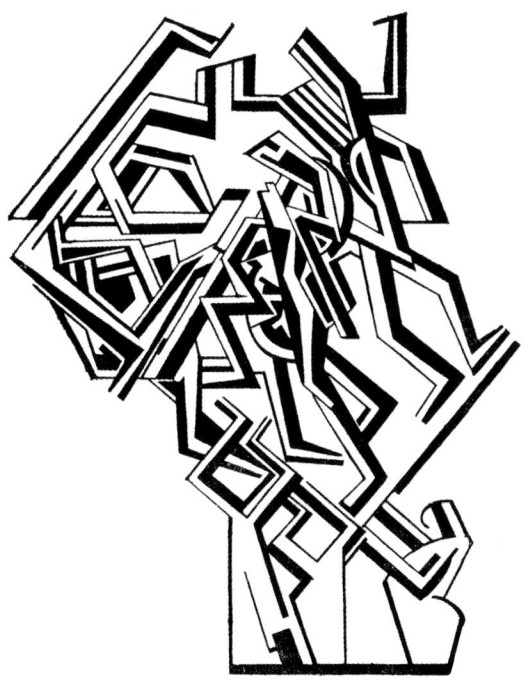

William Roberts, *Combat*, 1915, linecut. *Blast 2*, p. 55.

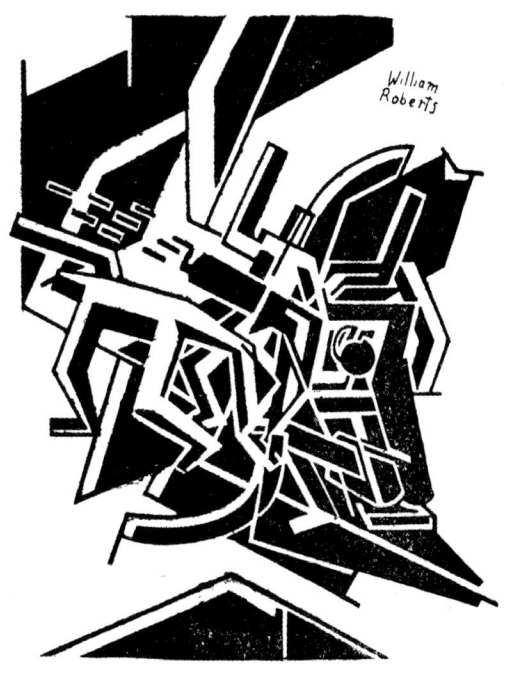

William Roberts, *Drawing*, 1915, linecut. *Blast 2*, p. 87.

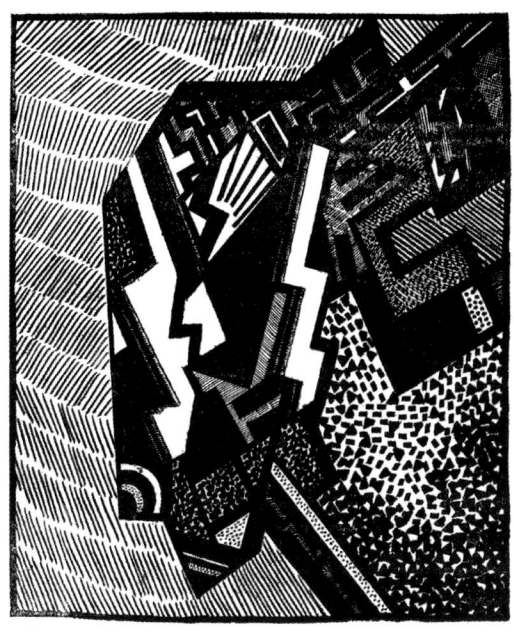

Edward Wadsworth, *War-Engine*,
1915, linecut. *Blast 2*, p. 61.

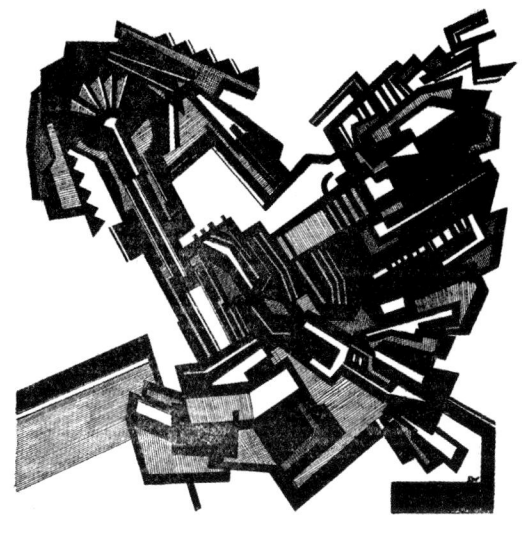

Helen Saunders, *Island of Laputa*,
1915, linecut. *Blast 2*, p. 8.

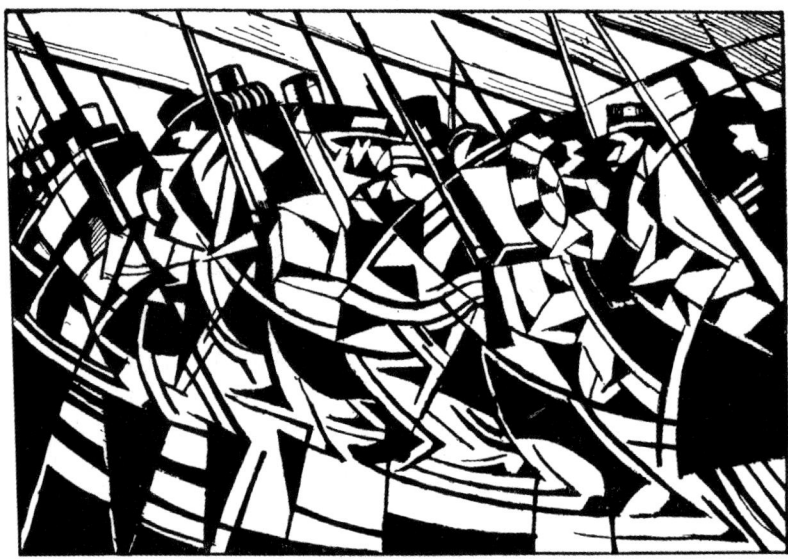

C.R.W. Nevinson, *On the Way to the Trenches*, 1915, linecut. *Blast 2*, p. 89.

showing a machine gun firing to the left. Wadsworth's *War-Engine* is an aerial view of an instrument of destruction. Also an aerial view, Saunders's *Island of Laputa* provided an examination of the flying island described in *Gulliver's Travels*, where the Laputans had developed a highly mechanized society but had no real understanding of what they had accomplished. Whether examining the intricacies of machinery or providing aerial views of a mechanized society, these images, like Lewis's *The Crowd* (p. 136), underscore how humane values have been exterminated by the war.

The presence of Nevinson's *On the Way to the Trenches* (the woodcut version of *Returning to the Trenches*) would have given Lewis smug pleasure. As a result of his experience in France, Nevinson was reconsidering his allegiance to Futurism. Lewis evaluated this work as possessing 'a hurried and harassed melancholy and chilliness that is well seen'.[13] In fact, Nevinson was in the process of rejecting Futurism and embracing naturalism. He told *The Studio* in December 1919: 'The immediate need of the art of today is a Cézanne, a reactionary, to lead art back to the academic tradition . . . and save contemporary art from abstraction.'

T. S. Eliot had been fascinated by Lewis's *Timon* illustrations when Pound showed them to him. Impressed, he submitted four poems for *Blast 2*: 'Preludes', 'Rhapsody on a Wintry Night', 'Bullshit' and 'The Ballad for Big Louise'.

Having encountered censorship problems with a poem by Pound in *Blast*, Lewis declined the last two. The others were Eliot's first poems to appear in England.

In including Saunders, Dismorr and Dorothy Shakespear, Lewis stealthily enacted a volte-face. Without stating so, he moved away from the phallic-dominated aspect of Vorticism. Why Lewis did this is unknown. At this point, only Gaudier had enlisted and Lewis would not appear to have been short of male contributors – in addition to Eliot, there were submissions from Pound, Ford and Gaudier.

Lewis may have felt the need to add other voices to his own in the new *Blast* and thus decided to include a poem, a series of short prose-poems and a prose piece by Dismorr, a long poem by Saunders, and five illustrations by Dismorr, Saunders and Shakespear. He may have felt forced into a decision against his own belief system – he did offer his usual chauvinist remarks about women in *Blast 2*. If he thought his back was pressed against the wall and that he had to include women in this issue, it was a breakthrough in the citadel of Vorticism. Previously, he had thought of Dismorr and Saunders as ancillary figures upon whom he could impose.

Shakespear, the daughter of the novelist Olivia Shakespear, had no formal training in art and entered the Vorticist circle through her husband, Ezra Pound. Before visiting the Rebel Art Centre, she had painted traditional watercolour landscapes but changed direction under the influence of Lewis, who gave her 'a shove out of the Victorian'. She never exhibited with the Vorticists, but her surviving work displays her own take on the movement. She began dextrously employing broad swatches of highly saturated colours

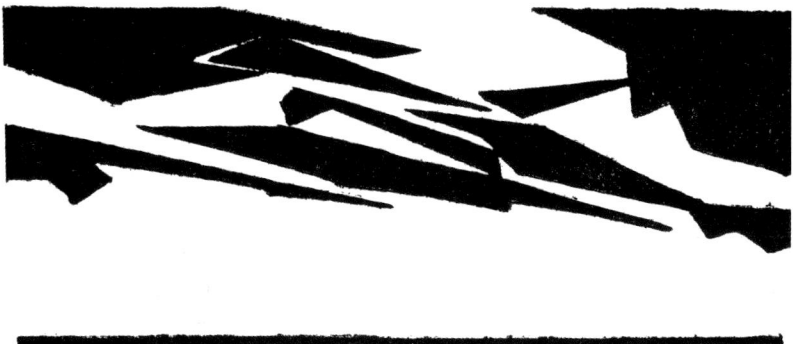

Dorothy Shakespear, *Snow-Scene*, 1915, linecut. *Blast 2*, p. 35.

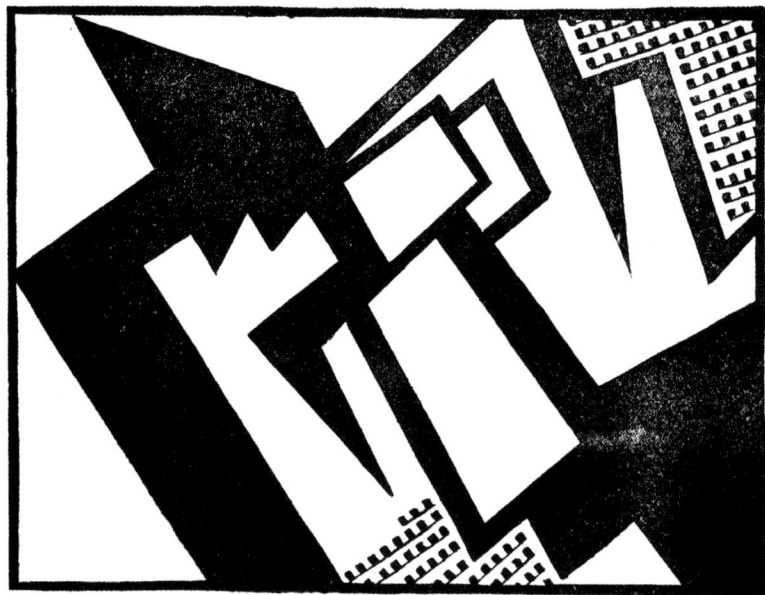

Jessica Dismorr, *The Engine*, 1915, linecut. *Blast 2*, p. 27.

to depict landscapes. Her dust jackets and illustrations to her husband's books became a perfect accompaniment to his Imagist verse.

Dismorr's bold *The Engine* places shards of black against negative space. This work may not be as intricate as Wadsworth's *War-Engine*, but it is both more abstract and more astringent in its contrast of shapes. In her verse, she introduced an aspect of Vorticism not sufficiently articulated in the work of her colleagues: metropolitanism. She may well have shared Lewis's view, as expressed in *Blast 2*, of London as 'the great modern city' – 'an up-to-date and iron Jungle'.[14]

For better or worse, Vorticism was resolutely London-based and in her 'London Notes' Dismorr reflected this. As a woman, she found the city intimidating but also a place of liberation. For her, it encompassed beauty as well as ferocity. In prose fragments indebted to Imagism, she compressed her urban experience into sharp, direct reflections.

HYDE PARK

Commonplace, titanic figures with a splendid motion stride
across the parched plateau of grass, little London houses only
a foot high huddle at their heels.

READING-ROOM [AT THE BRITISH MUSEUM]
This colossal globe of achievement presses upon two hundred cosmopolitan foreheads, respectfully inclined.

FLEET STREET
Curiously exciting are so many perspective lines, withdrawing, converging; they indicate evidently something of importance beyond the limits of sight.[15]

In Dismorr's short story 'June Night', Rodengo calls upon the unnamed narrator at her 'little dark villa'. She has an ardent admiration for him, but he is 'too conspicuous for day-light: but on a night of opera, this night of profound mutterings and meaningless summer lightning you are an indispensable adjunct of the scenery'. They board the number 43 bus that takes them to Regent's Park. 'It is hot for a night in June,' she observes. Then she informs her companion: 'you have a beautiful tenor voice, but you bore me. Your crime is that I can no longer distinguish you from the rest of the world.' She has had enough to do with romantics. 'At the next arret I leave . . . you Rodengo with a rose in your ear.' She wanders in 'mews and by-ways', and 'in the precincts of stately urban houses'; finally, she reaches 'the pool of silence . . . of unplumbable depths'. She comes to the realization, 'I must get back to the life of the thoroughfares to which I belong.' Rodengo has disappeared. She thinks of his charms without regret. 'The homeward-going buses are now thronged. Should I see you, I shall acknowledge you with affections. But am not returning that way.'[16]

This short narrative is about a woman's search for her own place in a male-dominated society. She will find her own way in all the intricacies of urban life; she will become a flâneur – someone who explores the city on her own. At the outset of the narrative, she allowed a male companion to travel with her, but she soon realized that she could discard him.

The poem 'Monologue' contains a harrowing account of what it is to be a woman in her culture: 'My niche in nonentity still grins –/ I lay knees, elbows pinioned, my sleep mutterings blunted against a wall.'[17] She wants to give birth to her identity as a woman, but this parturition is excruciatingly painful.

Saunders's 'Vision of Mud' takes its setting and resultant images from what she had heard about life in the trenches. The speaker contrasts her struggles as a woman with the battles fought by the soldiers.

I lie quite still: hands are spreading mud everywhere: they
plaster it on what should be a body.
They fill my mouth with it. I am sick. They shoved it all back
again . . .
I try to open my eyes a little . . .
My eyes are shut down again.
A giant cloud like a black bladder with holes in it hovers
overhead.[18]

Perhaps despite Lewis's intention, *Blast 2* contained a strong feminist presence. In the images and poetry of Saunders and Dismorr, the lonely plight of women who would become artists can be witnessed.

This raises an important issue. Why did Saunders and Dismorr remain faithful to Vorticism during their time at the Rebel Art Centre and afterwards? Women remained outsiders in the art establishment – women who practised advanced art doubly so. Despite the misogyny they endured, they believed fervently that this form of abstract expression conveyed the modern experience more than any other option open to them.

On the surface, the smaller *Blast 2* might seem a less significant publication than *Blast 1*: its BLAST and BLESS pages are each only a page, but it contains a very different kind of energy – a more pent up one. Lewis's definition of Vorticism is for the most part articulate and decisive. The illustrations are more coherent – as an album, they display various approaches to Vorticism's combination of large-part abstraction with hints of representation – the images of Lewis, Wadsworth, Roberts, Saunders and Dismorr demonstrate that common thread. More importantly, Lewis had adjusted his role of impresario to allow entry to the previously uninvited – the voices of Saunders and Dismorr resonate loudly.

20

OTHER SPACES:
THREE DESIGN PROJECTS

In 1914–15, much of Lewis's time was spent on the two *Blasts* and on organizing the Vorticist exhibition. Always strapped for cash, he took on three major
interior design projects in addition to all his other activities. The wealthy
Chicago-born painter and novelist Mary Borden Turner asked him to design
furniture for and further embellish her drawing room in Park Lane. Nothing
survives of this endeavour.

At the end of 1914, Violet Hunt, Ford Madox Ford's companion, engaged
Lewis to renovate the writer's stodgy study at South Lodge and make it into a
showpiece for Vorticism. This installation no longer exists, but Douglas
Goldring provided a description of how Lewis constructed a 'large abstract
decoration [above the mantelpiece] with the accompanying red paint on the
doors and skirting boards which gave the room its special character'.[1] Hunt
remembered 'three brick red coloured tapestry window curtains'. Rebecca West
recalled 'a huge abstract work over the fireplace, very violent and explosive, and I
remember Ford saying in his quizzical way that he "found it extremely restful."'[2]

The third decorating assignment (also not extant), done in association
with Saunders, was to transform a small dining room for the wealthy and for
artists' gatherings at the Restaurant de la Tour Eiffel. Roberts remembered
that Lewis was given carte blanche to do what he saw fit by the restaurant's
congenial owner, the Viennese-born Rudolph Stulik, who had once been
chef to Emperor Franz Josef.

Unlike his compatriot Madame Strindberg, Stulik's demeanour was
equitable, but he shared with her a passion for contemporary art – and, in
his case, a great affection for artists. The food at his establishment was inor-
dinately expensive – destined for the mouths of the super-rich – but he had
a soft spot for artists and allowed those he approved of to eat for nothing.

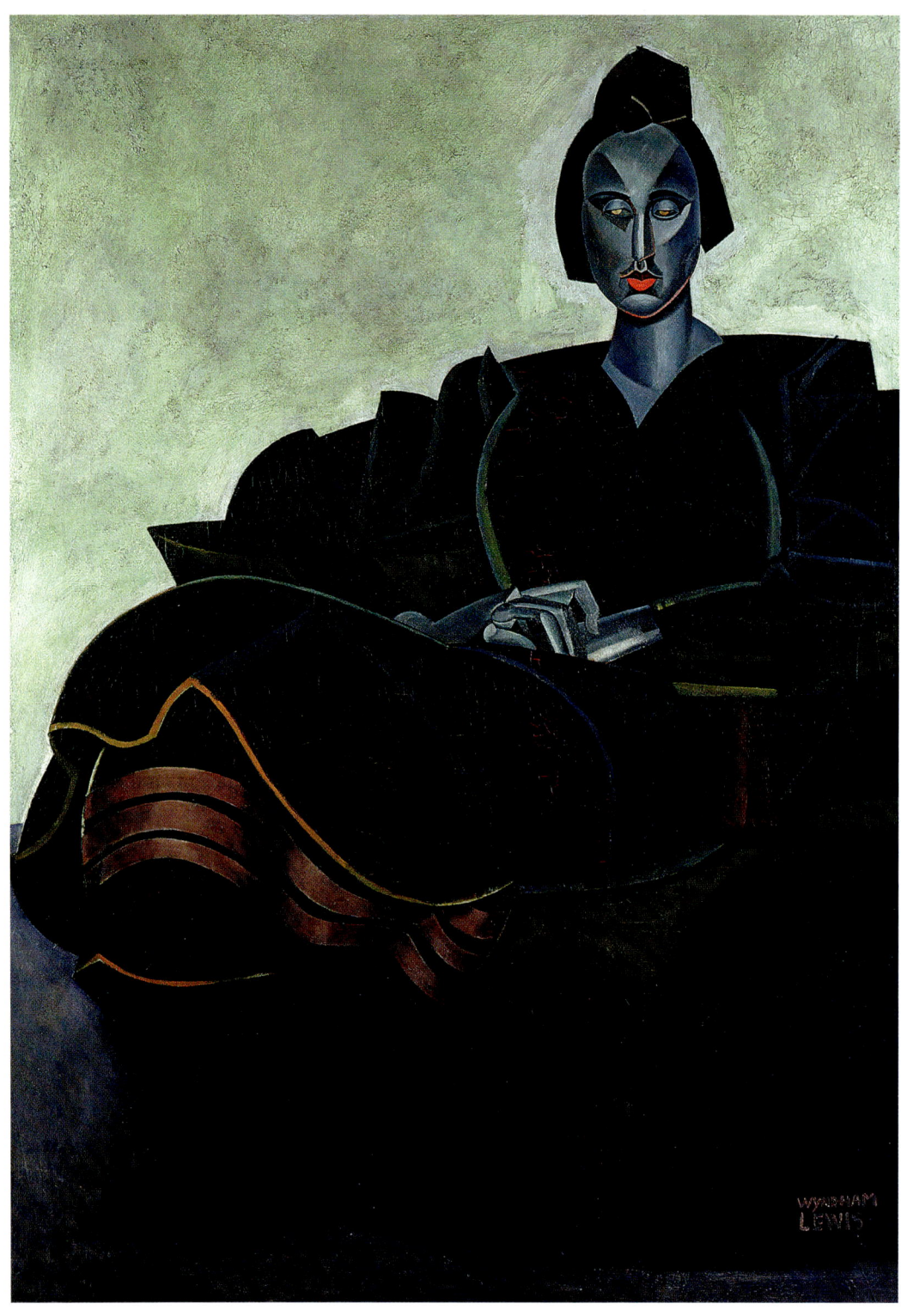

Wyndham Lewis, *Praxitella*, *c.* 1921, oil on canvas.

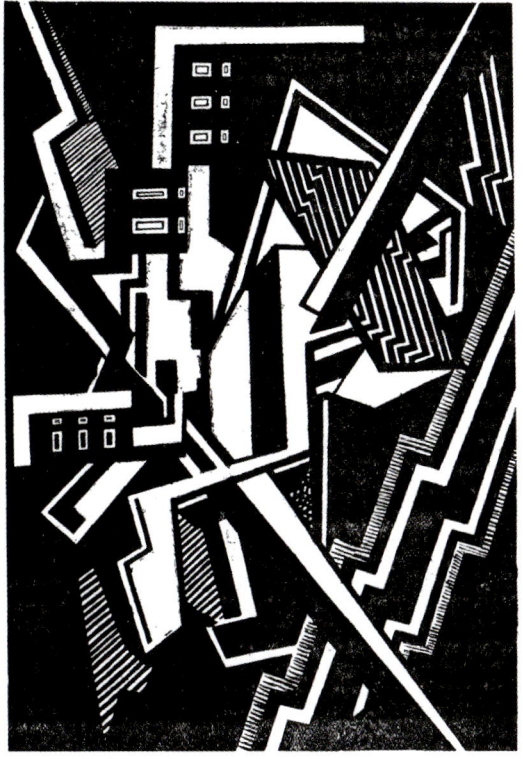

Helen Saunders, *Atlantic City*,
1915, linecut. *Blast 2*, p. 57.

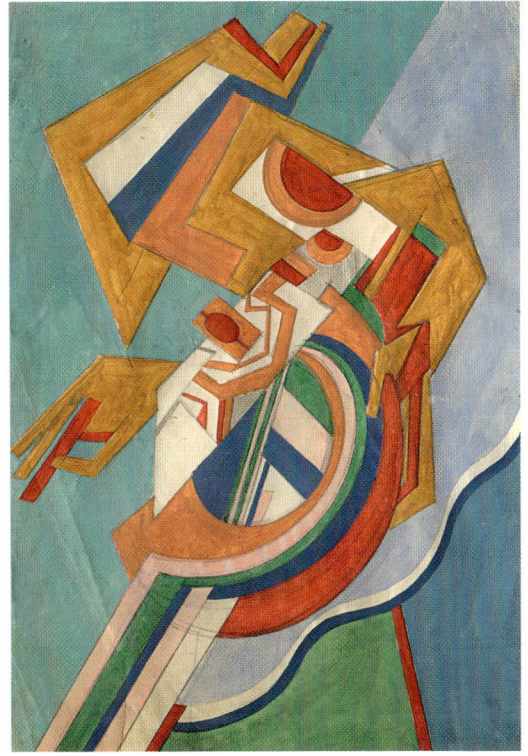

Helen Saunders, *Abstract Multicoloured Design*,
c. 1915, gouache, watercolour and graphite on paper.

Lewis lived at 4 Percy Street in 1914 – the Tour Eiffel was at 1 Percy Street. As he came to know his neighbour, Stulik determined he was a genius. Of course, Lewis helped him to come to that conclusion when he lavished his considerable charms upon him. Although many pictures by them graced the restaurant, Stulik determined to create a special room – a sanctuary – for his favourite artists, and commissioned Lewis to undertake it.

For Lewis and many of his cohorts, restaurants and cafés were an integral part of the urban experience. They met there, stayed there for hours at a time and discussed their projects into the night. Not wishing to disturb his regular clientele on the ground floor, Stulik asked Lewis to create the special dining room on the first floor at the front of the building.

One visitor, the painter Harry Jonas, remembered that the paintings were 'bright red and green' and 'very raw'. The redesigned space reminded him of a chapel or another place of worship: the 'subject matter of the pictures

I should describe as semi-abstract Buildings ... strong lines and flat patches of colour: a geometrical treatment'.³ Lewis's buildings looked like riffs on the skyscrapers in New York City, a place he had yet to visit.

The reviewer in the May 1916 issue of *Colour* magazine rhapsodized: 'Colour has been brought back to floors, walls, and ceilings, and is as asser-tive in draperies as it is in the furniture itself. The days of the dead level of mahogany' had vanished. 'We are entering a new realm of decorative fancy when we step into a London room whose floor is stained purple.' He also observed: 'Those outside the vortex may, in recovering from their giddiness, retain much of what is worth incorporating in our system of applied art. All the more so as the extreme violence of the rebels is not essential outside the battle area, within which we may occasionally desire to stray, though not caring to live there.'⁴

Saunders's role in decorating the dining room is unknown. It is possible that she did not want to be designated as having worked in a subordinate role on this project. This is probably not the case. Lewis had the habit of erasing the work of others. In *c.* 1921 he painted *Praxitella*, a portrait of the film critic Iris Barry. Only in 2022 did two students at the Courtauld – using X-ray and digital technologies – reveal that Lewis had painted over *Atlantic City*, a canvas by Saunders. Before that discovery, *Atlantic City* was known only by its appearance in *Blast 2*; the canvas had been shown at the 1915 Vorticist exhibition at the Doré Galleries and then disappeared.⁵

By 1921 Lewis had abandoned Vorticism. By rubbing out *Atlantic City* – a skeletal map-like representation of the popular resort in New Jersey employ-ing an assortment of Vorticist tropes – he was obliterating his own past and that of a former colleague.

If more information survived about the layout of the dining room at the Restaurant de la Tour Eiffel and the works of art hung there, more evidence about Saunders's contribution would be known, as Jo Cottrell has argued.⁶ A piece by Saunders such as *Abstract Multicoloured Design* might well have graced those walls.

21

THE VORTICIST EXHIBITION

The Vorticist Exhibition at the Doré Galleries opened on 10 June 1915, three weeks before the publication of *Blast 2*. The two launches were planned by Lewis to intersect. At the Doré the exhibitors were of two kinds: *Members* and *Those Invited to Show*.

Members were listed alphabetically:

Dismorr – four pictures
Etchells – two pictures, two drawings
Gaudier-Brzeska – six sculptures, two small objects
Roberts – four drawings
Saunders – four pictures, two drawings
Wadsworth – four pictures, four drawings, three woodcuts
Wyndham Lewis – four pictures, six woodcuts

The inclusion of the Invited group – Bernard Adeney (one landscape), Lawrence Atkinson (three paintings), Bomberg (three paintings, three drawings), Grant (two paintings, one still-life), Kramer (two paintings, two drawings) and Nevinson (three works) – diluted and slightly off-balanced the exhibition in the same way the inclusion of Kramer in *Blast 2* seemed off-kilter.

Lewis made the sweeping claim in the catalogue that 'the show includes specimens of every notable working at all in one or other of the directions,' but his assertion is puzzling. He may have thought that exposure to the work of the Invited might make the superiority of the work of the Members stand out.[1] He might also have thought the presence of the work of outsiders might normalize Vorticism and help integrate it into contemporary English art. Whatever his motives, he took a considerable risk in creating a hotchpotch.

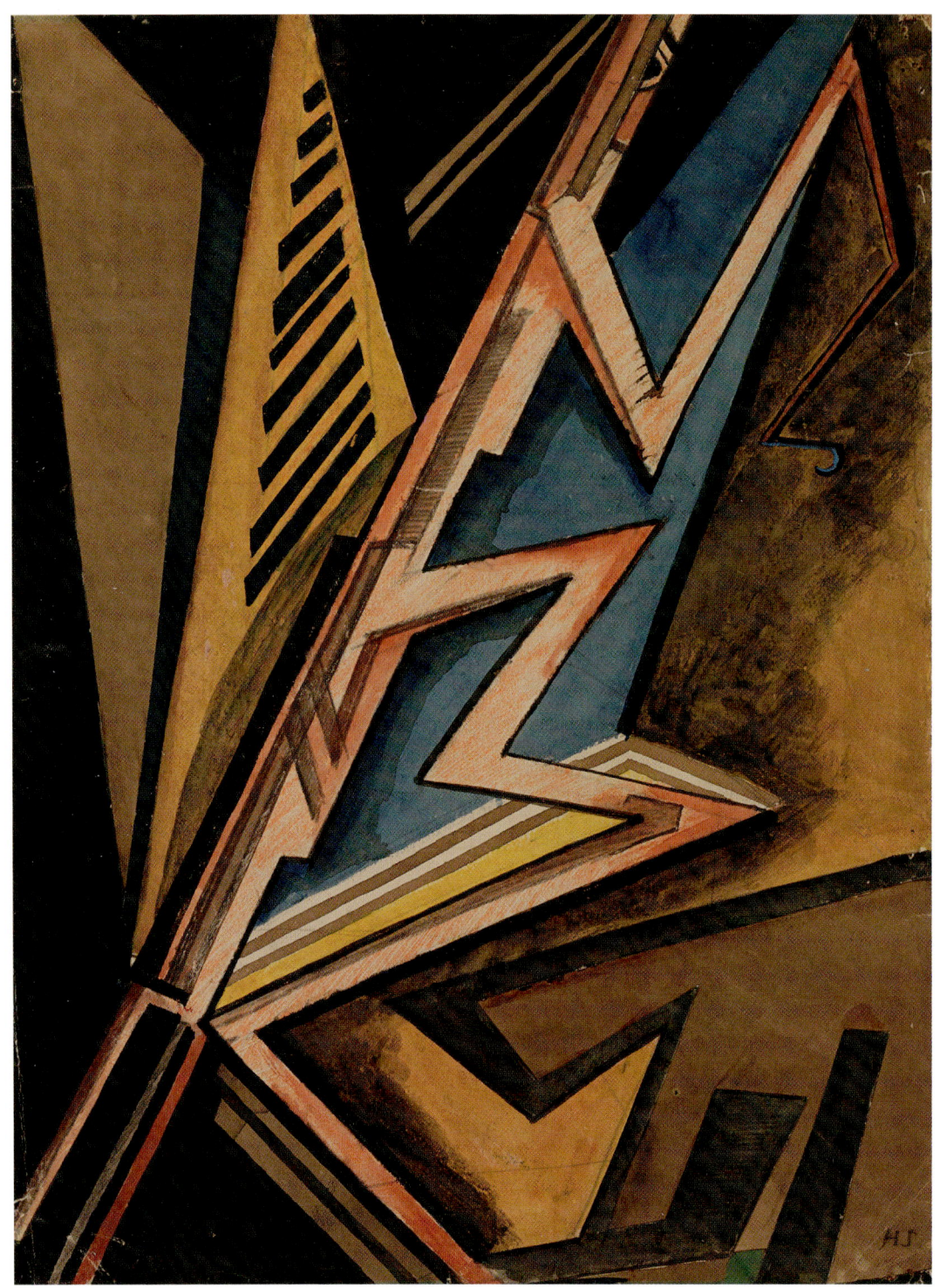

Helen Saunders, *Black and Khaki*, c. 1915, graphite, black ink,
watercolour, bodycolour and collage on paper.

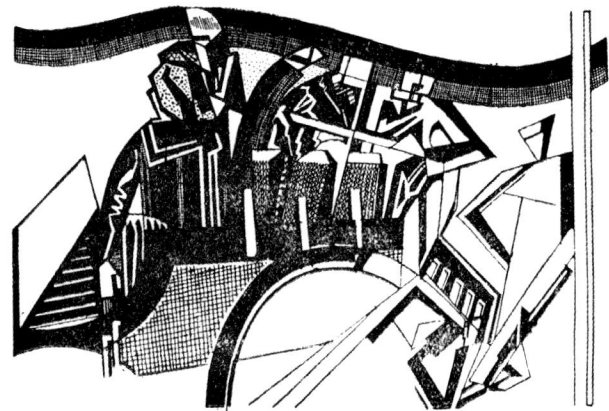

Frederick Etchells, *Hyde Park*, 1915, linecut. *Blast 2*, p. 17.

Lawrence Atkinson had signed the manifesto, and his submissions to the exhibition were indebted to Lewis and Wadsworth. Almost ten years older than Lewis, he had studied music in Berlin before becoming a concert performer and teacher of music in London and Liverpool. Then he abandoned music in favour of painting. He studied at La Palette and afterwards exhibited with Dismorr at the Stafford Gallery in October 1912. Lechmere, who studied music with Atkinson and painted with him and the other British Fauves in Normandy, thought his work was transformed after he saw Lewis's work at the Rebel Art Centre. She recalled that Atkinson was 'a regular visitor at Great Ormond Street [where] Lewis took a special interest in him'.[2]

Atkinson's three paintings blended into the work of the Members, but the same cannot be said of Bernard Adeney, one of the founders of the London Group. Adeney had painted *Toy Sailing Boats* (1911), which formed part of a seven-piece collection of panels painted for Borough Polytechnic under the direction of Roger Fry, who included him in the 'Second Post-Impressionist Exhibition'. Etchells, one of the other artists who painted the murals at the Polytechnic, possibly suggested Adeney to Lewis.

According to Lewis, when he had reviewed the second London Group exhibition earlier in 1915, Adeney's landscapes were 'pallid and solidified [and] bring us back to the "Fauves"'. His contributions, however, were not very much like a wild beast: 'His gentle logic plays round the heaviness of Cézanne like summer-lighting. These pale green meditations in form have great personal charm.'[3] Adeney's work is reminiscent of the work of Duncan

Grant, who had painted some extremely abstract compositions. Grant may have been included on that basis. In any event, the link to Vorticism was weak.

The inclusion of two paintings and two drawings by Kramer is as mysterious as his appearance in *Blast 2*. As he had done with Adeney, Lewis had offered Kramer some back-handed compliments in the second London Group show: 'he shows us a new planet risen on our horizon . . . It is still rather molten, and all sorts of objects and schools are in its melting pot. It has fine passages of colour, and many possibilities as a future luminary.'[4]

Nevinson insisted that the designation '(Futurist)' be inserted after his name. He had allowed a version of *On the Way to the Trenches* to be included in *Blast 2* and Lewis would have welcomed the exhibition of that oil because it reflected Nevinson's growing detachment from Futurism.

Most surprising is the appearance of Bomberg. When a repentant Lewis called on him several times to contribute illustrations to *Blast 1* and *Blast 2*, these requests were rejected. At first, Bomberg wanted nothing to do with that publication but, perhaps flattered by Lewis's repeated request, he replied that he would have to be 'adequately represented and demanded that five drawings be included in the publication [*Blast 2*] – or none'.[5] That condition was unacceptable to Lewis.

Although no illustration by Bomberg appeared in either publication, the relationship between the two was sufficiently restored that Bomberg agreed to exhibit in the separate room reserved for *Those Invited to Show*. He might have hoped that such exposure would lead to much-needed sales.

Although a list of all the works on display exists, it is difficult to reconstruct the exhibition because the whereabouts of many works are not known and the titles – when provided – are often not the ones later assigned. However, it is possible to gauge what a viewer would have seen by isolating at least one work by each member that was certainly – or most likely – shown. Dismorr – *Abstract Composition*, Etchells – *Hyde Park*, Gaudier-Brzeska – *Red Stone Dancer*, Roberts – *Twostep II* (p. 111), Saunders – *Black and Khaki*, Wadsworth – *Rotterdam* (p. 137), Lewis – *Workshop* (p. 110).

Saunders's *Black and Khaki* resembles Lewis's *Workshop*, but her use of a more aerial perspective forces the spectator's eye to look down into what resembles a staircase whereas the viewer looks more directly into *Workshop*, which is more representational of an interior space. In *Dance*, another contribution

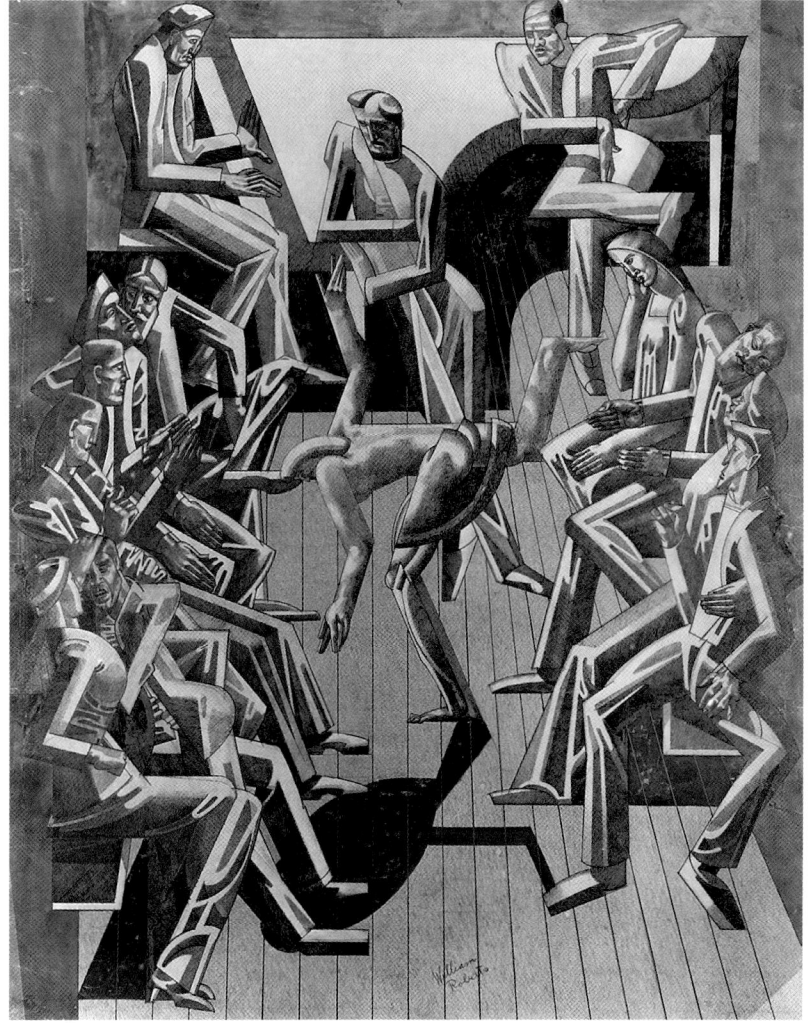

William Roberts, *The Toe Dancer*, 1914, pen, ink and gouache.

to the exhibition, Saunders, as Brigid Peppin has observed, took up a theme common in the work of other Vorticists: she was 'uniquely successful in capturing the convention-shattering body movements characteristic of popular dances' when she 'evokes the wiggles, contortions, romping, flounces of new popular dances like "Grizzly Bear" and "Turkey Trot"'.[6]

In Wadsworth's *Rotterdam*, the aerial view of the city below is interrupted by the thin white and black lines that force the eye upwards so that two perspectives are established.[7] In Roberts's *Twostep II*, the dancers are

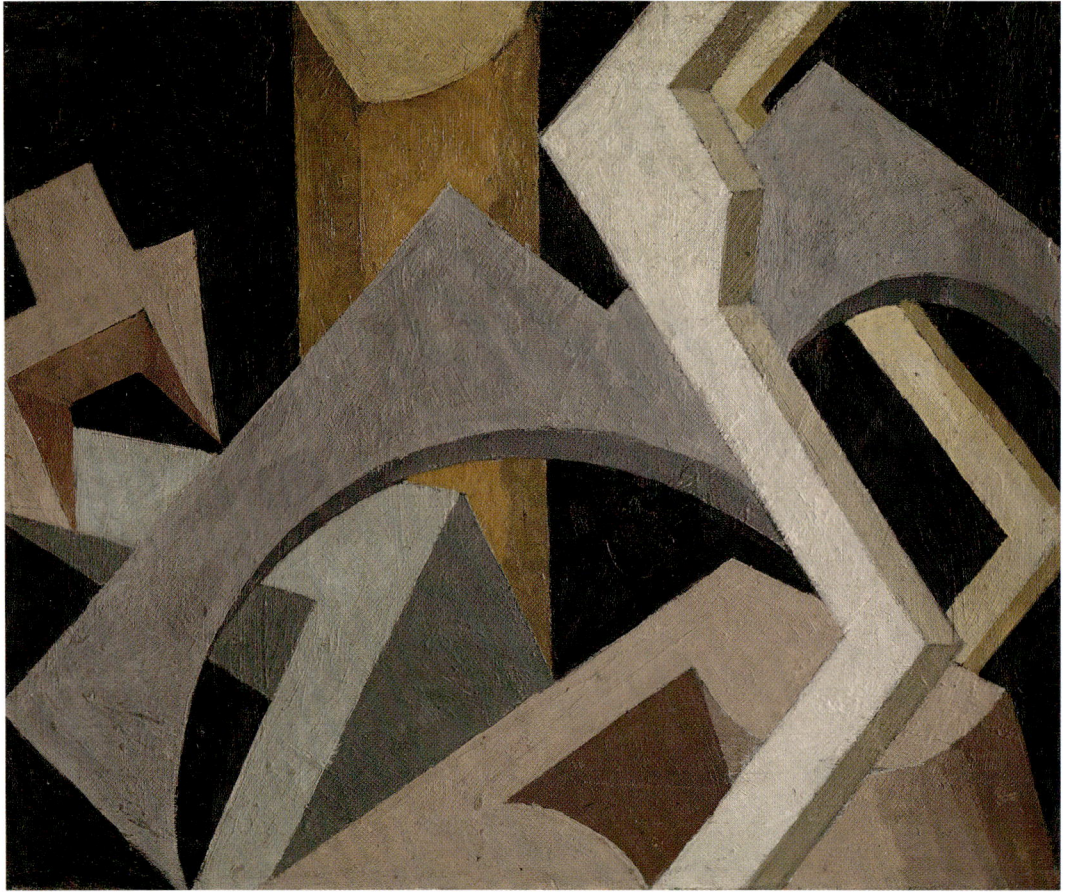

Jessica Dismorr, *Abstract Composition*, c. 1915, oil on wood.

represented by abstract lines interweaving with each other. This radically different approach to the one he used in the significantly more representational *The Toe Dancer* the year before demonstrates the artist's mixed feelings about abstraction versus representation. In *Hyde Park*, Etchells's skill as an architect is evident because he provides a side view – much like a blueprint – of all the components of the park.

Red Stone Dancer is Gaudier's most impressive experiment in Vorticism: the figure is a perfectly balanced arrangement of abstraction and representation. It can be compared to Mary Shelley's description of the Creature from *Frankenstein* – a composite of human anatomy with grotesquery. Pound considered *Red Stone Dancer* to be his protégé's finest use of pure form.

'The "abstract" or mathematical bareness of the triangle and circle are fully incarnate, made flesh, full of vitality and of energy.'[8]

Dismorr's *Abstract Composition* varied dramatically from Lewis's Vorticist images by depicting architectural fragments floating and interacting with each other. Her work bears a slight resemblance to Bomberg's in its use of interlocking forms, but she ventures further than he in the direction of pure abstraction. In the instance of this painting, she made her own distinct contribution to Vorticism.

Bomberg's six entries are now impossible to identify, but his work at that time had moved as close to pure abstraction as it ever would in his entire career. At that time, human figures – a characteristic of his previous work – had been at the point of disappearing. This is what Rebecca West recalled when in 1915, in company with Lewis, she saw Bomberg's white paintings.[9] A reviewer of the Vorticist exhibition stated: 'Mr Bomberg has a very pretty watercolour design of pseudo-calligraphic character.'[10] The closest to calligraphy of Bomberg's works at this time was his chalk drawing *Zin*. Bomberg's submissions in no way resembled those of the Vorticists. He staunchly remained one of *Those Invited to Show*.

The Athenaeum's reviewer of the Doré exhibition argued that Lewis's influence overwhelmed the other exhibitors. In speaking of Lewis and Wadsworth, he provided a precise explanation of what he meant: the Vorticists

> certainly fill their canvases with systems of interacting move-
> ment, the co-ordinations, and antagonisms of which are admirably
> stressed by a use of colour very similar to that of any other capable
> designer. Their designs are now virtually rectilinear, the small sharp
> curve occasionally introduced as a kind of knot being used not
> for purposes of transition, but rather to envenom the clash of
> opposing forces.[11]

What the visitor to the exhibition would have seen were prime examples – by Members – of the Vorticist mixture of abstraction with representation and its emphasis, in various ways, on capturing a single, defining moment within chaos. As such, the exhibition provides a snapshot of the sameness and diversity within the movement in 1915. It suggests, moreover, that this faction had reached a plateau from which the various members could move in different directions to redefine and expand its form of art. That never occurred. The exhibition became a moment frozen in time.

22

MEMORIAL:
THE PENGUIN CLUB EXHIBITION

By the time works by the Vorticists were shown at the Penguin Club exhibition in New York City in 1917, the movement had died. The New York show was a failed attempt to resuscitate the movement – in reality, it was a wake.

Ezra Pound was the person responsible for the Penguin Club exhibition. If Lewis was Vorticism's impresario, Ezra Pound was its major-domo. Rude, abrasive and cantankerous, like Lewis, Pound also shared with him the desire to reform language and art. Pound believed that verse could be revolutionized if language was pared down to its essence and outmoded means of expression were eradicated. He believed in concentrated vivid imagery.

He did not think verse could become abstract, but he firmly believed that abstract art could display strong images of a reality beyond representation and, in this way, influence poetry. In this regard, he saw the Vorticist-inspired art of his wife, Dorothy Shakespear, as the perfect accompaniment to his writing.

Pound and Lewis sometimes differed on aesthetic issues, but their bond remained strong. Aware of the potential of the war to stifle modernist art – especially Vorticism – Pound placed an advertisement in *The Egoist* on 2 August 1914 for a 'Preliminary Announcement of the College of Arts'. By November, he printed a leaflet aimed at attracting American students. This college would offer 'contact with artists of established reputation, creative minds, men for the most part who have already suffered in the cause of their art'.[1] The faculty was to include Lewis, Gaudier, Wadsworth and himself. Saunders was to be in charge of the Painting Atelier.

The death in 1915 of Gaudier – one of the proposed instructors – haunted Pound. He told a friend, 'the arts will incur no worse loss from the war than this . . . We have lost the best of the young sculptors, and the most promising.' In commemoration of his friend, he began work on a memoir about him:

'I am . . . writing it very much as I should have written it if he had lived, save that I have not him leaning over my shoulder to correct me and to find incisive, good-humoured fault with my words.' He added: 'I should in any case have written some sort of book upon vorticism.'[2] For Pound, Gaudier was the perfect Vorticist because he created sculptures that are both imagistic and abstract, and, in doing so, he encapsulated the interiority of any subject to which he turned.

In addition to writing a book about Gaudier, Pound felt that the Vorticists – most of whom were at the front – needed a patron who could use his largesse to keep their flame alive. He decided to approach John Quinn, a prosperous lawyer in New York who was a voracious collector of modern art. For Pound's purpose, Quinn had an astounding pedigree. He had helped organize the Armory Show in New York in 1913 and bought almost $6,000-worth of the works shown there.

As was his wont, Pound was combative in approaching Quinn. In an article in the *New Age* in January 1915, the poet lambasted 'American collectors buying autograph MSS. of William Morris, faked Rembrandts and faked Van-dykes. One looks out on a plutocracy and on the remains of an aristocracy who ought to know by this time that keeping up the arts means keeping up living artists; that no age can be a great age which does not find its own genius.'[3] Stung, Quinn complained to Pound: he had long been collecting Cézanne, Gauguin, Picasso, Matisse and Duchamp. He also owned six Epsteins. Intrigued by Pound's voluminous praise of Gaudier, he asked how he could acquire work by the Frenchman. The trap had been sprung.

When he learned of Gaudier's death, Quinn informed Pound: 'Poor brave fellow. There is only the memory of a brave gifted man. What I can do I will do.'[4] He asked Pound to get his hands on any available work, ordered twenty issues of each *Blast* and promised to finance an exhibition of Vorticist art in New York City.

When he was told that Sophie Brzeska forbade the export of any her partner's work to the States, Quinn was crestfallen and informed Pound he was cancelling the scheduled exhibition at the Montross Gallery. On 23 August 1915 Pound attempted to mollify Quinn by suggesting he concentrate on acquiring works by Lewis. He reminded the attorney that he had become devoted to Vorticism solely because of Lewis and Gaudier, and he pointed out that Vorticism would never have existed without Lewis, who was a genius: 'the vitality[,] the fullness of the man! Nobody knows it. Nobody has *any* conception of the volume and energy and the variety.' To whet Quinn's appetite, he praised Lewis's drawings as 'stupendous'.[4] In order to fortify his case, he downplayed Wadsworth, who did 'occasional good things. Etchells does desultory good things. Miss Saunders has done one, but I can't say that they feed me (i.e. my mind). And I can most certainly say that without Lewis there would be no vorticist school, no vorticist painting.'[5]

Intent on closing a deal, Pound perhaps forgot that he had suggested to Quinn twelve days earlier that he might want to purchase a Saunders: 'The things I personally would buy if I had the cash are Saunders' "Island of Laputa" (tendency to placidity in upper right ¼ of picture counteracted by great energy in her waves convention)' (p. 143). In his opinion, this image was strong because of Lewis's influence: 'This is Miss S. with Lewis, so to speak.'[6]

Pound warned Quinn in no uncertain terms that the show had to go on: 'I simply CANT [*sic*] top it now. The boys have sent in the stuff, and if it don't go, I can never look anybody in the face again.'[7] Browbeaten into submission, Quinn agreed to receive the work, but when the shipment arrived in New York in June, the Montross Gallery had decided not to host the putative show. Saddled with the cost of packing, insurance and freight, Quinn stored the works in his apartment. When he showed them to two friends, they were disdainful. He wondered, he told Pound, if they had been overly sentimental about Gaudier. Pound diplomatically replied that these artists did not care about sales: they would be satisfied that Quinn had looked at their works. Quinn then spent £438 on pieces by Etchells, Roberts, Lewis and Wadsworth; in September he spent a further £46 on ones by Dismorr and Saunders.[8]

Quinn managed to arrange an exhibition at the Penguin Club, an artists' society at 5 East 15th Street. There were 75 works in the exhibition: 46 by Lewis, 9 by Etchells, 4 by Roberts, 4 by Dismorr, 4 by Saunders and 8 (woodcuts and drawings) by Wadsworth. Since Quinn had gone on a shopping spree of the works he had received, 52 were not for sale. The exhibition may have been more focused than the one in 1915, but nothing by Bomberg or Gaudier was on display. (Quinn eventually evaded Brzeska's embargo and acquired work by the sculptor.)

There were several conundrums. The exhibition could easily have carried a secondary title: 'Works by Wyndham Lewis and Associates'. Some of the

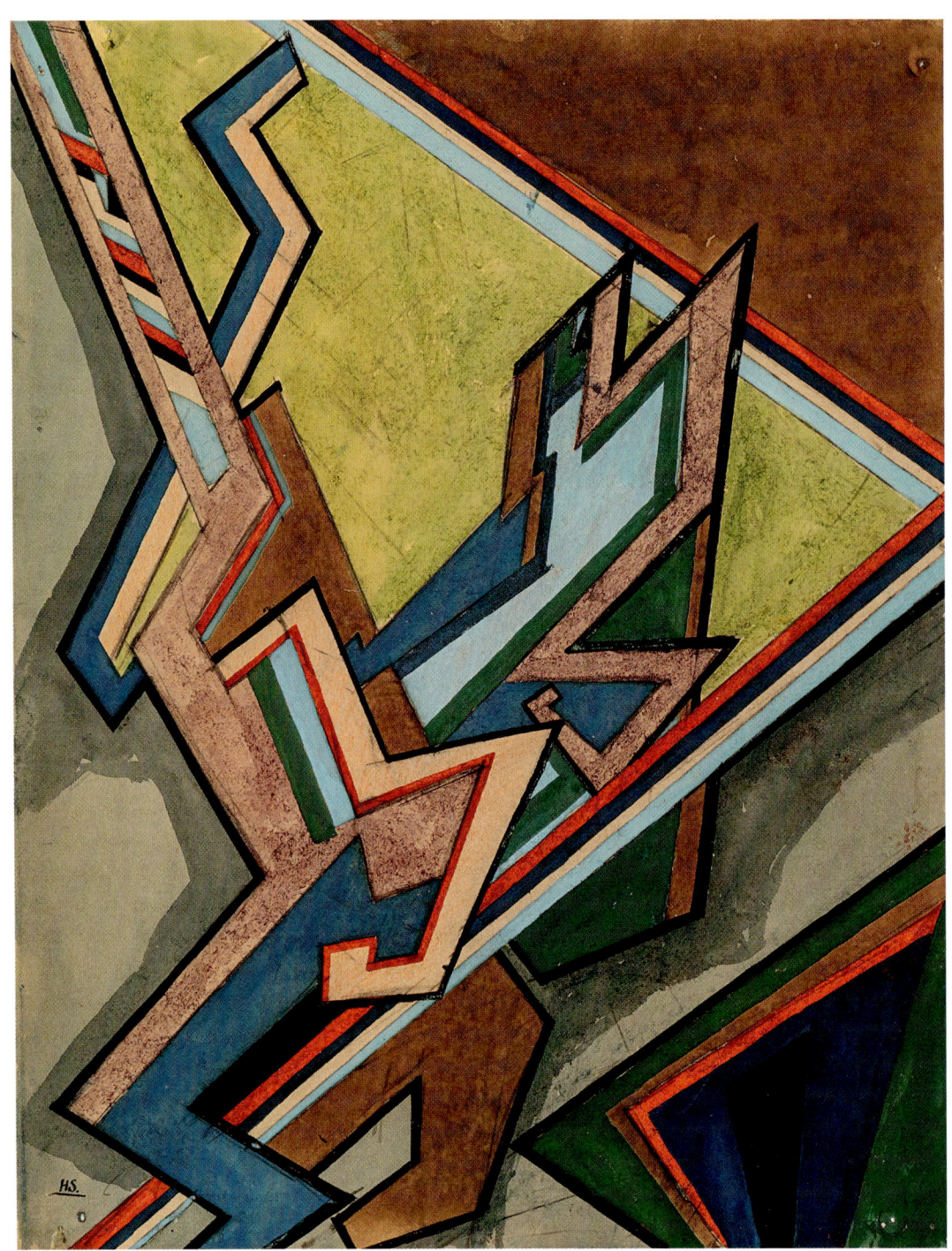

Helen Saunders, *Dance, c.* 1915, graphite and gouache on paper.

works by Lewis went back to 1912 and even earlier in contrast to the more recent work by his colleagues. Any would-be collector would have been dismayed that only 23 items were for sale. Another major difficulty was the scant but hostile attention given to the show by the press. *Art World* claimed that 'Vorticism is the result when Cubism and Futurism rush into a vacuum from opposite sides, meeting in the centre.' Referring to the Armory show, the notice continued:

> Tendencies that had meteoric vogue some years ago, and were supposed to have run their course for pictorial purposes are revived . . . The walls are brilliant with hangings in which intricacy of design and color harmonies and contrasts are effectively shown. Such work was long ago recognized by the public as ingenious. It failed to win enduring favor because it belongs to mechanical or ornamental design rather than to art.

The article, lumping Cubism and Vorticism together, correctly claimed that the arrival of the Vorticists in New York 'seems to be belated'.[9]

The Penguin Club exhibition was the second and last Vorticist exhibition (although Lewis tried to revive the movement with the Group X exhibition in 1920). Although all the works on display – with the glaring exception of Lewis – were recent, the Penguin Club was essentially a Vorticist Retrospective; very much a last hurrah.

Various reasons can be given for the short lifespan of Vorticism. Some of the artists fought in the war and were not, as a result, producing as much art as they had before. Bomberg enlisted with the Royal Engineers in November 1915 but was transferred to the King's Royal Rifles, where he was listed as a sapper. In June 1916 he was sent to the front in France. Lewis joined the Royal Artillery in February 1916 as a gunner and eventually became an officer in the Royal Garrison Artillery. He served in France from May to November 1917. In February 1916 Roberts volunteered for the Royal Artillery and served in France from August 1916 to April 1918. Wadsworth served in the Royal Navy Volunteers Reserve from August 1916 to August 1917. Hulme was killed in action on 28 September 1917. Gaudier had died two years before.

War brought chaos, and Vorticism is about the containment of chaos at the still point of the vortex; to many, unrelenting pandemonium seemed to be the real state of human affairs and so the idea that it could be tamed went against the zeitgeist. Moreover, there was a move by some of the Vorticists towards representation, especially in art commissioned by governments to represent the war.

All the above contributed to the disintegration of Vorticism, but there are other factors. English art remained resistant to abstraction and envisioned all the new modernisms as a kind of national threat. This issue can be stated more positively. For the brief time it existed, Vorticism demonstrated that a distinctly English avant-garde art could create its own unique form of modernism.

The movement survived – considerably subdued and mutated – in the art of the Rebels. The tyros, having immersed themselves in Vorticism, had become fully fledged artists. Then they reinvented themselves. Although all of them with one exception – Jessica Dismorr – moved away from abstraction, their later work, especially up to about 1925, remained rooted in their previous incarnations as Vorticists.

PART THREE:

AFTERSHOCKS

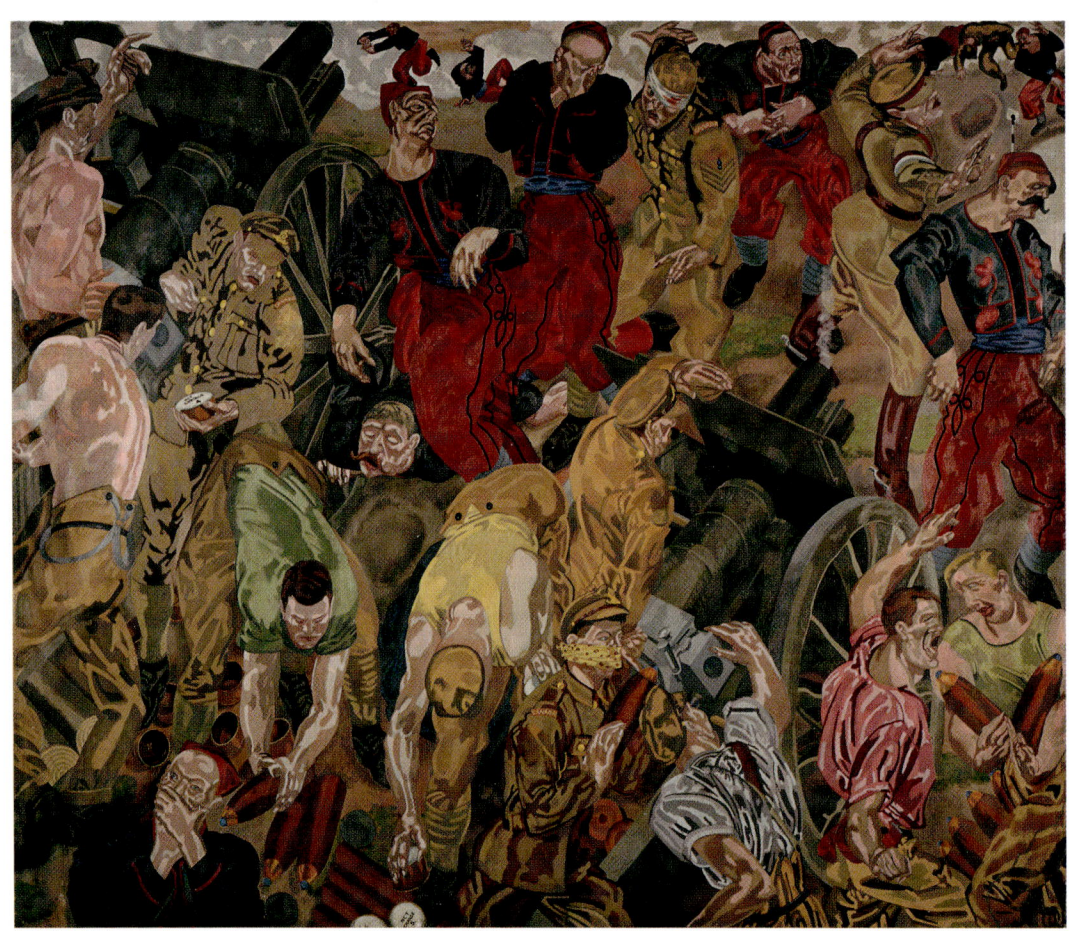

William Roberts, *The First German Gas Attack at Ypres*, 1919, oil on canvas.

23

'LESS CUBISM':
WILLIAM ROBERTS

Although he wrote at length about his early years, Roberts glided over his association with Vorticism. 'From the autumn of 1914 till the end of 1915 . . . I continued my Cubistic painting, associating with the artists who had once been a part of Roger Fry's Omega Workshop Group. However, in March 1916 an end was put to these activities, by my entry into the Royal Field Artillery.'

Roberts, a reluctant Vorticist from the outset, insisted his early work was Cubistic. He also described Vorticism 'as a kind of exotic growth nurtured later by certain cultivators in the hope that it would overgrow and supplant . . . flowering Cubism.'[1] Late in life, feeling overshadowed by Lewis, he attempted to disassociate himself further from him. The ex-Vorticist to whom he felt most akin remained Bomberg, a person who, like himself, resisted being placed in any box.

In 1915, however – whether he ever admitted it to himself – in a piece such as *Study for Twostep II* (p. 111) his work had come to resemble that of Wadsworth, Saunders, Etchells and Lewis. He would have eventually broken away from their influence, but the war considerably hastened the process.

In August 1916 he arrived at Vimy Ridge. The Somme offensive, in which many Englishmen had lost their lives, had started two months earlier. Like many others he was traumatized by the senselessness and futility of what he witnessed: 'I believe I possess the average amount of hope and patience, but this existence beats me.' He added: 'I am feeling very bitter against life altogether just at present.'[2] His battery was relocated at the end of 1916 to Ypres, but in the spring of 1917 the 51st Brigade headed south for the build-up to the Battle of Arras. When that advance was finally halted, over 160,000 British lives had been lost.

At the end of 1917 Roberts, serving as a 4.5 Howitzer gunner, had been in France for almost seventeen months and was given a two-week leave back in England. He fondly recalled, 'First World War London was a great place to spend one's leave. At night in the black-out the streets of Soho were filled with groups of roving soldiers in search of a good time.' He took a room at the Eiffel. 'One night, as a change from the Eiffel's cuisine, I dined in the company of Augustus John at Pagani's in Great Portland Street, where John, perhaps because he was the Official War Artist of the party, amused himself by drawing on his serviette between courses. If this had happened at the Eiffel, I feel sure Stulik would have framed the serviette.'[3]

Back in France late in 1917 Roberts received a letter from a friend who wrote:

> 'Lewis is back here on leave, and has been made an Official
> War Artist. Do some drawings at once and send them to Konody,
> he is choosing artists to do war paintings for the Canadian War
> Records Office.' Situated as I was at the time, it was extremely
> difficult to find the opportunity or the materials to make a drawing
> of any kind. Fortunately the battery was resting for a few days, and
> I was able to slip away at odd times to a small unoccupied army
> hut that formed part of the camp. There, on a sheet of newspaper,
> I made a drawing whose subject I cannot recall at this date.[4]

The Canadian-born Max Aitken, later Lord Beaverbrook, had made his fortune in his native land before emigrating to England in 1910, where he became a press baron, a Member of Parliament and a knight; he was elevated to the peerage in 1915. Using his own money, he established the Canadian War Memorial Fund in 1916 to commission official war artists to paint the war effort of the troops from Canada. The programme eventually employed close to 120 artists, most of them British or Canadian, who created nearly 1,000 works.

P. G. Konody, the critic, commissioned the artists and then vetted their submissions. The Hungarian-born Konody, who wrote for the *Daily Mail* and *The Observer*, liked to think of himself as up-to-date but, unlike his colleague Frank Rutter, had never been partial to abstraction and actively disliked Vorticism. He preferred clear, uncluttered art or, as he put it, 'diversity kept under control'.[5]

Emboldened by this news, but aware of Konody's predilections, Roberts wrote the journalist and craftily insinuated he had wandered far from his old ways but was willing to amend that.

> I will send you some more things that will have less 'Cubism' in them, but should a meeting of your Committee take place before they reach you, will you only exhibit those that you think would not puzzle too much for this meeting? Perhaps some of my earlier and slightly more finished drawings could be brought together . . . Tonks has one . . . And Professor Brown at the Slade has a drawing which would be good to view.

During his time in France, he discovered fond memories of his days at the Slade: 'Happy home for illusions! An artistic nursery.'[6]

Konody was sufficiently placated that Roberts received a letter on 17 December from the Canadian War Records Office that told him it

> would be glad to know whether, providing you are given the necessary facilities and leave, you are prepared to paint the picture at your own risk . . . The reason for this request is that the Art Advisor informs us he is not acquainted with your realistic work and Cubist work is inadmissible for the purpose . . . if the picture is accepted you would be paid between £250 to £300.[7]

As soon as he was on leave again in London – and enticed by the huge sum on offer – Roberts called on Konody

> for further information. He showed me a list of the artists who were being employed and the subjects they were to paint. He said that all except one had been allocated and that concerned the first gas attack upon the Canadians at Ypres. Although I was without experience of that kind of cloud gas warfare, and told Konody so, I accepted the commission.[8]

To paint *The First German Gas Attack at Ypres*, he was transferred or, as he put it,

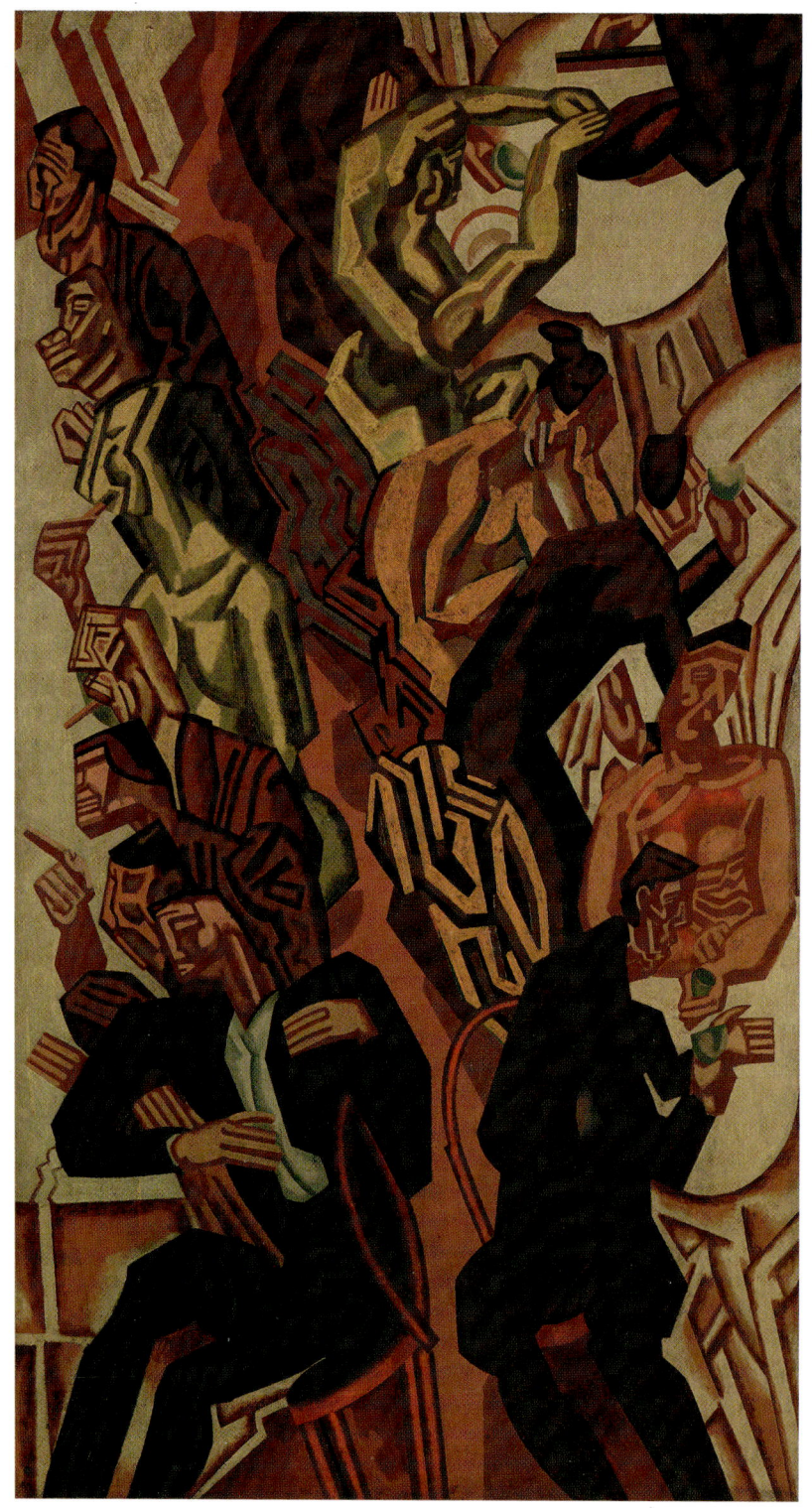

William Roberts, *The Diners*, 1919, oil on canvas.

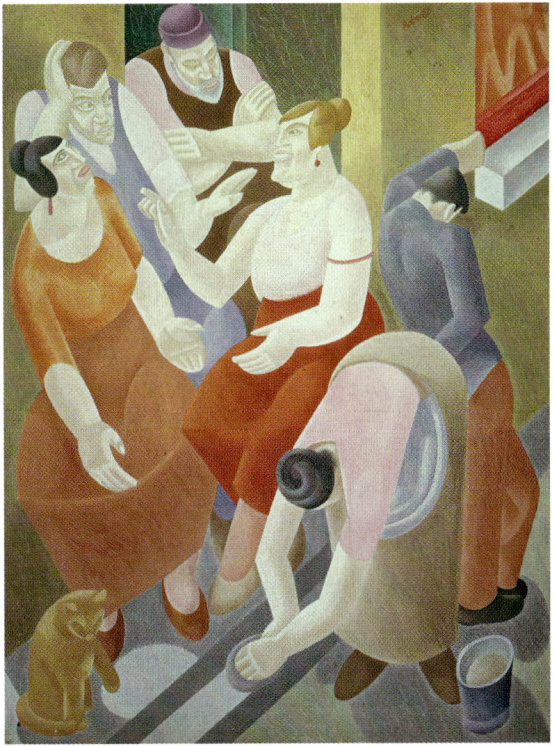

William Roberts, *The Char*, 1924, oil on canvas.

'Loaned' perhaps would be a better word, to the Canadians for
six months. I continued to wear my Royal Field Artillery uniform,
but lived free from military duties, as a civilian, and at my own
expense. I took a studio in Flood Street, Chelsea (rent paid by the
Canadians) and spent the summer of 1918 working there on my
12 by 10-foot canvas. Later in the year, the collection of Canadian
War Paintings was exhibited at the Royal Academy. When I had
finished with the Canadians, I did not return to France because the
British Ministry of Information, who had their own War Records
organization, commissioned me to do for them *A Shell Dump,
France.* For this I was paid by monthly instalments, but before
this picture was finished the war was ended.[9]

As much as he could, Roberts eliminated any hints of Cubism or
Vorticism from *First German Gas Attack.* The resulting enormous vividly

coloured canvas, in which eighteen stricken soldiers writhe in pain and gasp for air, relates much more to German Expressionism than any other modernism. This crowded painting is also excessively melodramatic, with the interlaced figures competing for the viewer's attention and cut off at the edges of the canvas.

After the war ended, in August 1919 Stulik, recently released from internment, asked Roberts to decorate the lobby leading to the Vorticist Room. Although the restaurateur reimbursed him only in meals, Roberts was glad to get away from his cramped living quarters to work in a larger space. For this project, Roberts painted three panels placed in a row along a wall above a dining table. During his time at the Slade, Tonks had invited him to assist in decorating the walls in a girls' school in Fulham and so Roberts had some experience working on such an installation.

In accepting this commission, Roberts did not continue in the direction of *First German Gas Attack* but revisited the style of his work from 1913–14, as in *The Return of Ulysses*. He may have done this to please Stulik or to blend his work with that of Lewis and Saunders in the Vorticist Room. The figures in the two surviving panels – *Study for Dancers* and *Study for Diners* – are squeezed together. Both canvases could be illustrations to Dante's *Inferno*, and, as such, resemble the figures in *First German Gas Attack*. Roberts had always been fascinated by dancing figures and he returned to this theme here. The figures may interweave here, but in a melancholic, desultory way. They are suffering, trapped. The diners are not taking any pleasure in the food on offer, and the dancers are linked in macabre embraces.

In his later work, Roberts abandoned this type of painting, although he always retained a strong sense of geometrical composition and angularity as a holdover from his Vorticist years. His figures became monumental in a way reminiscent of Fernand Léger's and like the French artist he often depicted members of the working class.

Slade classmates and friends Roberts and Bomberg were much alike in possessing fiery temperaments – and in venting their feelings. Like Roberts, Bomberg also worked for the Canadian War Record Office. His experience proved traumatic.

24

'METHODIC DISCORD':
DAVID BOMBERG

At the outset of the war, Roberts and Bomberg obtained accommodation at a derelict house in Osmonde Terrace overlooking Primrose Hill. The house had been purchased by a friend of Augustus John, Stewart Gray, who had once been a lawyer in Edinburgh who had 'led a contingent of "hunger marches" to London'. Convinced by John those young artists needed a refuge, the house was purchased by Gray 'so they might be able to carry on, despite war conditions and to keep themselves free from the need to join up as a means of livelihood. As well as painters, singers and dancers whose work had been stopped by war conditions were offered a home.'[1] This habitation was primitive: no gas, no electricity, no running water. Gray, who was reputed to resemble Tolstoy, looked after his charges. Roberts was mesmerized by Gray's wife, whose acrobatic choreography he immortalized in *Toe Dancer* (p. 157).

Bomberg, who became infatuated with another resident of the house, Maria Wajda, a Russian ballet dancer, painted a series of abstracts emphasizing movement. These paintings demonstrate he was also aware of all the excitement generated by Diaghilev's Ballets Russes, especially by its costumes and stage designs.

Perhaps surprisingly, Bomberg's dancers are much more abstract than those by Roberts. In speaking of his dancer images in the Chenil exhibition in 1914, Bomberg had appealed 'to a *sense of Form* . . . I am *searching for an Intenser* Expression.'[2] In his previous work, the separation of figures from their backgrounds was clear. Now the figures are difficult to discern.

Demoralized by attempting to survive in London, Bomberg thought that time in the army might make his life more endurable, although he soon found barrack life barely tolerable. But he managed to spend time drawing.

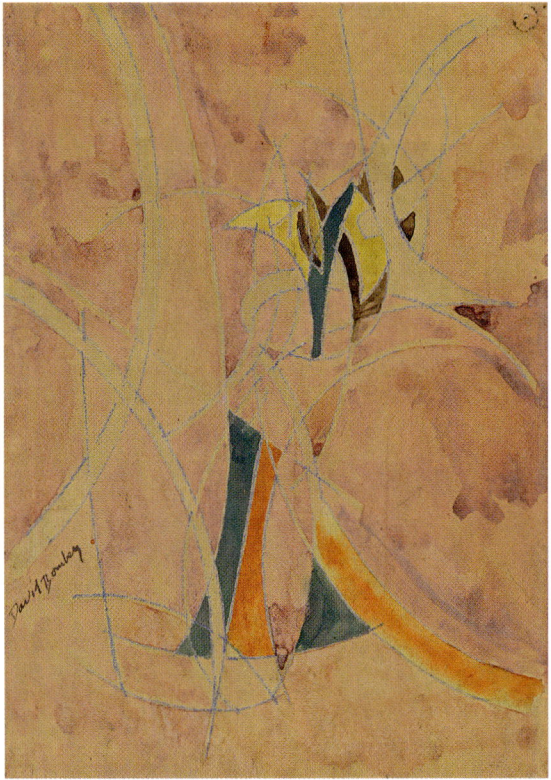

David Bomberg, *The Dancers*, 1914, watercolour, crayon, graphite and ink on paper.

At the front, life in the trenches did not provide such opportunities and, in fact, he became both crestfallen and depressed, as can be seen in jottings such as these: 'Assassins! Figurantes waiting in the wings! Hidden guns. And guns that you cannot hear at all – flashing in fast rotation – fantastically . . . jerky marionettes, snow-clad.' He also spoke of the barrage balloons: 'Isolated, a curling string. Swollen, blown-out toads with piercing eyes – gloating in dripping lakes of boundless clouds, over desolated tracts of wasted ground.'[3] The imagery in these passages may be vivid and poignant but they reveal the stress that was grinding Bomberg down. He was further downtrodden when he heard of the death of Hulme – the critic who had possessed a profound understanding of his work.

Having reached breaking point, the distraught artist put a gun to his foot and pulled the trigger. Some nearby soldiers bandaged his wound and rushed him to hospital. When he told the adjutant that he had deliberately

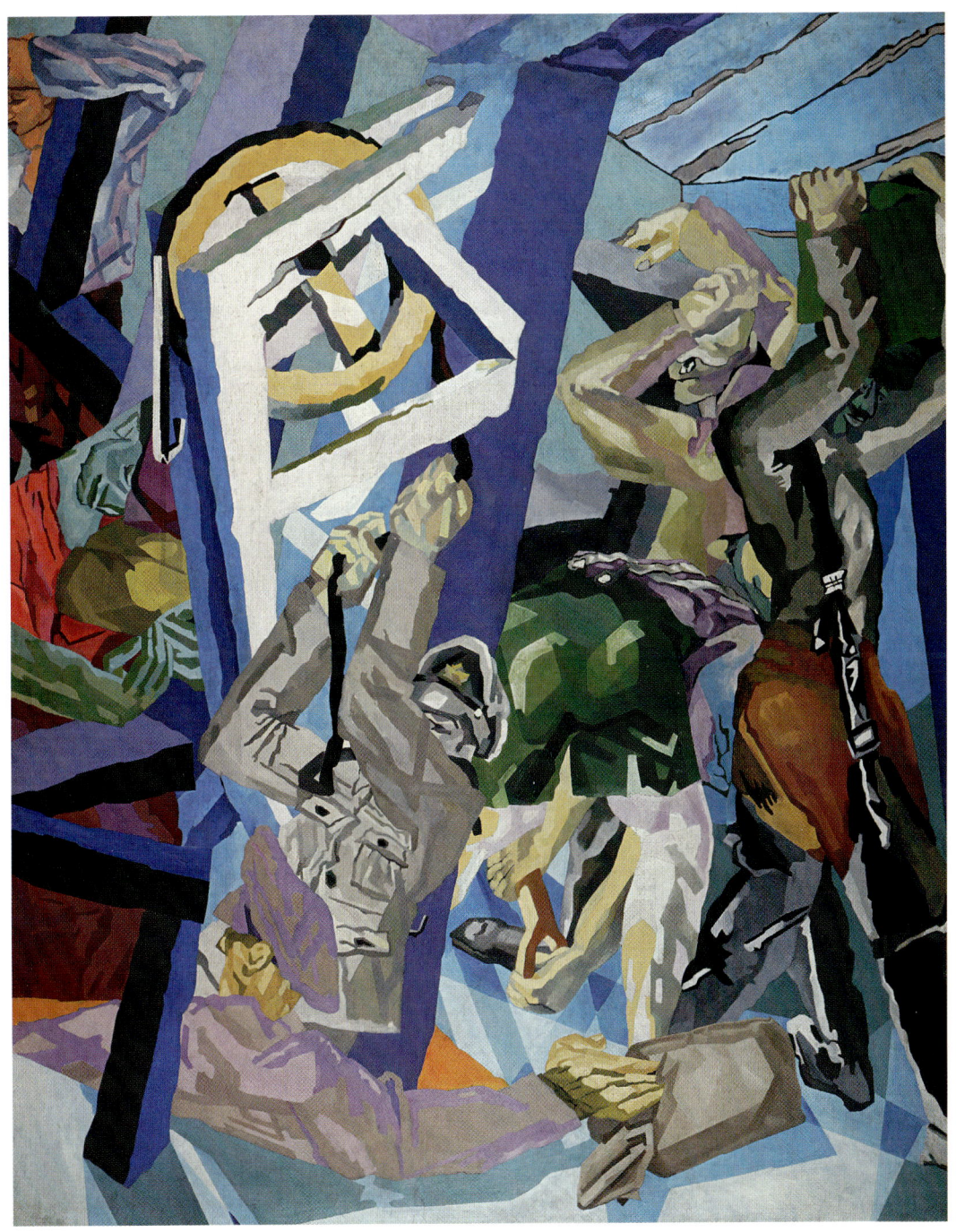

David Bomberg, *Study for Sappers at Work: A Canadian Tunnelling Company,*
Hill 60, St. Eloi, c. 1918–19, oil on canvas.

wounded himself, he received a stern lecture and a request to claim that he had injured himself by accident. When Bomberg refused, his superior informed him that his cowardice did not merit the firing squad.

Having taken his stand and then been assigned the role of runner, he was able to come to grips with the remainder of his stay at the front. Subsequently, he was allowed to withdraw from active service. He summed up his experience poignantly: 'They live a thousand intermittent lives, these trenchmen, with liquid acid freezing on their hearts.'

When, back in London, Bomberg applied to the Canadian War Memorial Fund for a commission, he was told, like Roberts, that he would have to undertake the project at his own risk because Konody was 'not acquainted with your realistic work, and cubist work would be inadmissible'.[4] Bomberg, who had always refused to place his work under any banner, agreed. He chose to depict a Canadian tunnelling company at work under Hill 60 near St Eloi. This topic allowed him to show a group of men interlocked in a communal exercise. As he envisioned it, *Sappers at Work* would not be unlike *The Mud Bath* or even *Ezekiel*. He began work in spring 1918 and worked on the canvas until that autumn.

In *The Mud Bath* (p. 109), the figures and their surroundings are reduced to abstract elements that blend harmoniously. Bomberg could not really do this in *Sappers*, but he thought of several compromises. One study depicts the sappers very much like the figures in *The Mud Bath*. However, he showed several sketches done in a representational way to Konody, who gained the impression that the finished painting would be what he was hoping for. Knowing that the critic would reject a 'Cubist' work, Bomberg prepared an amalgam – a compromise – between representation and abstraction.

When Bomberg took the result to Konody, the critic was aghast: 'You submit to me the most wonderful drawings ... and you bring me this futurist abortion.'[5] When a tearful Bomberg told his wife, Alice, of the altercation, she confronted Konody, who, somewhat mollified, agreed that Bomberg could begin work on a new canvas as long as she assured him that she would supervise her husband so that not a hint of Cubism or Futurism would remain on the substitute canvas.

The rejected painting is daunting – a work that captures the horror of war by the dissonance established in a variety of powerful passages. The blue and white vertical structure running down the middle is reinforced by the soldier reaching out from it. The left side of the painting is calm as opposed to the writhing forms on the left. At the very bottom, the extended hand of the soldier in mauve intersects with the space of the soldier above him. The result is utterly chaotic but reflects discord and confusion in no uncertain terms. The amended, second version portrays the sappers at work and the massive structures over their heads. It is an impressive, dramatic piece of work, but it is not in the kind of style that adequately expressed Bomberg's talent – or that he was comfortable with.

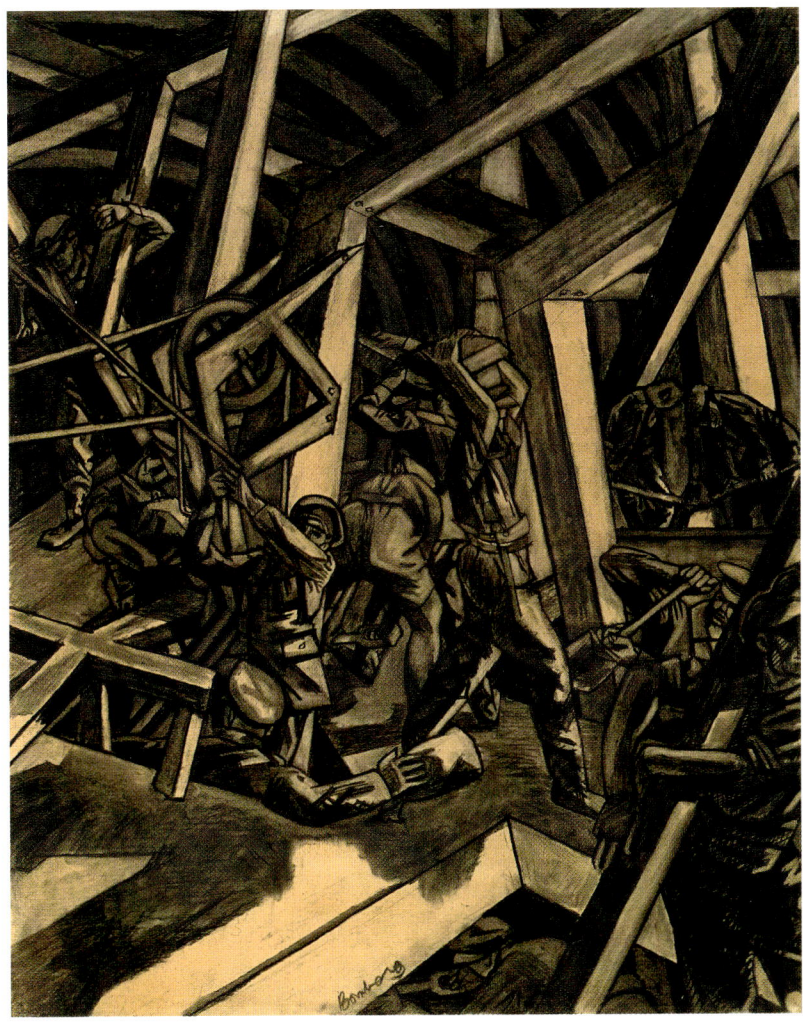

David Bomberg, *Sappers at Work: Canadian Tunnelling Company,*
R 14, St. Eloi, c. 1918–19, charcoal on paper.

In large part because of the *Sappers at Work* contretemps, Bomberg did not know what direction to take. Did Konody's rejection of one painting and eventual acceptance of a substitute mean that he should abandon any hint of abstraction? In 1919 he made a series of pen and ink drawings in which he tried to balance the two modes of expression. When Frank Rutter – a critic diametrically opposed to Konody – saw them, he was so impressed that he displayed over a hundred at his newly established Adelphi Gallery in 1919. Herbert Read thought 'a high standard of formal beauty is attained.' Moreover, his

> *ideas* are always good. Perhaps the fact that Mr Bomberg has ideas is his most remarkable peculiarity. And the way he will explore all the possibilities of an idea in a series of drawings seems to indicate that his mind is of that objective, scientific sort that alone is capable of wonders. Mr Bomberg is possibly a great artist.[6]

Despite the generous accolade, Bomberg remained deeply unsure of himself. *Barges*, which he submitted to the London Group exhibition in

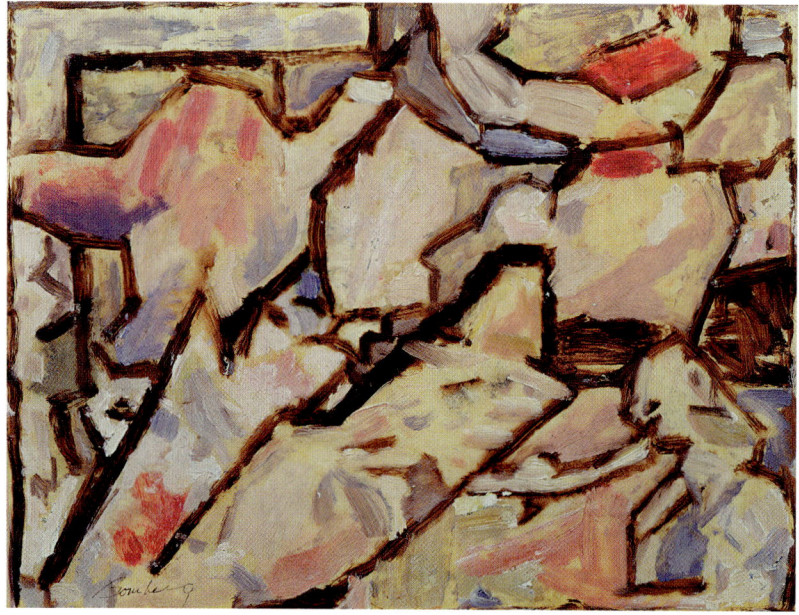

David Bomberg, *Imaginative Composition: The Tent*, c. 1920–23, oil on paper.

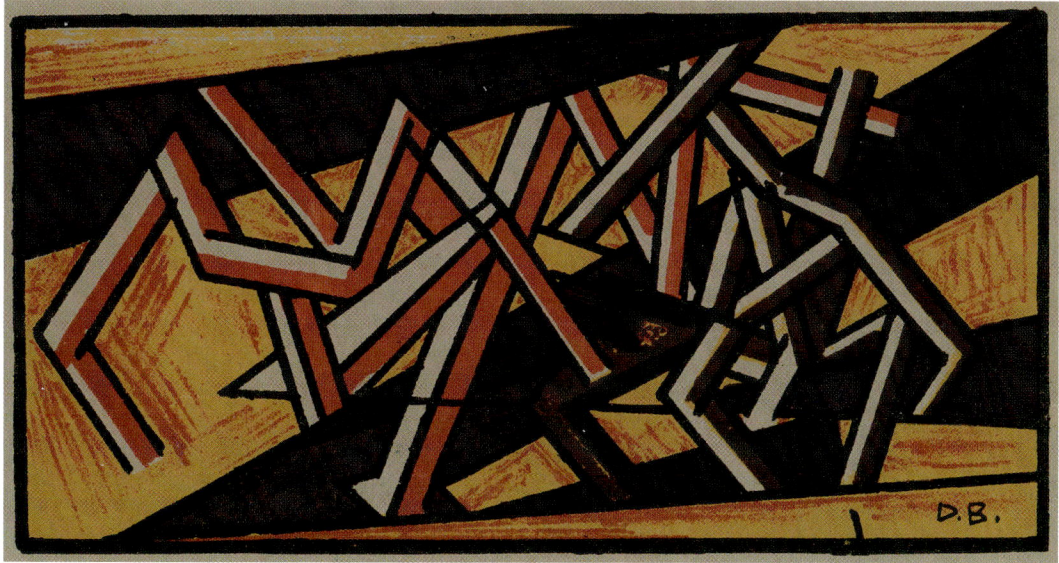

David Bomberg, *Russian Ballet*, c. 1914–19, lithograph.

1919, demonstrates this. The barges themselves are painted in a representational manner whereas their shadows are abstract shapes. In *The Tent*, it is not possible to discern the object supposedly depicted – instead, there is a melange of undefined passages.

Bomberg may have wanted to continue in the style of images like *Ezekiel*, but he was frightened to do so. In 1919, in six small lithographs for the booklet *The Russian Ballet*, he reprised the subject-matter of his early paintings. He also wrote an accompanying poem worthy of Ezra Pound's best efforts in constructing an Imagist text.

Methodic discord startles . . .
Insistent snatchings drag fancy from space,
Fluttering white hands beat – compel. Reason concedes.
Impressions crowding collide with movement around us –
the curtain falls – the created illusion escapes.
The mind clamped fast captures only a fragment for new illusion.

To raise money, Bomberg had one hundred copies of the booklet printed and attempted to sell them at the Alhambra Theatre, where the Ballets Russes performed. Hearing of this, Diaghilev put a stop to it. So, Bomberg took all the booklets to Henderson's Bomb Shop at Charing Cross Road, where they were put up for sale. About ten were sold before Henderson determined they were unsaleable.

The three small pieces show light infiltrating darkness. The three larger pieces are more varied. In the one shown here, very much in the manner of *Mud Bath*, the dancers intersect with each other in a highly choreographed moment. Another is an overhead view of the dancers. The smallest shows a conflict between two abstract forces, one brown, one black. This portfolio, which displays a mixture of approaches Bomberg had used when he was associated with Vorticism, became a farewell to his early life and art.

Bomberg had always held himself apart from Vorticism – he was only ever tangentially a member of the group – but these images from 1919 are of arrested moments in which time has come to a stop and intimations of the vortex can be glimpsed.

From 1923 to 1927 Bomberg painted landscapes in Palestine, then in Spain and Cyprus, and, upon returning to England, in Cornwall. Traces of his Vorticist years can be seen in the strong architectural lines that under-score his subsequent compositions. At the outset of his career, he had been adventurous in discovering ways to represent transcendent states of mind. He never lost that urge.

25

'COLD-BLOODED PERSISTENCE': EDWARD WADSWORTH

Ezra Pound once observed: 'I cannot recall any painting of Mr. Wadsworth where he seems to be angry.'[1] On this point, Jonathan Black has pointed out that

> Wadsworth's version of Vorticism appeared to lack the bite, the venom and the weighty power that all too potently radiated from Lewis's abstractions . . . In his own way, Wadsworth did develop a formula of geometric abstraction that confidently anticipated the following challenge in the July 1915 second *Blast*: 'You must catch the clearness and logic in the midst of contradictions: not settle down and snooze on an acquired, easily possessed and mastered satisfying shape.'[2]

Black's claim has considerable merit: Wadsworth's work has a tranquil, soothing presence completely absent in Lewis's work. He was never an angry person like Lewis.

Moreover, he was not volatile like Roberts and Bomberg, and he was never as overly demanding, outrageous and self-serving as Lewis. At the Slade, Wadsworth took delight in exploring his unruly side. Later, he became a faithful friend to his fellow Vorticists.

At the outset of the war, Wadsworth was assigned to the Anti-Aircraft Gun Crew in Paddington. In June 1916 he sailed from Southampton for the eastern Mediterranean to serve as a sub-lieutenant (intelligence officer) on the island called Ispathio off Mudros in the north Aegean, where he remained during the summer of 1917. From there, he wrote to John Quinn to ask about the Penguin Club exhibition: '[I] am entirely separated from most of the things

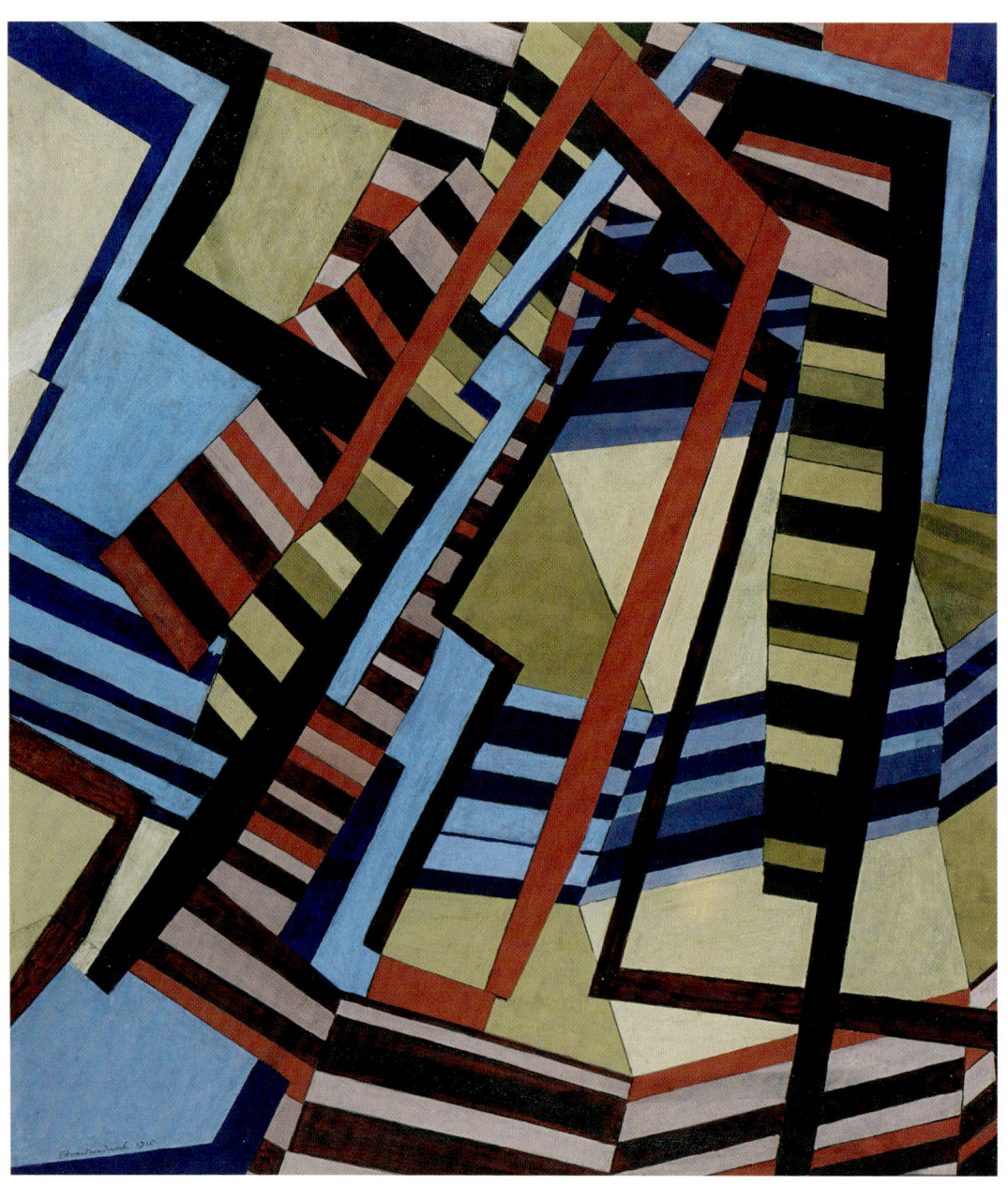

Edward Wadsworth, *Enclosure*, 1915, gouache, ink pencil, and painted paper on paper.

that interest me, consequently I have no idea of what sort of reception the Vorticist pictures had.'[3] Woefully, Quinn told him that the exhibition 'was not, I am sorry to say, a great success'. He was frank in telling Wadsworth that he liked his woodcuts but did not care for the drawings. He found the paintings merely 'interesting'. He added: 'But I imagine that when the war is over and you get back to work, a different thing will come out of it.'[4]

Wadsworth responded, 'To a certain extent I agree with you: I think [the woodcuts] are probably the best in that they are the most complete.' He then explained what he meant by 'complete'. Their 'means of expression is in a more complete accordance with the thing expressed *in them* than some of the other things which are perhaps more experimental and less mature. [The woodcut as a genre] leaves nothing to accident.'

He remained uncertain where he was going in his art and whether a 'different thing will come out of it all when I get back after the war . . . certainly things will develop like all healthy children. I don't anticipate, though, that my work will in the near future be in any way reactionary – at least I don't feel like that now.'[5]

For Wadsworth, the drawing *Enclosure* – which was shown in New York – was decidedly experimental. Using collage, he constructed this drawing by overlapping planes of vibrant colours. The strong verticals moving to the right bestow the sense of confinement indicated in the title. This composition is pure abstraction whereas the woodcuts always clearly hint at their subject-matter: landscapes, towns, engines – often from an aerial perspective. The intricate *War-Engine* in *Blast 2* shows him in this mode (p. 143).

Wadsworth had a much easier time than Roberts and Bomberg with his commission from the Canadian War Records Office; in fact, the project was perfect for him. The danger from German U-boats had been catastrophic in 1917 and so the Admiralty decided to have more than 2,300 ships dazzle-painted. Early in 1918 Wadsworth was sent on a course devoted to camouflage. In April he was stationed in Avonmouth and Bristol and by July he was sent to Liverpool to act as a supervisor. He served under Norman Wilkinson, a marine painter and poster designer who had devised dazzle camouflage. This technology was intended to mislead the enemy, not make the vessels invisible. At times, as many as one hundred ships were in harbour to be painted. Wadsworth was responsible for the application of the paint to the ships.

He remained in Liverpool until the end of 1918 and, a month later, was in London waiting to be demobilized.

In the spring of 1919, he painted *Dazzle-Ships in Drydock at Liverpool* for the Canadian War Records. He also made seven woodcuts of the ships. In November the Royal Academy held a camouflage exhibition at which four of Wadsworth's dazzle-ship woodcuts were on display. The reviewer in the *Evening Standard* was impressed: 'The "dazzle" section illustrates amusingly an inversion of some of the principles of Post-Impressionism – how to destroy form instead of emphasising it – and the woodcuts of ships by Mr Edward Wadsworth, are by far the best things artistically in the exhibition.'[6]

Earlier, in March 1919, Frank Rutter gave Wadsworth a one-man show of his woodcuts at the Adelphi Gallery. The exhibition received strong notices, including Bernadette Murphy's in the *Arts Gazette*:

> the simple black cuts are the most uncompromising abstraction
> we have had since the Vorticist show in 1914. They are akin to the
> most cubic cubes of Picasso . . . these prints, demanding great
> care in registration, are each produced from several blocks . . .
> Wadsworth is acquiring his place in contemporary art by
> cold-blooded persistence, the quiet assertion of his work.[7]

At the very same time he was being hailed by critics like Murphy, Wadsworth had turned in a new direction: pen and ink drawings and lithographs of the Black Country, the area in the Midlands where he had been born. It had been heavily transformed during the Industrial Revolution by coal mines, iron foundries, glass factories and steel mills that produced such strong pollution that many parts of it were blackened by soot. Lewis recalled Wadsworth once 'taking me in his car on a tour of some of Yorkshire's cities. In due course we arrived on a hill above Halifax. He stopped the car and we gazed down into its blackened labyrinth. I could see he was proud of it. "It's like Hell, isn't it?" he said enthusiastically.'[8]

For Wadsworth, his daughter Barbara recalled, this area was 'superb visual excitement – beauty in contrast of form as well as related form, beauty in the relentless vigour of man-made landscape'.[9] He recognized that the land had been corrupted by man's intrusion but for him the result was a remarkable

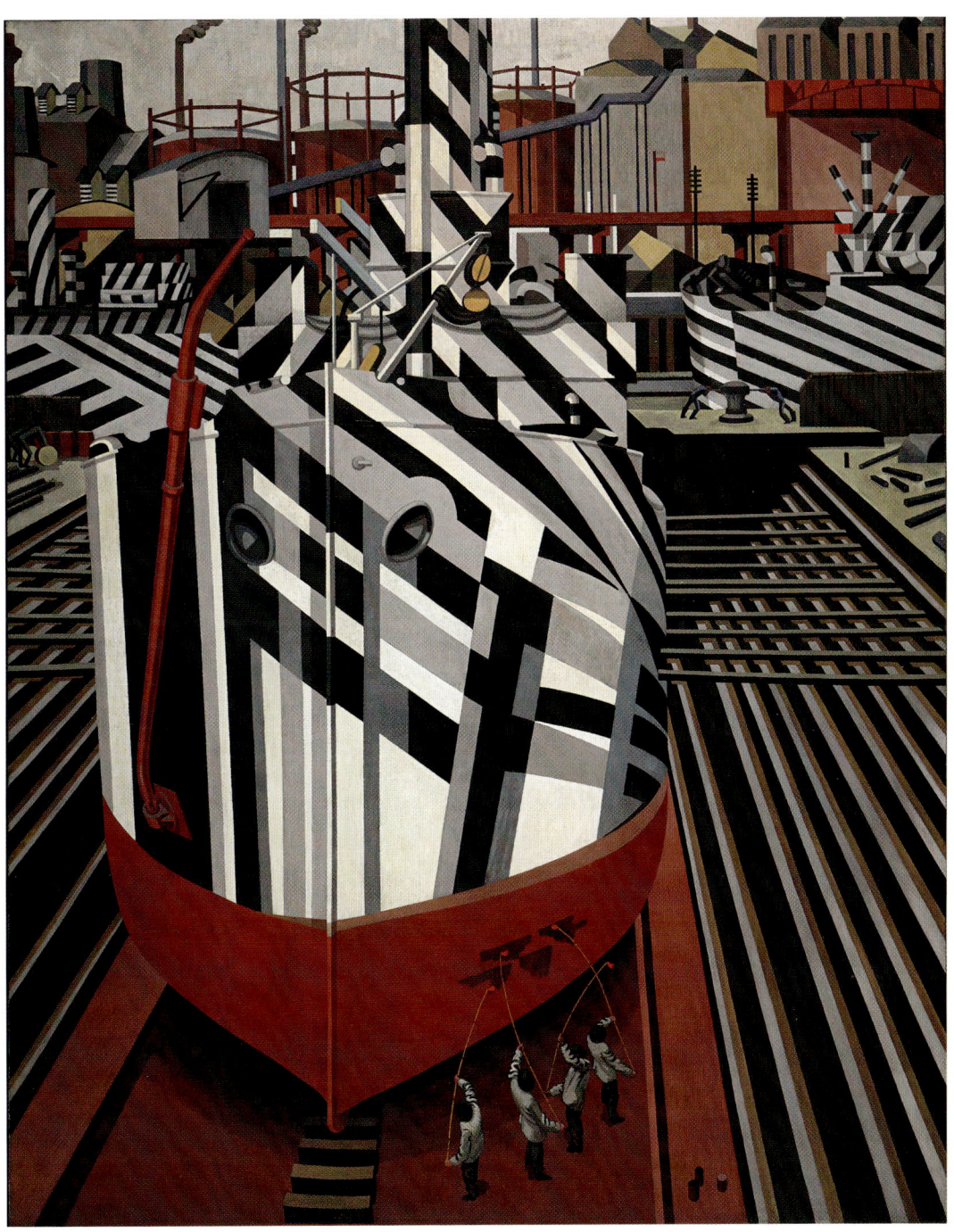

Edward Wadsworth, *Dazzle-Ships in Drydock at Liverpool*, 1919, oil on canvas.

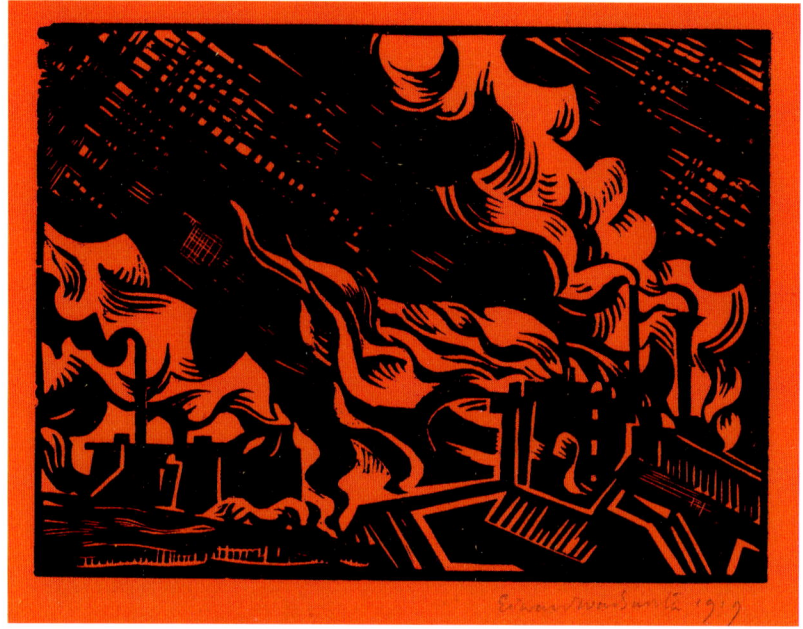

Edward Wadsworth, *Black Country, Blast Furnace*, 1919, woodcut.

combination of man and nature and, as such, worthy of exploration. Quiet –
even phlegmatic – in his outer life, Wadsworth unleashed his inner demons
in these new works.

The resulting images – often close-ups – are confrontational. The viewing
angles are so intimate that the viewer is forced to see into the devastated landscapes. Wadsworth's previous predilection for abstraction is clearly depicted
because the shapes are rendered in jagged contrasting passages of verticals
and horizontal passages. When the Black Country exhibition (37 drawings)
opened at the Leicester Galleries in January 1920, Konody claimed that
Wadsworth 'had distilled art of the highest order out of material that to the
ordinary painter would not only be unpromising, but positively forbidding'.[10]
Alan Clutton-Brock was impressed with 'the terrific energy of the whole
industrial process', which Wadsworth showed 'as energy [that] can only be
represented in rhythmical and orderly forms'.[11] O. R. Drey perceived how
the artist 'transformed the waste places of industrialism . . . into fields of
sombre and, sometimes sinister romance'.[12] Wadsworth recognized that he
had derived enormous benefit from his abstract work that he could put to
use in his more representational images.

Not shown at the Leicester Galleries were the various versions of the woodcut *Blast Furnaces*. This image differs from the drawings and lithographs because the viewer looks directly at the furnaces – the cause of the landscapes being black – rather than being placed at a safe distance, as in the landscapes. In the hand-coloured red versions especially of this woodcut, Wadsworth displayed the source of pollution in a semi-abstract, highly visceral manner that recalls his Vorticist works. It is an image of the hell he had proudly told Lewis about. Wadsworth had been born in this region and loved it. He also knew that it was a landscape blighted by man. And in *Blast Furnaces*, he captured the beauty of evil. He never returned to such disturbing imagery in the remainder of his career.

In 1920, when his father died, Wadsworth inherited a quarter of a million pounds that made him worry-free financially. That year, he began painting in tempera many years after being introduced to that medium by Fry. He also returned to the type of painting he had done seven years before that; in both, there is a delicate balance between abstraction and representation, and in both, volume is constructed in a Cézanne-like manner but broken into carefully delineated passages that blend with each other.

Outwardly Wadsworth had been a faithful disciple of Lewis. Their work in 1913–14 shared many similarities, although Wadsworth often deviated from his mentor. He remained grateful for Lewis's tutoring and wished to be as faithful to him as he had been to Gaudier.

Although he abandoned Vorticist stylization and later worked in a surrealist mode, Wadsworth never intended to throw aside Lewis, who remained an expert in cadging money from his friends. He expected Wadsworth to support him. Eventually, their relationship disintegrated when Wadsworth refused to tolerate Lewis's insults and threats. His admiration of Lewis the artist did not vanish: at his home in Kensington one 'room, known as [his] "den", was entirely filled with pictures' by Lewis.[13]

26

THE UNINVITED: HELEN SAUNDERS

In *Blast 2*, the Doré Galleries exhibition and the Penguin show, Saunders's fierce attachment to Vorticism is evident. Although her work encompassed the stylistic attributes of the movement, she injected her own point of view. She also collaborated with Lewis in the Vorticist Room, although he effaced her involvement with the project when it was completed.

After Lewis joined the army in March 1916, she continued her friendship with him. She even rented rooms for him, moved his belongings there and then sent him the keys. She typed his novel *Tarr* and other manuscripts – correcting his mistakes. In September 1917 Lewis asked her to get a quotation from Leveridge – the printer of *Blasts 1* and *2* – for a new *Blast* (that was never published).

She also kept in touch with some of her former colleagues – she and Dismorr remained close friends. She met for lunch with William Roberts at the Eiffel and with Ezra Pound and Dorothy Shakespear at Pagani's. She may have visited with Lewis when he was hospitalized with double pneumonia in the winter of 1917. By the next summer, to her distress, he refused to see her. This estrangement lasted until mid-1922.

Saunders refused an offer of marriage from Walter Sickert. In severely reduced circumstances, she lived with a friend, Blanche Caudwell, from 1933 until Caudwell's death in 1950. Saunders's subsequent painting returned to its earlier representational leanings. To a degree, she may have seen Vorticism – for her – as a misstep.

Years earlier, Lechmere had been certain Saunders was infatuated with Lewis. She implied that such feelings may have led her to act in a subservient way towards him. Lewis was adept at using his charms to manipulate others, and this is what he may have done, she felt, with Saunders. Frederick Etchells recalled that she 'was completely potty about Lewis. If Lewis had painted Kate Greenaway pictures, Saunders would have done them too.'[1]

Such a reading is problematical because it is both reductive and dismissive; it also assigns no sense of agency or artistic integrity to Saunders, whose accomplishments belie Lechmere's and Etchells's put-downs. Saunders had been infatuated with Lewis, but there is another, more credible way of looking at her involvement with Vorticism: she became intrigued by it, determined to explore it, and made her own strong contributions to it.

Saunders showed two paintings with the London Group in 1916, but most of her time was eaten up working full time during the war in a government office. The place of a woman in an art world controlled by men was, she felt, a dubious proposition. She told Dismorr:

> I suppose Art only really comes naturally out of an excess too great for ordinary life. Certainly, I have not got that. Perhaps no woman has. But I should very much like the chance of doing some quite representative painting, as literal as Van Gogh. It would give one a chance I feel of 'finding my level' in Art, and perhaps inventing something.[2]

This letter suggests that Saunders wondered if women could gain any kind of status in the art world. Although discouraged, she wanted to return to representational art in the hope that she could rekindle some sort of inspiration. Of course, she had attempted something similar in her time as a Vorticist.

Saunders possessed an intricate understanding of herself – and of what she considered her limitations:

> I am still a solitary by nature – and I still find it difficult to get much out of actual things except retrospectively and imaginatively – what I fear more than anything else is the monotonous stampede of other people's thoughts through my mind when my own thoughts are too tired or dissipated to give battle to the invaders.[3]

In the 1920s she painted at L'Estaque, a village near Marseilles in southern France which inspired Cézanne and later Georges Braque. Her renditions

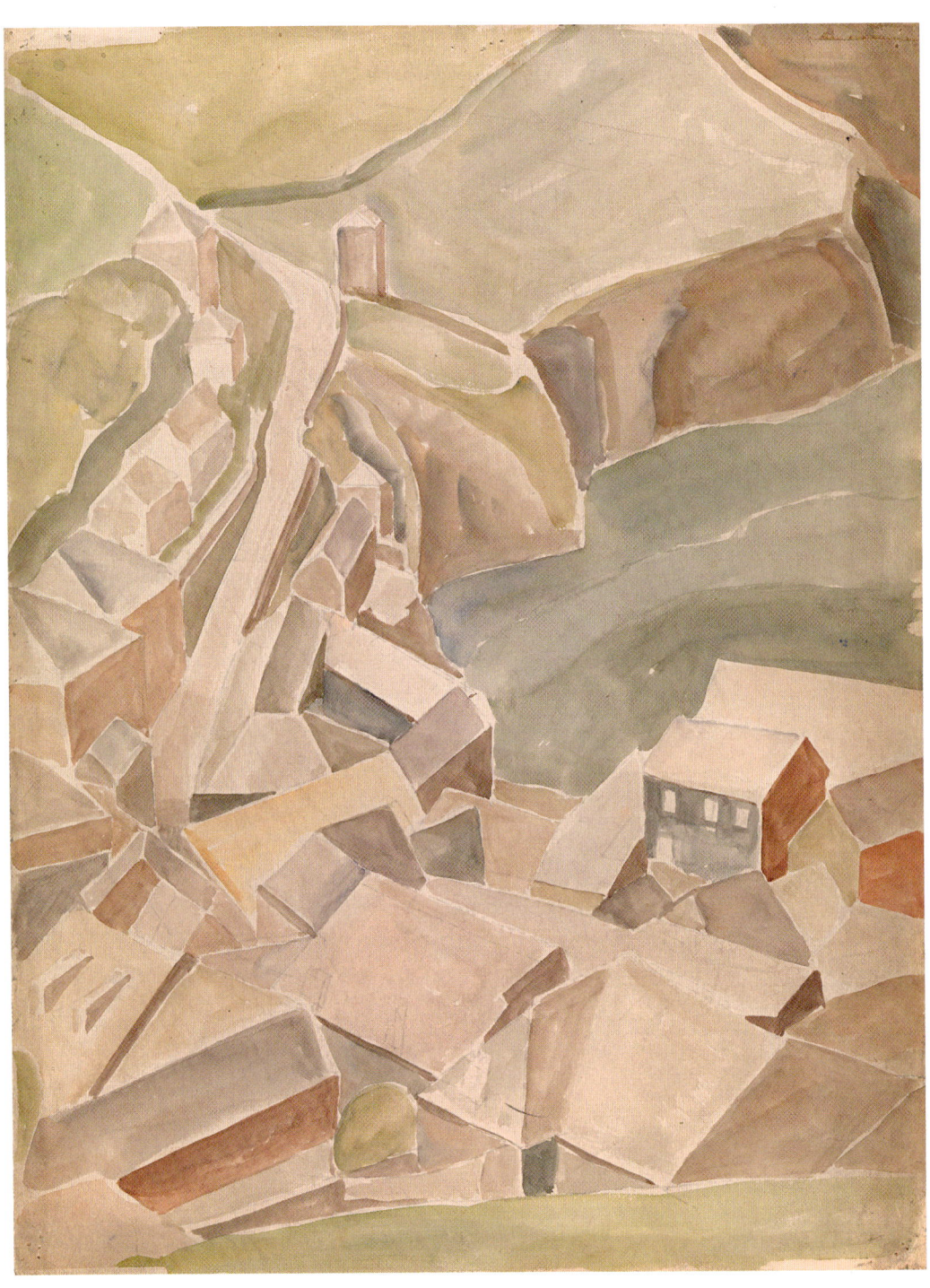

Helen Saunders, *View of Port Isaac*, 1930s, graphite and watercolour on paper.

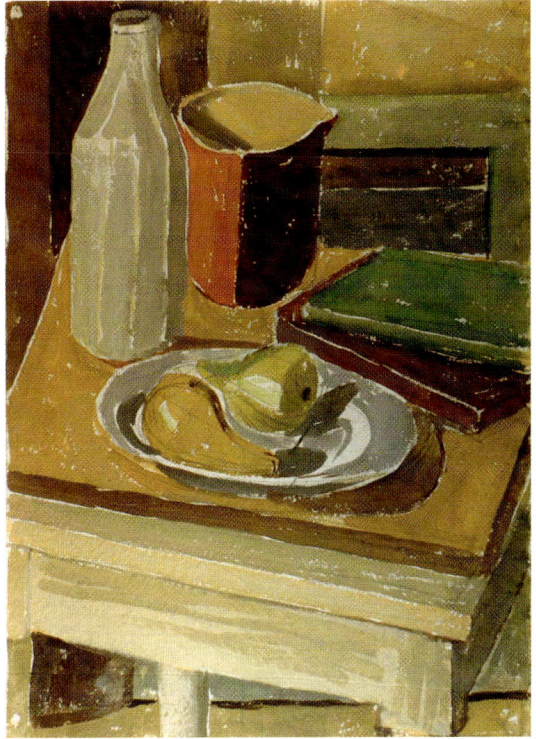

Helen Saunders, *Still-Life*, 1925–30, gouache on paper.

of that place show an indebtedness to Cézanne's concern with volume and stolidity. They also display an adherence to her teacher Rosa Waugh's theory of 'Natural Perspective' where multiple vantage points are emphasized. Another locale she frequented was the picturesque fishing village Port Isaac in Cornwall. These watercolours have a strong affinity with those done in France. In both, her previous incarnation as a Vorticist can be witnessed in the strong geometrical construction in these 'representational' works and in how individual passages in the depiction of the houses emerge from abstract shapes.

Often discouraged when her submissions to exhibitions were rejected, she remained committed to her art: 'I don't really paint "in order to keep well", but rather try to keep well "in order to paint".'[4]

27

THE UNWANTED:
JESSICA DISMORR

The Group X exhibition at the Mansard in 1920 was an attempt to restart Vorticism. Cuthbert Hamilton's aptly named *Reconstruction* (1919–20) moves resolutely in that direction. Dismorr was the only female exhibitor. In the *Self-Portrait* reproduced in that catalogue, she showed herself in the process of disintegration. That year Lewis offered her sensible advice when she told him that she had been advised to take a 'rest cure' to rid herself of depression: 'I think that the doctor's theory that you should not paint is all rubbish. They probably think that your paintings are very pathological, & that has made you ill. I should think that a bit later on when you are stronger, that the best possible distraction for you would be to paint.'[1]

In May 1925 Lewis asked Dismorr to buy some of his drawings. In reply she told him she was short of money and could not assist him. His reply was cruel and disparaging: 'I would much rather not receive letters from you holding out those tantalizing prospects every few months or weeks. I have meant to suggest to you for some time past that the moment had arrived for our acquaintanceship to terminate and avail myself of the opportunity to do so.' He then offered her a brutal assessment of her character: 'I find you a dull person, and the fact that I have known you for so long does not release me, in your company, from a sense of oppression. The fact that you are possessed of a fixed idea that everybody . . . is *after your money*, does not improve matters.'[2] Despite this caustic missive, Dismorr remained loyal to Lewis and sent him £30 in 1928. Two years later she told a friend: 'Don't treat him as a friend or think he'll do anything for you – he only makes use of people – and he'll throw you over.'[3]

Lewis's startling dismissal in 1925 probably arose because he was furious when he learned that the progressive Mayor Gallery had held an exhibition

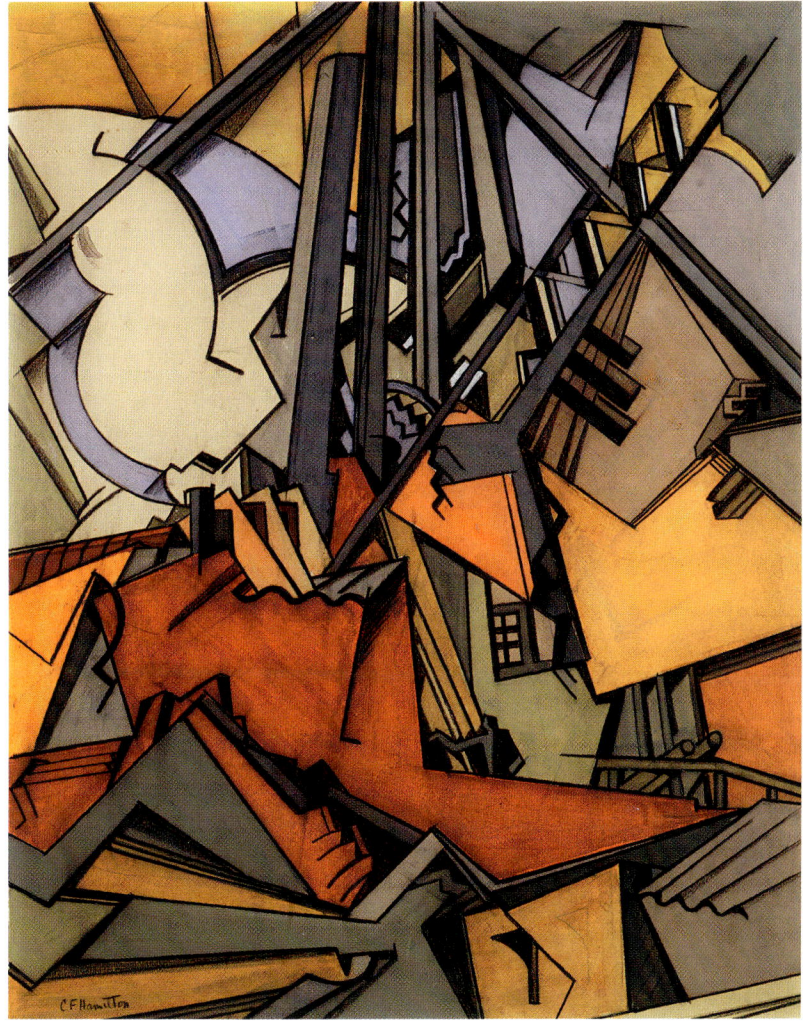

Cuthbert Hamilton, *Reconstruction*, 1919–20, graphite, crayon and gouache on paper.

of Dismorr's watercolours. In the *Sunday Times*, Frank Rutter wrote that her 'deliberation in three-dimensional design, coupled with an intense simpli-fication of forms, gives an appearance of great strength to Miss Dismorr's work, and the longer it is studied, the more evident will its merits become.' He added: 'The exhibition should be seen by all interested in the modern movement.'[4]

In addition to the Mayor exhibition, she showed her work at the London Group regularly, was elected to the Seven and Five Society and in 1936

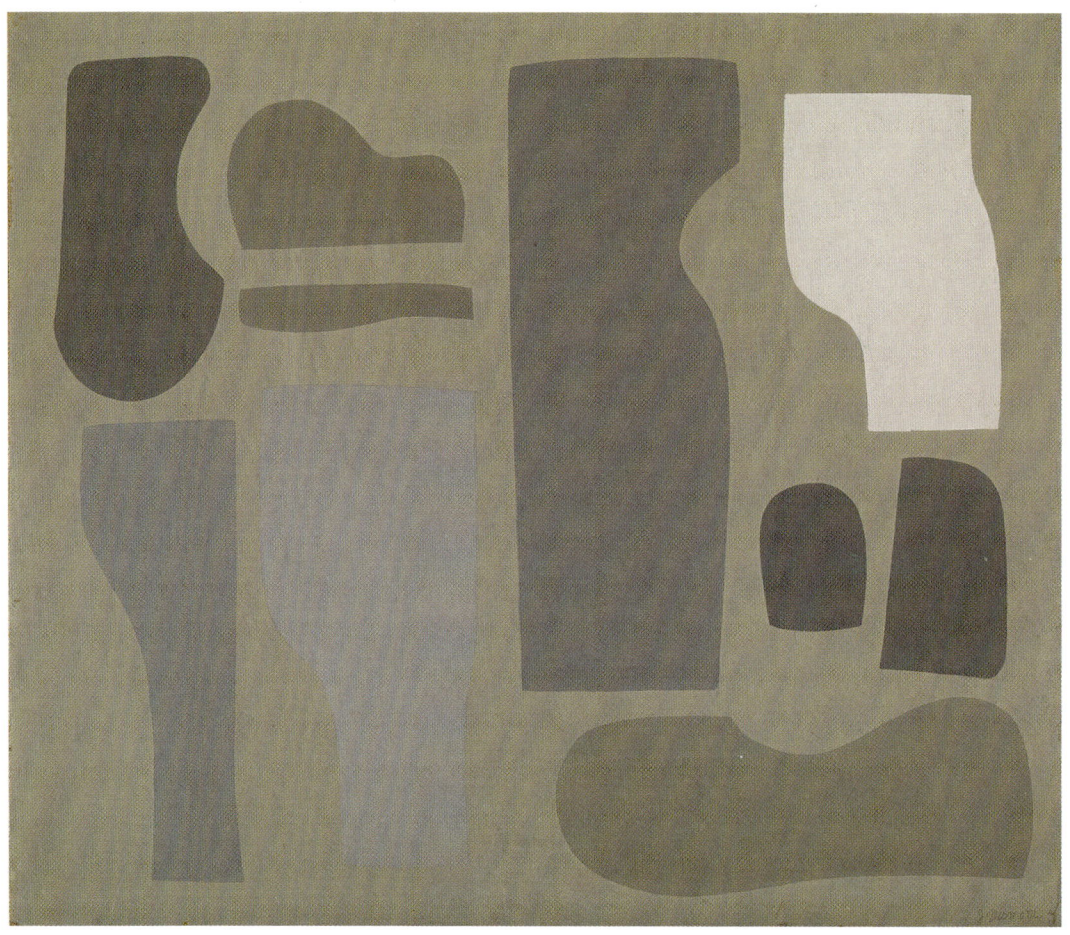

Jessica Dismorr, *Related Forms*, 1937, tempera on board.

contributed to 'De Olympiade Onder Dicatuur' in Amsterdam, an exhibition to counter Joseph Goebbels's display of Nazi art at the 1936 Berlin Olympiad. The following year, she contributed to the Artists' International Association for Peace, Democracy and Cultural Development. Politically, she was at odds with Lewis, who supported the Third Reich.

Dismorr's artistry extended to plays and poems, some of which appeared in the *Little Review* and the *London Mercury*. In the *Little Review* in September 1919, she declared: 'Art that is one step beyond the level of taste charms like a novelty, art that is two steps ahead hurts like an outrage.' In another statement in the same essay, she observed: 'Great art at first sight is often austere and repellent, and if it is an advance in a strange direction must be so.'[5] Both these declarations can be read as commentaries on Vorticism and her own adherence to its aesthetics.

Throughout her career, Dismorr reverted time and again to abstractions clearly derived from her work in the 1915 Doré exhibition. The colour palette in a 1937 abstraction is the same as in an earlier one from 1915 that looks like an assortment of architectural elements disconnected from each other (p. 158); in 1937 similar forms have been carefully detached from each other, as in a jigsaw puzzle. She also experimented with a series of sombre, powerful portraits and in Expressionist-like compositions in which the female figures are significantly larger than the male ones. The suggestion is that women must perform more stridently than men because their opinions are often taken as valueless.

Dismorr's later work, divided between pure abstractions and representational works – the latter nodding in the direction of Surrealism – shows a relentless nature exploring various paths. She was the only Vorticist who, in her later career, remained committed to exploring abstraction.

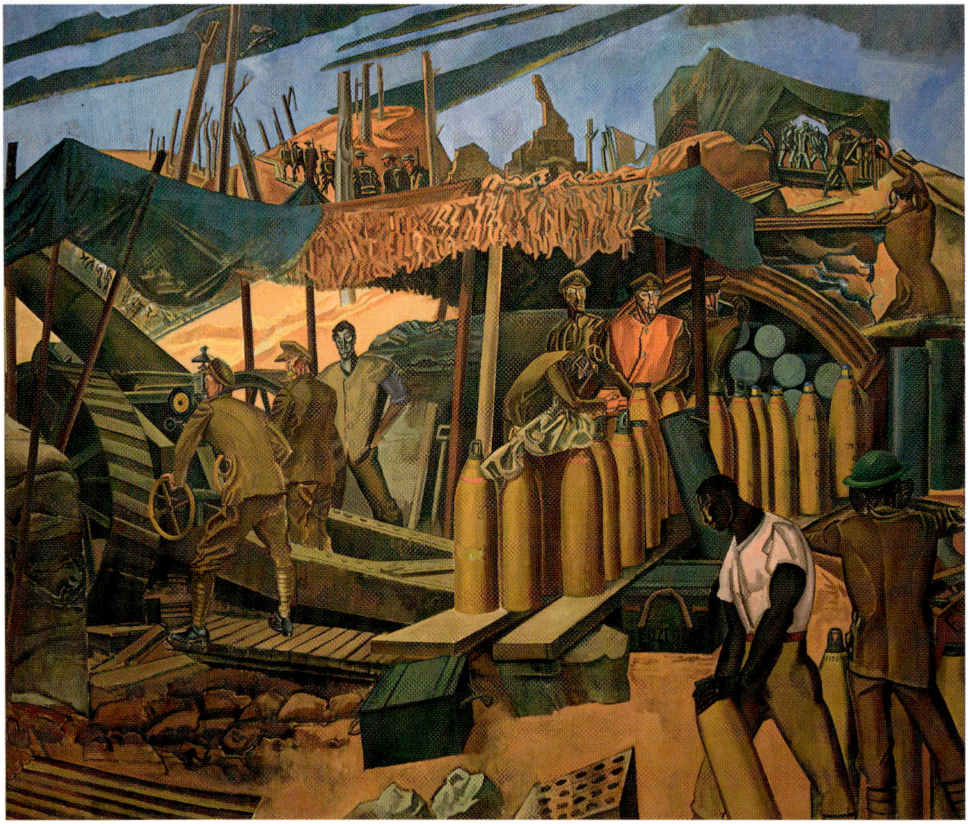

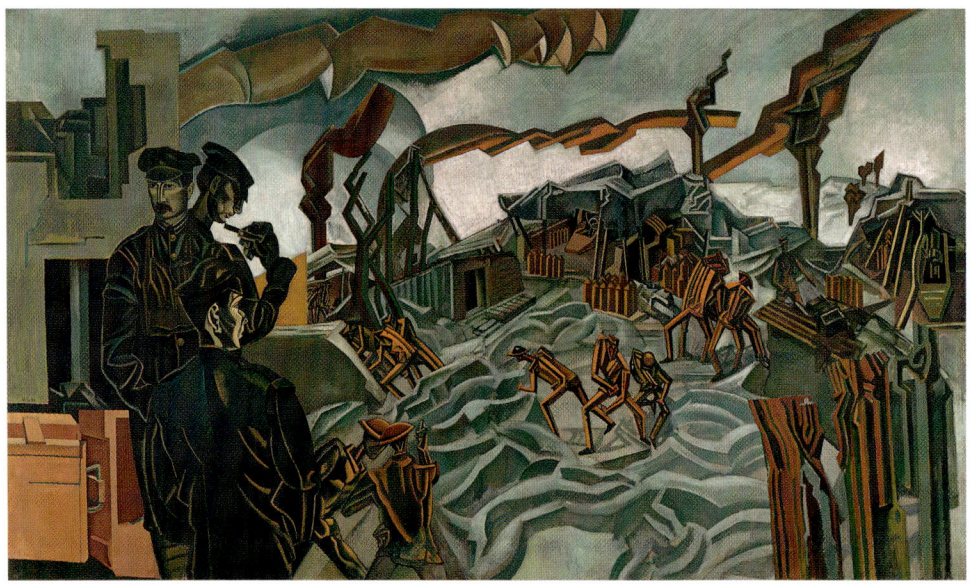

Wyndham Lewis, *A Canadian Gun-Pit*, 1918, oil on canvas.

Wyndham Lewis, *A Battery Shelled*, 1919, oil on canvas.

28

IN TRANSITION:
WYNDHAM LEWIS

When Lewis approached Konody in December 1917 to obtain a commission from the Canadian War Records, he was stunned when the critic received him warmly. 'When I asked him if he had among his artists an artillery-artist, to paint howitzers, he shouted NO! When I said I knew all about howitzers – how would it be for me to paint one? – he screamed OF COURSE!'[1]

A year later, he complained to Herbert Read that when he looked 'at my Canadian painting today I came to the conclusion that Konody had succeeded in making me paint one of the dullest good pictures on earth ... What a nightmare this wicked war has been!'[2] As was his habit, Lewis placed the blame on someone else for what he considered his own inept production.

When he saw *A Canadian Gun-Pit*, Augustus John commented on the inherent contradictions in the result. Lewis 'was painting his gun-pit and striving to reduce his "Vorticism" to the level of Canadian intelligibility – a hopeless task'.[3] The painting is an uneasy mix of styles in which representation defeats abstraction. Lewis's drawings in his one-man exhibition at the Goupil Gallery in February 1919 were in the same vein: 'I have attempted here only one thing, namely, in a direct ready formula to offer an interpretation of what I took part in in France.'[4]

The more dramatic *A Battery Shelled* commissioned by the Imperial War Museum is also a deeply conflicted painting. On the right-hand side, the fragments in the air, the mud and the robotic figures contain distinct Vorticist elements; on the left, the three soldiers, in dark colours in contrast to the blues in the central picture area, look like uneasy voyeurs who have been glued on to the canvas.

The divide in Lewis can be explained in part by the fact that the more he explored prose fiction, the more he realized that writing did not lend itself to abstraction. In his foreword to his one-man exhibition at the Goupil in February 1919, he claimed he had 'tried to do with the pencil and brush what story tellers like Tchekov and Stendhal did in their books'.[5] Perhaps as an attempt to reconcile the two parts of his creativity, he took leave of abstraction.

Later in life Lewis attempted to justify himself. He had once been fascinated with what he termed 'geometrics' but, as he got older, he found them bleak and empty. Always a person of extremes, Lewis cut himself off from the modernism he had in large part invented. Lewis's change of heart was not as sudden as he suggested. He tried his best to revive Vorticism in the Group X exhibition in 1920. That group's first and only exhibition took place at the Mansard Gallery from 27 March until 24 April 1920. The objective of Group X was to recreate the pre-war fervour of the Vorticists – in that aim, it failed.

In the Group X catalogue Lewis stressed the social importance of Vorticism:

> Let us give a direct example of how this revolution will work in popular ways. In poster advertisements by far the most important point is a telling design. Were the walls of London carpeted with abstractions rather than the mass of work [on display there] ... Public taste could thus be educated in a popular way to appreciate the essentials of design better than picture galleries have ever done.[6]

He knew that this attempt was doomed to failure:

> the members of this group have agreed to exhibit together twice annually, firstly for motives of convenience, and with no theory or dogma that would be liable to limit the development of every member. Each member sails his own boat and may lift his sails to any wind that may seem ... to promise a prosperous cruise.[7]

Despite the bravado, a canvas such as *Praxitella* (p. 150) clearly demonstrates that by 1921 only remnants of Vorticism can be seen in Lewis's work. The sharp pointed lines used in its construction betray its lingering influence.

In the *Burlington Magazine*, Clive Bell labelled English painting after the war hopelessly provincial and claimed, 'The French know enough of Vorticism to know that it is a provincial and utterly insignificant contrivance which has borrowed what it could from Cubism and Futurism and added nothing to either.'[8] There can be no doubt that the war brought about a sense of retrenchment – the adventurous spirit in which Fry had launched both his landmark exhibitions had vanished. Lewis also retreated.

Lewis blandly provided an explanation for his retrenchment when he claimed that 'war, and especially those miles of hideous desert known as "the Line" in Flanders and France, presented me with a subject matter so consonant with the austerity of that "abstract" vision I had developed, that it was an easy transition.'[9] In another reflection, he observed that the war had been a ghastly dream in which 'I was visited by images of an order very new to me. Upon waking I found an altered world; and I had changed too, very much. The geometrics that had interested me so much before, I now felt were bleak and empty. They wanted *filling*.'[10]

In many ways, Lewis's remarks were face-saving. According to him, Vorticism had been a necessary stage in introducing modern art to England – but it had remained merely a scaffolding, a prop to be tossed aside. He was suggesting that it had been essential that representational art be purged by Vorticism so that it could re-emerge with its faults eradicated.

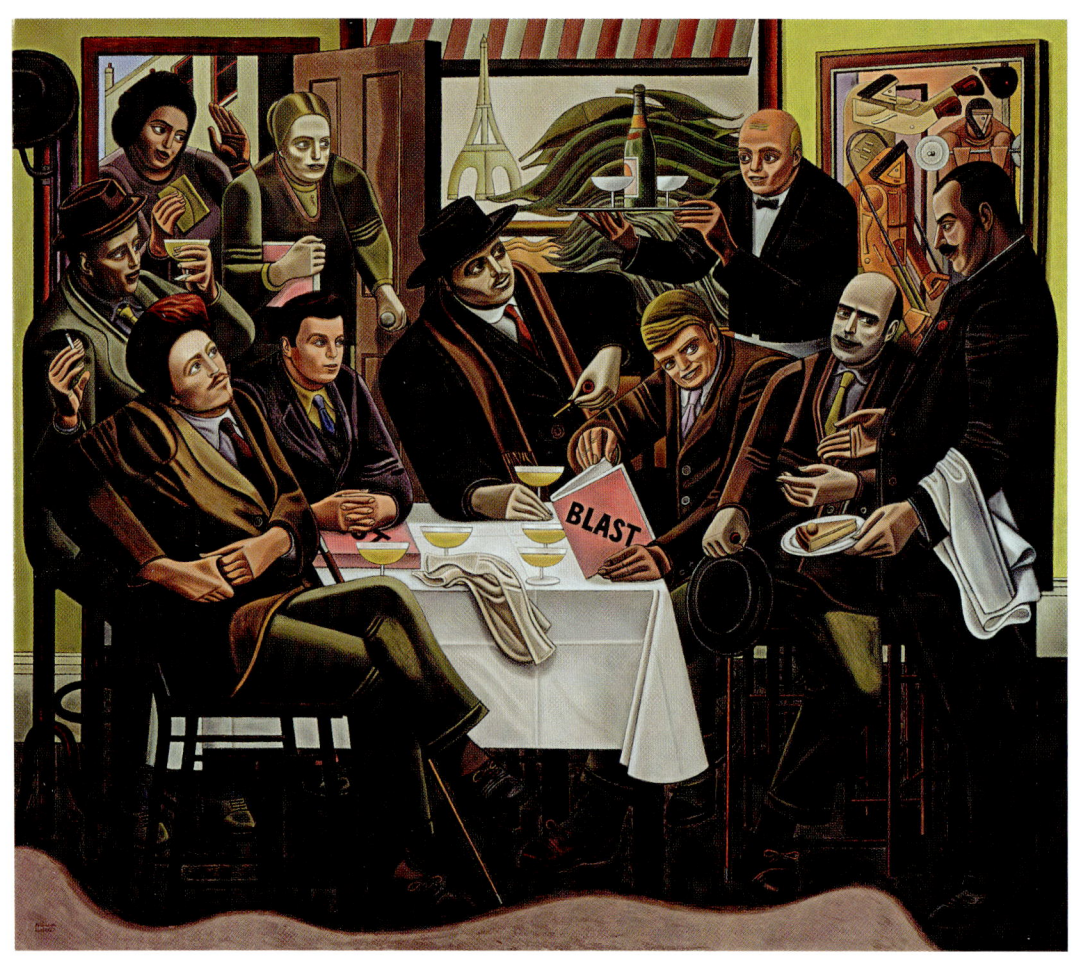

William Roberts, *The Vorticists at the Restaurant de la Tour Eiffel, Spring, 1915*, 1961–2, oil on canvas.

EPILOGUE:
THE LAST SUPPER

In 1956 the Tate Gallery staged the retrospective 'Wyndham Lewis and Vorticism'. Work by Roberts was included, but the exhibition was firmly centred on Lewis. In the catalogue, Lewis was quoted: 'Vorticism, in fact, was what I, personally, did and said at a certain period.' Although Roberts had always been resistant to defining himself as a Vorticist, he felt that the exhibition was incorrectly rewriting the history of modernist art in England. In a series of vitriolic pamphlets, he claimed that he had been experimenting with Cubism well before he was associated with the Rebel Art Centre. He distanced himself from that place and claimed that his two drawings in *Blast 1* had been reproduced without his consent.

Roberts was reworking the past to suit himself and, in that spirit, he painted five years later *The Vorticists at the Restaurant de la Tour Eiffel, Spring, 1915* as a further attempt to justify his early life as an artist.[1] In making an 'imaginative reconstruction of a typical rebel dinner', he parodied Leonardo's *Last Supper*.[2] Wearing his customary sombrero and leaning backwards, Lewis is the Christ in the centre of this composition. Next to him on his right is Roberts, whose hands are clasped on top of *Blast 1*; he appears much more boyish than any of the other artists. To his right is a proud, paternal-looking Pound, leaning backwards like Lewis. To Lewis's left sits Etchells – who displays his copy of *Blast 1* – and next to him, a weary-looking Wadsworth. Joe the waiter stands behind Lewis while his boss, Stulik, offers the diners a piece of cake. At the back of the composition are Roberts's fanciful recreations of the decorations made by Lewis and Saunders. For Roberts, *Blast 1* is a closed book whereas Etchells ingratiatingly flaunts his copy.

At the left of the image, the worried, apprehensive faces of Dismorr and Saunders – who have apparently just opened the door apparently shut to them – indicate that they are uncertain whether they are welcome in this all-male enclave. No notice is taken of them. They might as well be invisible. Roberts obviously still believed that the Vorticists had – or should have – excluded women. The posture of the two women is stooped, as if to suggest they existed in a different realm from their colleagues. Saunders clasps a copy of *Blast 1*, the only hint that she has a right to be in the room.

Roberts idealized his own face but broadly caricatured those of his associates. He looks like an innocent stranded among a band of thieves, although he is the Judas figure.

The Vorticists is in some ways a revenge piece that allowed Roberts to construct his early activities as time badly spent. He was putting his male colleagues down while insisting women had no right to sit at the table. This painting has been often reproduced as the standard or 'official' portrayal of the long-disbanded group, but its status should not be iconic. It is a piece of propaganda by Roberts, who was rewriting his history and that of the group to which he had belonged.

In this canvas, Roberts created a false narrative, one suited to his 'version' of his early life. As the painting suggests, Lewis and Pound might have been the kingpins in the creation of Vorticism but a more accurate way of recreating that past is found in the interactions among the artists.

Wadsworth subtly marked his distance from Lewis, a fallible leader. Bomberg and Roberts were attracted and repulsed by the group's aesthetics. The crucial roles of Saunders and Dismorr have often been erased. Although Roberts cannot be criticized for omitting Gaudier, Bomberg and Hulme, no evidence of their impact on the group is evidenced. In fact, the diners look like a group of businessmen pleased with themselves. The Vorticists were conspirators in advancing their version of modernity, but the painting reduces them to a group of strange-looking individuals at a celebratory dinner in which they are caricatured by the artist, who sits smugly among them.

Although short-lived, Vorticism was an attempt to transform and radicalize modernist English art. In spirit the group was revolutionary. And for that reason alone, it should be applauded.

REFERENCES

INTRODUCTION

1 Ezra Pound to William Carlos Williams, 19 December 1913, in *The Letters of Ezra Pound, 1907–1941*, ed. D. D. Paige (London, 1951), p. 65.

2 Pound was not a Vorticist because he was not a visual artist. However, he was closely aligned to the aims of the Vorticists and attempted to appropriate the group's aesthetics to Imagism.

3 Violet Hunt, *I Have This to Say* (London, 1926), p. 211.

4 T. E. Hulme, 'Modern Art. II – A Preface Note and Neo-Realism', *New Age*, 26 March 1914.

5 Karin Orchard, '"A Laugh Like a Bomb": The History and the Ideas of Vorticism', in *Blast: Vorticism 1914–1918*, ed. Paul Edwards (London, 2000), p. 22.

1 THE WOULD-BE CUBIST: WILLIAM ROBERTS

1 Roberts's *Sketch of His Early Life* written in 1977 – and published after his death as William Roberts, *Early Years* (London, 1982) – is the source for the autobiographical passages in this chapter.

2 Lynda Morris, *Henry Tonks and the Art of Pure Drawing* (Norwich, 1985), p. 8.

3 Joseph Hone, *The Life of Henry Tonks* (London, 1939), p. 41.

4 Stanley Spencer to Sydney Spencer, 1911. Quoted by Richard Carline, 'Stanley Spencer: His Personality and Mode of Life', in *Stanley Spencer RA* (London, 1980), p. 11.

5 Hone, *The Life of Henry Tonks*, p. 103.

6 Randolph Schwabe, 'Three Teachers: Brown, Tonks and Steer', *Burlington Magazine*, LXXXII/483 (1943), pp. 141–6.

7 Roger Fry, *Vision and Design* (London, 1920), p. 202.

8 'An English Cubist: William Roberts and Vorticism's Year' appeared as the preface to Roberts's *Some Early Abstract and Cubist Work, 1913–1920* (London, 1957).

9 Richard Cork, *Art Beyond the Gallery in Early 20th Century England* (New Haven, CT, and London, 1985), p. 126.

10 My description is of the *Study* reproduced here; the oil painting is at Nottingham Castle.

2 THE DISSIDENT: DAVID BOMBERG

1 William Roberts, *Early Years* (London, 1982), pp. 10–11.

2 This information is recorded in May C. Staveley, *The Housing Problem in Birmingham* (Birmingham, 1903), pp. 8–9.

3 Back-to-back front houses have only a front door (opening on to a yard) and no back door; the houses at the back have only a front door (opening on to an alley).

4 Kitty Newmark, interview with Richard Cork, in Richard Cork, *David Bomberg* (New Haven, CT, and London, 1987), p. 7.

5 Ibid.

6 John Bomberg, interview with Richard Cork, ibid.

7 Joseph Leftwich, interview with Richard Cork, ibid.

8 Roberts, *Early Years*, p. 13.

9 Jean Liddiard, *Isaac Rosenberg* (London, 1975), p. 77.

10 Ibid.

11 Bomberg's earlier *Island of Joy* (*c.* 1912) bears a close resemblance in its arrangement of figures to Roberts's *Ulysses*.

12 Vanessa Bell to Roger Fry, 26 December 1913. Tate Gallery Archives.

3 THE COSTER: WILLIAM WADSWORTH

1 Barbara Wadsworth, *Edward Wadsworth: A Painter's Life* (Salisbury, 1989) provides a detailed account of her father's early life, and I have quoted from and summarized her findings.

2 Ibid., p. 12.

3 Bruce Lockhart, *My Scottish Youth* (New York, 1937).

4 C.R.W. Nevinson, *Paint and Prejudice* (London, 1937), p. 26.

5 He may also have known of Thomas Phillips's *Lord Byron in Albanian Dress* (1813).

6 Wadsworth, *Edward Wadsworth*, p. 72.

4 THE UNSEEN: HELEN SAUNDERS

1 Mengting Yu, *London's Women Artists, 1900–1914: A Talented and Decorative Group* (Singapore, 2020) provides a wealth of information on this subject.

2 Virginia Woolf, *Moments of Being* (New York, 2002), p. 17.

3 Deborah Cherry, *Painting Women: Victorian Women Artists* (London and New York, 1993), p. 9.

4 Brigid Peppin, 'Helen Saunders (1885–1963): Mapping a Career', in *Helen Saunders: Modernist Rebel*, exh. cat., The Courtauld Gallery, London, ed. Rachel Sloan (2023), p. 11.

5 Rose Waugh, undated letter to Kate Gliddon, cited by Brigid Peppin, *Helen Saunders, 1885–1963* (Oxford and Sheffield, 1996), p. 7.

6 Peppin, *Helen Saunders*, p. 7.

7 Peppin, 'Helen Saunders', p. 11.

8 This canvas was previously titled *Litlington*. See ibid.

9 Richard Cork, *Vorticism and Abstract Art in the First Machine Age* (London, 1976) p. 150.

5 THE OVERLOOKED: JESSICA DISMORR

1 Also, as Faith Binckes has argued, Dismorr may have been utilizing the pages of the magazine to create provocative female nudes to subvert how women's bodies were usually portrayed: *Modernism, Magazines, and the British Avant-Garde* (Oxford, 2010). In her illustration for 'Le Petit Compatible', Dismorr eschews the notion of the hairless female nude, makes the body of the woman shapeless and has the woman putting her hands over her breasts.

2 Lewis Hind, 'Two Visions of Art: The Straightforward and the Eerie', *Daily Chronicle*, 16 October 1912.

3 P. G. Konody, 'Art and Artists: English Post-Impressionists', *The Observer*, 27 October 1912.

6 THE PROVOCATEUR: WYNDHAM LEWIS

1 Wyndham Lewis, *Tarr* (London, 1951), p. 22.
2 Unpublished vita, 1959, cited by Jeffrey Meyers, *The Enemy: A Biography of Wyndham Lewis* (London, 1980), p. 8.
3 Cited ibid., p. 9.
4 William Rothenstein, *Men and Memories, 1900–1922* (London, 1922), p. 27.
5 Quoted in Richard Cork, *Vorticism and Abstract Art in the First Machine Age* (London, 1976), p. 3.
6 Wyndham Lewis, *Rude Assignment: A Narrative of My Career Up-to-Date* (London, 1948), p. 119.
7 Wyndham Lewis, 'William Rothenstein', in *Wyndham Lewis on Art*, ed. W. Michel and C. J. Fox (London, 1969), p. 416.
8 *Blast 2* (1915), p. 38.
9 Ibid., p. 40.
10 *The Times*, 11 December 1911.
11 *The Times*, 30 July 1912.
12 Ashley Gibson, *Postscript to Adventure* (London, 1930), p. 103, quoted in Richard Cork, *Art Beyond the Gallery in Early 20th Century England* (New Haven, CT, and London 1985), p. 67.
13 Augustus John, *Chiaroscuro: Fragments of Autobiography* (London, 1952), p. 117.
14 Quoted in Michael Holroyd, *Augustus John: A Biography* (London, 1976), p. 480.
15 'The Cabaret Theatre Club', *The Times*, 27 June 1912.
16 See Lisa Tickner, 'Wyndham Lewis: Dance and the Popular Culture of *Kermesse*', in *Modern Life and Modern Subjects: British Art in the Early Twentieth Century* (New Haven, CT, and London, 2000), pp. 79–116.
17 Kate Lechmere was the model.
18 Fredric Jameson describes the two kinds of Timon images as the 'round' and the 'square' in a form of power struggle. 'What do they struggle for? For mastery of the space itself, for its complete saturation and domination by their own specific logic . . . But neither side exists in a pure state, altogether free from the infection (or the gravitational) pull of the other.' 'Wyndham Lewis's *Timon*: The War of Forms', in *Vorticism: New Perspectives*, ed. Mark Antliff and Scott W. Klein (Oxford, 2013), pp. 27–8.
19 Lewis, *Rude Assignment*. p. 120.
20 Ford Madox Ford, *Return to Yesterday: Reminiscences, 1894–1914* (London, 1941), p. 407.
21 Cited by Meyers, *The Enemy*, p. 117.
22 Douglas Goldring, *Odd Man Out: The Autobiography of a 'Propaganda Novelist'* (London, 1935), p. 100.

7 THE IDEALIST: HENRI GAUDIER-BRZESKA

1 Cited by Paul O'Keeffe, *Gaudier-Brzeska: An Absolute Case of Genius* (London, 2004), p. 6.
2 Ibid., p. 33.
3 Ibid., p. 30.
4 Ibid., p. 58.
5 Ibid., p. 68.

6   Ibid.
7   Gaudier to Brzeska, October 1912, cited in Roger Cole, *Burning to Speak: The Life and Art of Henri Gaudier-Brzeska* (Oxford, 1978). H. S. Ede, *Savage Messiah* (London, 1931), p. 256.
8   Enid Bagnold, *Autobiography (from 1899)* (London, 1969), p. 66.
9   Gaudier to Dr Uhlemayr, 18 June 1912, cited in Cole, *Burning to Speak*.
10 *Blast 2* (1915), p. 34.

8 THE ITALIAN CONNECTION

1   All citations are taken from the Sackville Gallery catalogue, March 1912, which reprints 'Initial Manifesto of Futurism', 'Futurist Painting' and 'The Exhibitors to the Public'.
2   André Gide, *Journals*, trans. Justin O'Brien (New York, 1947), pp. 103, 129.
3   Douglas Goldring, *South Lodge: Reminiscences of Violet Hunt, Ford Madox Ford and the English Review Circle* (London, 1943), p. 64.
4   Jonathan Black, 'Taking Heaven by Violence: Futurism and Vorticism as seen by the British Press, *c.* 1912–20', in *Blasting the Future! Vorticism in Britain, 1910–1920* (London, 2004), p. 29.
5   Wyndham Lewis, *Anglosaxony: A League that Works* (Toronto, 1941), pp. 41–2.
6   William C. Wees, *Vorticism and the English Avant-Garde* (Toronto, 1972), p. 90.
7   *Evening News*, 2 March 1912.
8   P. G. Konody, *The Observer*, 3 March 1912.
9   Walter Sickert, 'The Futurist "Devil among the tailors"', *English Review* (April 1912).
10 Sackville Gallery catalogue.
11 Lewis Hind, *Daily Chronicle*, 20 March 1912.
12 Frank Rutter, *Sunday Times*, 10 March 1912.
13 Cited by Charles Harrison, *English Art and Modernism, 1900–1939* (London, 1981), p. 87.
14 Cited by Black, 'Taking Heaven', p. 29.
15 Richard Cork, *Vorticism and Abstract Art in the First Machine Age* (London, 1976), p. 50.
16 Richard Cork, *David Bomberg* (New Haven, CT, and London, 1987), p. 64.

9 AN IDEAL HOME? THE OMEGA WORKSHOPS

1   *The Times*, 9 July 1913.
2   Richard Cork, *Vorticism and Abstract Art in the First Machine Age* (London, 1976), p. 90.
3   See James King, *Interior Landscapes: A Life of Paul Nash* (London, 1987), p. 66.
4   Leonard Woolf, *Beginning Again* (New York, 1964), p. 95.
5   Lewis to Fry, August–September 1913. Tate Gallery Archives.
6   See Quentin Bell and Stephen Chaplin, 'The Ideal Home Rumpus', *Apollo* (October 1964).
7   Ibid.
8   Vanessa Bell to Fry, 13 October 1913. Tate Gallery Archives.
9   Quoted in Cork, *Vorticism*, p. 93.
10 Wadsworth to Lewis, 22 December 1913, cited ibid., p. 94.
11 Lewis to Clive Bell in a probably unsent letter in November 1913. Quoted by Cork in Vorticism, p. 95.
12 Fry to Gore, 9 October 1913, cited ibid., p. 95.
13 Fry to Simon Bussy, 28 December 1913, cited ibid., p. 146.
14 Winifred Gill to Duncan Grant, 29 August 1966. Tate Gallery Archives.

10 THE OTHERS

1 Foreword to the catalogue at the Doré Galleries, October 1913.
2 Frank Rutter, *Revolution in Art* (London, 1910), p. 48.
3 Clive Bell, *The Nation*, 25 October 1913.
4 Ibid.
5 The existence of the canvas of *Radiation* is known only from a photograph reproduced in *Blast 1*. The whereabouts of the canvas of *Cape of Good Hope* are also unknown; the study provides an indication of the appearance of the finished painting.
6 Richard Cork, *Vorticism and Abstract Art in the First Machine Age* (London, 1976), p. 215.
7 Ezra Pound, *The Egoist*, 16 March 1914.
8 *Blast 1* (1914), p. 122.
9 Quoted by Cork, *Vorticism*, p. 110.
10 Introduction to the Catalogue.
11 Ibid.
12 Quoted by Richard Cork, *David Bomberg* (New Haven, CT, and London, 1987), p. 136.
13 Ibid.
14 Foreword to the Catalogue.
15 Quoted by Cork, *Vorticism*, pp. 82–3.

11 A NEW ROOM

1 *The Nation*, 25 October 1913.
2 Undated letter in the collection of the Rare Books division of Cornell University Library.
3 Kate Lechmere in an interview with Richard Cork. See Cork, *Vorticism and Abstract Art in the First Machine Age* (London, 1976), p. 125.
4 Lord Drogheda, *Double Harness: Memoirs* (London, 1978), p. 12.
5 Ibid., p. 5.
6 *Vanity Fair*, 25 June 1914.
7 *Athenaeum*, 7 March 1914.

12 ROOMS OF ONE'S OWN

1 Quoted by Jeffrey Meyers, *The Enemy: A Biography of Wyndham Lewis* (London, 1980), p. 52.
2 Jeffrey Meyers, 'Kate Lechmere's "Wyndham Lewis from 1912"', *Journal of Modern Literature*, X/1 (1983), pp. 158–66.
3 Quoted by Meyers, *The Enemy*, p. 52.
4 Kate Lechmere in an interview with Richard Cork. See Cork, *Vorticism and Abstract Art in the First Machine Age* (London, 1976), p. 147.
5 *Vanity Fair*, 25 June 1914.
6 Ibid.
7 Kate Lechmere interview with Cork, *Vorticism*, p. 148.
8 Helen Saunders, undated letter to Lewis in the Lewis Collection at Rare Books division of Cornell University Library.
9 Helen Saunders, undated letter in the collection of the Wyndham Lewis Trust.
10 Jessica Dismorr, undated letter to Lewis in the Lewis Collection at Rare Books division of Cornell University Library.
11 Wyndham Lewis, undated letter to Dismorr, *c.* 1914–15, in the Lewis Collection at Rare Books division of Cornell University Library.
12 Roger Fry, *The Nation*, 20 July 1912.

13 The title of this work was assigned by Richard Cork.

14 Miranda Hickman, 'The Gender of Vorticism', in *Vorticism: New Perspectives*, ed. Mark Antliff and Scott W. Klein (Oxford, 2013), p. 125.

16 Gaudier, *The Egoist*, 15 June 1914.

17 Richard Cork, *Art Beyond the Gallery in Early 20th Century England* (New Haven, CT, and London, 1985), p. 200.

18 'Rebel Art Centre Prospectus'.

19 Kate Lechmere, interview with Richard Cork, *Vorticism*, p. 76.

20 William Roberts, 'Wyndham Lewis, the Vorticist', *The Listener*, 21 March 1957.

21 'Rebel Art Centre Prospectus'.

13 THE TURNCOAT

1 Michael J. K. Walsh in *C.R.W. Nevinson: The Cult of Violence* (New Haven, CT, and London, 2002) points out that although Nevinson portrayed himself as a 'rebel, the anti-establishment standard bearer of intellectualism' (p. 14), this was a facade that allowed him to conceal his acute sense of vulnerability.

2 C.R.W. Nevinson, *Paint and Prejudice* (London, 1937), p. 56.

3 Ibid., p. 43.

4 Ibid., p. 56.

5 Ibid., p. 57.

6 Ibid.

7 Quoted by Richard Cork, *Vorticism and Abstract Art in the First Machine Age* (London, 1976), p. 223.

8 P. G. Conody, 'Side-Splitting Art Humour, Conscious and Unconscious 'Isms in East End', *Daily Express*, 8 May 1914.

9 Cited in Introduction to *Twentieth-Century Art: A Review of Modern Movements* (May–June 1914).

10 *Jewish Chronicle*, 8 May 1914.

11 *Jewish Chronicle*, 15 May 1914.

12 As reported in the *Daily Sketch*, 23 May 1914.

13 Wyndham Lewis, *Blasting and Bombardiering* (London, 1937), pp. 37–8.

14 Ibid.

15 Ibid., pp. 36–7.

16 *The Observer*, 14 June 1914.

17 Bomberg signed his name on condition that it carried a postscript stating that he signed 'the letter not as a member of the Art Rebel Centre (being unconnected with that group), but independently'.

18 The term also appeared in the *New Age* on 18 June 1914 and the *Evening News* of 8 August 1914.

14 'GREAT SILENT PLACE': DEFINING VORTICISM

1 As a student, Bomberg visited the National Gallery regularly and knew many of its masterpieces well. His early work is both informed and influenced by that knowledge. For Richard Cork, 'several of the most heartfelt moments in *Vision of Ezekiel* occur when the risen figures clasp each other.' He argues that this aspect of the canvas 'suggest[s] Bomberg had gained inspiration from Botticelli's *Mystic Nativity*, a highly personal work that the Renaissance master may well have used as solace in his most private devotional moments'. *Young Bomberg and the Old Masters* (London, 2019), p. 21. Cork links *The Mud Bath* to Michelangelo when he emphasizes an incident that

took place in December 1914, as recorded in Alice Bomberg's unpublished memoir about her husband: while waiting for a bus, David 'informed me that we were going to see a *real* picture. That's all he would tell me, so we sat quietly till the bus took us to the National Gallery. He hurried me through the rooms . . . We came to Michael Angelo's 'Entombment' (of Christ). He pointed out to me the wonderful composition of the picture and marvellous proportions of the figures and other details . . . David explained . . . that the modern pictures that were such a revelation to me, had their beginning with the Old Masters and Michael Angelo was the chief of these.' Cork then argues persuasively that the 'formal arrangement' of Christ's body in *The Entombment* may have influenced Bomberg in the planning and execution of *The Mud Bath*. *David Bomberg* (New Haven, CT, and London, 1987), pp. 89–90.

2 *Blast 2* (1915), p. 91.
3 'Vorticist Exhibition at the Doré Galleries', *Athenaeum*, 19 June 1915.
4 Ezra Pound, *Gaudier-Brzeska: A Memoir* (New York, 1970), p. 50.
5 Wyndham Lewis, 'Early London Environment', in *T. S. Eliot: A Symposium*, ed. Richard Marsh and Tambimuttu (London, 1948), p. 27.
6 Wyndham Lewis, *Blasting and Bombardiering* (London, 1937), p. 277.
7 'Ezra Pound, A Few Don't's by an Imagiste', *Fortnightly Review* (March 1913).
8 With obvious approval, Pound, in *Ezra Pound: A Memoir*, p. 134, is quoting a passage from Laurence Binyon's *The Flight of the Dragon: An Essay on the Theory and Practice of Art in China and Japan* (London, 1911).

15 THE FIRST EXPLOSION: *BLAST 1*

1 Douglas Goldring, *South Lodge* (London, 1943), p. 67.
2 See Robert Hewison, '*Blast* and the Work of Art in the Age of Mechanical Reproduction', in *The Vorticists: Manifesto for a Modern World*, ed. Mark Antliff and Vivien Greene (London, 2011), p. 69.
3 Saunders once stated that she did this 'in deference to my conventional home background'. Letter to William Wees, 1 September 1962. However, her surname was pronounced 'Sarnders'. Richard Aldington, in his capacity as an Imagist, signed to indicate his solidarity with Pound. Malcolm Arbuthnot, an experimental photographer, was sympathetic to Lewis. The artist Lawrence Atkinson was a member of the Rebel Art Centre and produced work similar to Lewis's.
4 The four illustrations by Wadsworth (*Cape of Good Hope*, *A Short Flight*, *March* and especially *Radiation*) suggest movement in a manner not dissimilar from Futurist practice. His work from 1915 is more static and more like Lewis's.
5 *Blast 1* (1914), p. 150.
6 Ibid., pp. 112–13.
7 Kate Lechmere interview with Richard Cork, *Vorticism and Abstract Art in the First Machine Age* (London, 1976), p. 243.
8 *The Egoist*, 15 June 1914
9 Ibid., p. 119.
10 Ibid., p. 124.
11 Ibid., p. 122.
12 Ibid., p. 125.
13 Ibid.
14 Cited by Barbara Wadsworth, *Edward Wadsworth: A Painter's Life* (Salisbury, 1989), p. 208.
15 C.R.W. Nevinson, *The Observer*, 12 July 1914.

16 *New York Times*, 9 August 1914.

17 Kate Lechmere, interview with Richard Cork, *Vorticism and Abstract Art*, p. 237. On 23 July Helen Saunders became involved in a stand-off between Lewis and Lechmere when the latter demanded forty copies of the magazine be returned to her. Saunders told Lechmere that was not Lewis's intent. 'Miss Saunders was then told that if she did not hand over the *Blasts* forthwith Miss Lechmere would exercise her power as co-director and shut up the Rebel Art Centre . . . Miss Saunders capitulated': Paul O'Keeffe, *Some Sort of Genius: A Life of Wyndham Lewis* (London, 2000), p. 160.

16 THE THEORIST: T. E. HULME

1 T. S. Eliot, *Criterion II*, 7 April 1924.

2 David Bomberg to Alan R. Jones, 23 December 1953, quoted by Jones in *The Life and Opinions of T. E. Hulme* (London, 1960), p. 116.

3 T. E. Hulme, *Speculations: Essays on Humanism and the Philosophy of Art*, ed. Herbert Read (London, 1924), p. 82.

4 John Middleton Murry, 'Aims and Ideals', *Rhythm* (June 1911).

5 T. E. Hulme, *New Age*, 26 March 1914.

6 Ibid.

7 *The Nation*, 14 March 1914.

8 David Garnett, *The Golden Echo* (London, 1953), p. 237.

17 JULY 1914

1 Interview with Kate Lechmere in Richard Cork, *Vorticism and Abstract Art in the First Machine Age* (London, 1976), p. 161.

2 Ibid.

3 The exact date of the row between Hulme and Lewis is difficult to determine. It likely took place in late June or early July 1914.

4 Kate Lechmere, 'Recollections of Vorticism', *Apollo*, January 1971.

5 See Jonathan Wood, 'Ornaments, Talismans and Toys: The Hand-Held Sculptures of Henri Gaudier-Brzeska', in *Blasting the Future! Vorticism in Britain, 1910–1920* (London, 2004), pp. 41–7.

6 Robert Ferguson, *The Short, Sharp Life of T. E. Hulme* (London, 2002), p. 180.

7 *Daily Chronicle*, 25 June 1914.

8 Interview with Alice Bomberg, in Cork, *Vorticism*, p. 204.

9 T. E. Hulme, *New Age*, 9 July 1914.

10 *Pall Mall Gazette*, 25 June 1914.

11 Jacob Epstein, *Let There Be Sculpture* (New York, 1940), p. 74.

12 Ezra Pound, *Guide to Kulchur* (London, 1968), p. 63.

13 Cork, *Vorticism*, p. 247.

14 Interview with Etchells in Cork, *Vorticism*, p. 247.

15 William Roberts, *Cometism and Vorticism: A Tate Gallery Catalogue Revised*, *Vortex Pamphlet No. 2, July–August 1956*, unpaginated.

16 Wyndham Lewis, *Blasting and Bombardiering* (London, 1937), pp. 50–51.

18 THE WAR

1 Cited by Richard Cork, *Vorticism and Abstract Art in the First Machine Age* (London, 1976), p. 268.

2 Cited by Richard Cork, *Wild Thing: Epstein, Gaudier-Brzeska, Gill* (London, 2010), p. 156.

3 *The Egoist*, 15 June 1914.
4 Cited by Barbara Wadsworth, *Edward Wadsworth: A Painter's Life* (Salisbury, 1989), p. 58.
5 Ibid., p. 60.
6 Ibid.
7 *Blast 2* (1915), p. 78.
8 Jacob Epstein, *Let There Be Sculpture* (London, 1940), p. 56.
9 Cork, *Vorticism*, p. 472.
10 Unsent draft of a letter to William Roberts. See Cork, *David Bomberg* (New Haven, CT, and London, 1987), p. 88.
11 C.R.W. Nevinson, *Paint and Prejudice* (London, 1937), pp. 71–8.
12 Frank Rutter, *Sunday Times*, 21 March 1915.
13 Cited by Wadsworth, *Edward Wadsworth*, p. 58.
14 *Blast 2*, pp. 33–4.

19 THE SECOND EXPLOSION: *BLAST WAR NUMBER*

1 Letter is quoted in Barbara Wadsworth, *Edward Wadsworth: A Painter's Life* (Salisbury, 1989), p. 54.
2 Ibid.
3 Lewis experienced recurrent illness from autumn 1914 until well into 1915. This may have impeded his work on *Blast 2*. See Paul O'Keeffe, *Some Sort of Genius: A Life of Wyndham Lewis* (London, 2001), pp. 163–5.
4 *Blast, War Number, July 1915*, ed. Wyndham Lewis (London, 1915), p. 5.
5 Ibid., p. 5.
6 Ibid., p. 16.
7 Ibid., p. 38.
8 Ibid., p. 40.
9 Ibid.
10 Ibid., p. 45.
11 Ibid., p. 78.
12 In *Blast 1*, the images are designated as 'Illustrations'; in *Blast 2*, they are 'Designs'. The distinction may be because there are photographic reproductions of paintings in *Blast 1* and none in *Blast 2*. The 22 illustrations in addition to tailpieces were reproduced photomechanically in *Blast 1*. Nineteen were reproductions of existing paintings and drawings by members of the group. *Blast 2* contained seventeen credited images, only one of which is a photograph reproduced in half-tone. The remainder were linecut reproductions.
13 *Blast 2*, p. 77.
14 Ibid., p. 9.
15 Ibid., p. 66.
16 Ibid., pp. 78–8.
17 Ibid., p. 65.
18 Ibid., p. 73.

20 OTHER SPACES: THREE DESIGN PROJECTS

1 Douglas Goldring, *South Lodge* (London, 1943), p. 13.
2 Richard Cork, *Art Beyond the Gallery* (New Haven, CT, and London, 1985), pp. 208–9.
3 Ibid., p. 221.
4 Ibid., pp. 229–30.

5 Brigid Peppin convincingly argues that *Atlantic City* may have been inspired by *New York* (1913), a canvas by the American painter Max Weber. *New York* had been shown in 1913 at the Grafton Group exhibition to which Saunders had been an invited participant. 'Helen Saunders as Vorticist – A Discreet Yet Revolutionary Spirit', in *Helen Saunders: Modernist Rebel*, , exh. cat., The Courtauld Gallery, London, ed. Rachel Sloan (2023), p. 13.

6 See ibid., pp. 33–42.

21 THE VORTICIST EXHIBITION

1 At some stage, Lewis may have invited Roger Fry to show in the second tier of exhibitors. See Richard Cork, *Vorticism and Abstract Art in the First Machine Age* (London, 1976), pp. 275–6.

2 Kate Lechmere, interview with Cork, in *Vorticism*, p. 156.

3 *Blast 2* (1915), p. 77.

4 Ibid.

5 Richard Cork, *David Bomberg* (New Haven, CT, and London, 1987), p. 105.

6 Rachel Sloan, ed, *Helen Saunders: Modernist Rebel*, exh. cat., The Courtauld Gallery, London (2023), p. 16.

7 The whereabouts of the painting are not known.

8 'Prefatory Note' to the catalogue of the Gaudier Memorial Exhibition in 1918.

9 Cork, *Bomberg*, p. 105.

10 *The Athenaeum*, 19 June 1915.

11 Ibid.

22 MEMORIAL: THE PENGUIN CLUB EXHIBITION

1 The pamphlet version of the 'Prospectus' was published in London at the Complete Press in November 1914.

2 *The Letters of Ezra Pound, 1907–1941*, ed. D. D. Paige (London, 1951), p. 106.

3 Ezra Pound, *New Age*, 21 January 1915.

4 Quinn to Pound, 17 December 1915, in *Letters*.

5 Pound to Quinn, 16 March 1916, ibid., p. 211.

6 Pound to Quinn, 23 August 1915, ibid., p. 212.

7 Pound to Quinn, 11 August 1915, ibid., p. 215.

8 Pound to Quinn, 18 March 1915, ibid., p. 216.

9 Don Marquis, 'The First Intelligible Answer', *Art World* (May 1917).

23 'LESS CUBISM': WILLIAM ROBERTS

1 'William Roberts, A Brief Discussion of the Vortex Pamphlets', in *Five Posthumous Essays and Other Writings* (Valencia, 1990).

2 William Roberts, *Memories of the War to End War, 1914–1918* (London, 1978–9).

3 William Roberts, *4.5 Howitzer Gunner, RFA 1916–1918* (London, 1978–9).

4 Ibid.

5 As quoted by Maria Tippett, *Art at the Service of War: Canada, Art, and the Great War* (Toronto, 1984), p. 32.

6 R. F. Wodehouse, *A Check List of the War Collections . . .*, Ottawa, National Gallery of Canada, n.d., p. 4.

7 Roberts, *4.5 Howitzer Gunner*.

8 Ibid.

9 Ibid.

24 'METHODIC DISCORD': DAVID BOMBERG

1 Etchells interview with Richard Cork, in *Vorticism and Abstract Art in the First Machine Age* (London, 1976), p. 379.
2 Foreword to the Chenil exhibition catalogue.
3 Cited by Richard Cork, *David Bomberg* (New Haven, CT, and London, 1987), p. 108.
4 Harold Watkins to Bomberg, 29 December 1917, cited ibid., p. 111.
5 Recounted by Alice Mayes in 'The Young Bomberg', cited ibid., p. 112.
6 Herbert Read, *Arts Gazette*, 13 September 1919.

25 'COLD-BLOODED PERSISTENCE': EDWARD WADSWORTH

1 Ezra Pound, *The Egoist*, 15 August 1914.
2 Jonathan Black, *Edward Wadsworth: Form, Feeling, and Calculation; The Complete Paintings and Drawings* (London, 2005), p. 23.
3 Bernadette Murphy, *Arts Gazette*, 30 April 1917.
4 Quoted in Barbara Wadsworth, *Edward Wadsworth: A Painter's Life* (Salisbury, 1989), p. 73.
5 Quoted ibid.
6 November 1919, quoted ibid., p. 77.
7 15 March 1919, quoted ibid., p. 89.
8 November 1919, quoted ibid.
9 Ibid., p. 88.
10 Cited ibid., p. 91.
11 Allan Clutton-Brock, 'Mr. Wadsworth's Realism', *The Times*, 10 January 1920.
12 O. R. Drey, *Westminster Gazette*, 27 January 1920.
13 Citation is from Frances Spalding, *The Real and the Romantic: English Art Between Two World Wars* (London, 2022), p. 281.

26 THE UNINVITED: HELEN SAUNDERS

1 Richard Cork, *Vorticism and Abstract Art in the First Machine Age* (London, 1976), p. 419.
2 Letter to Dismorr, November/December 1917, cited by Brigid Peppin, 'Mapping a Career', in *Helen Saunders: Modernist Rebel*, exh. cat., The Courtauld Gallery, London, ed. Rachel Sloan (2023), p. 18.
3 Ibid.
4 Saunders to Dismorr, 19 December 1962, cited ibid., p. 24.

27 THE UNWANTED: JESSICA DISMORR

1 Lewis to Dismorr, 17 October 1920, Cornell University Rare Book and Manuscript Collection.
2 Lewis to Dismorr, 13 November [1925], Cornell University Rare Book and Manuscript Collection.
3 Cited by Jeffrey Meyers, *The Enemy: A Biography of Wyndham Lewis* (London, 1980), p. 58.
4 Frank Rutter, *Sunday Times*, 29 November 1925.
5 Jessica Dismorr, *Little Review*, VI/6 (September 1919).

28 IN TRANSITION: WYNDHAM LEWIS

1 Wyndham Lewis, *Blasting and Bombardiering* (London, 1937).
2 Lewis to Read, 17 December 1918, in the Lewis Collection at Rare Books division of Cornell University Library.

3 Cited in Michael Holroyd, 'Damning and Blasting', *The Listener*, 6 July 1972.

4 Foreword to Goupil catalogue (February 1919).

5 Ibid.

6 Wyndham Lewis in the introduction to the catalogue of the Group X exhibition in 1920.

7 Ibid.

8 Clive Bell, *Since Cezanne* (London, 1929), p. 261.

9 Wyndham Lewis, *Rude Assignment* (London, 1951), p. 128.

10 Ibid., p. 137.

EPILOGUE: THE LAST SUPPER

1 Andrew Gibbon Williams in *William Roberts: An English Cubist* (London, 2004), provides an excellent overview of this thorny topic (pp. 125–7). He also quotes (p. 27) the artist's statement: 'My year's connection with Vorticism ended with the publication of my two line drawings *Combat* and *Machine Gunners* in the second *BLAST* in July 1915; that marked the close of the Vorticist episode. To the question: What was Vorticism? The answer could only be – a slogan. For as far as the character of the work of each artist forming the Group was concerned, this continued to be the same during Vorticism as after it, the varying development according to each talent, of Cubist and Futurist influences.'

2 Richard Cork, *Vorticism and Abstract Art in the Machine Age* (London, 1976), p. 554; Roberts's canvas may have also been an attempt to parody Henri Fantin-Latour's *Un atelier aux Batignolles* (1870), a homage to Manet, who, seated at his easel, is surrounded by admirers.

SELECT BIBLIOGRAPHY

Abstraction: Towards a New Art; Painting, 1910–1920 (London, 1980)

Antliff, Mark, and Vivien Greene, eds, *The Vorticists: Manifesto for a Modern World* (London, 2010)

Antliff, Mark, and Scott W. Klein, eds, *Vorticism: New Perspectives* (Oxford and New York, 2013)

Bagnold, Enid, *Autobiography* [1899] (London, 1969)

Beasley, Rebecca, '"A Definite Meaning": The Art Criticism of T. E. Hulme', in *The Camden Town Group in Context*, ed. Helena Bonett, Ysanne Holt and Jennifer Mundy (London, 2012)

Bell, Clive, *Since Cezanne* (London, 1929)

Bell, Quentin, and Stephen Chaplin, 'The Ideal Home Rumpus', *Apollo* (October 1964)

Binckes, Faith, *Modernism, Magazines, and the British Avant-Garde* (Oxford, 2010)

Black, Jonathon, 'Taking Heaven by Violence: Futurism and Vorticism as seen by the British Press, *c.* 1912–20', in *Blasting the Future!: Vorticism in Britain: 1910–1920* (London, 2004), pp. 29–39

—, *Edward Wadsworth: Form, Feeling and Calculation; The Complete Paintings and Drawings* (London, 2005)

Blast, Review of the Great English Vortex, ed. Wyndham Lewis (London, 1914)

Blast, War Number, July 1915, ed. Wyndham Lewis (London, 1915)

Blasting the Future! Vorticism in Britain, 1910–1920 (London, 2004)

Cherry, Deborah, *Painting Women: Victorian Women Artists* (London and New York, 1993)

Clarke, Jay A., and Jonathan Black, *Machine Art Modernism: Prints from the Daniel Cowin Collection* (Williamstown, MA, 2015)

Cole, Roger, *Burning to Speak: The Life and Art of Henri Gaudier-Brzeska* (Oxford, 1978)

Collins, Judith, *The Omega Workshops* (Chicago, IL, 1984)

Cork, Richard, *Vorticism and its Allies* (London, 1974)

—, *Vorticism and Abstract Art in the First Machine Age,* 2 vols (London, 1976)

—, *Art Beyond the Gallery* (New Haven, CT, and London, 1985)

—, *David Bomberg* (New Haven, CT, and London, 1987)

—, *David Bomberg* (London, 1988)

—, *Jacob Epstein* (London, 1999)

—, *Wild Thing: Epstein, Gaudier-Brzeska, Gill* (London, 2010)

—, *David Bomberg and the Old Masters* (London, 2019)

Drogheda, Lord, *Double Harness: Memoirs* (London, 1978)

Ede, H. S., *Savage Messiah* (London, 1931)

Edwards, Paul, ed., *Blast: Vorticism, 1914–1918* (Aldershot, 2000)

Epstein, Jacob, *Let There Be Sculpture: An Autobiography* (London, 1940)

Ferguson, Robert, *The Short, Sharp Life of T. E. Hulme* (London, 2002)

Foster, Alicia, *Radical Women: Jessica Dismorr and Her Contemporaries* (London, 2019)

Garnett, David, *The Golden Echo* (London, 1953)

Gibson, Eric, 'Between Two Worlds: The Art of David Bomberg', *New Criterion* (December 1988)

Goldring, Douglas, *Odd Man Out: The Autobiography of a 'Propaganda Novelist'* (London, 1935)

—, *South Lodge* (London, 1943)

Greenwood, Jeremy, *The Graphic Work of Edward Wadsworth* (Woodbridge, 2002)

Harrison, Charles, *English Art and Modernism, 1900–1939* (London, 1981)

Heathcock, Catherine Elizabeth, 'Jessica Dismorr (1885–1939): Artist, Writer, Vorticist', PhD thesis, University of Birmingham, 1999

Heffernan, Laura, 'Abstraction and the Amateur: De-Disciplining T. E. Hulme', *Modernism/Modernity*, XXI/4 (2015), pp. 881–98

Helmreich, Anne, and Ysanne Holt, 'Marketing Bohemia: The Chenil Gallery in Chelsea, 1905–1926', *Oxford Art Journal*, XXXIII/1 (2010), pp. 43–61

Hewison, Robert, '*Blast* and the Work of Art in the Age of Mechanical Reproduction', in *The Vorticists: Manifesto for a Modern World* (London, 2011), pp. 67–74

Hickman, Miranda, 'The Gender of Vorticism', in *Vorticism: New Perspectives* (Oxford, 2013), pp. 119–33

Hulme, T. E., 'Modern Art – A Preface Note and Neo-Realism', *New Age* (12 February 1914)

—, *Speculations: Essays on Humanism and the Philosophy of Art*, ed. Herbert Read (London, 1924)

Hunt, Violet, *I Have This to Say* (London, 1926)

Jameson, Fredric, 'Wyndham Lewis's *Timon*: The War of Forms', in *Vorticism: New Perspectives* ed. Mark Antliff and Scott W. Klein (Oxford, 2013), pp. 15–30

John, Augustus, *Chiaroscuro: Fragments of Autobiography* (London, 1952)

Jones, Alan R., *The Life and Opinions of T. E. Hulme* (London, 1960)

King, James, *Interior Landscapes: A Life of Paul Nash* (London, 1987)

Lewis, Wyndham, *Tarr* (New York, 1918)

—, *Blasting and Bombardiering* (London, 1937)

—, *Return to Yesterday: Reminiscences, 1894–1914* (London, 1941)

—, *Rude Assignment: A Narrative of My Career Up-to-Date* (London, 1951)

—, *Letters of Wyndham Lewis*, ed. W. K. Rose (London, 1963)

Lewison, Jeremy, ed., *A Genius of Industrial England: Edward Wadsworth, 1889–1949* (Bradford, 1990)

Liddiard, Jean, *Isaac Rosenberg* (London, 1975)

Lipke, William, 'A History and Analysis of Vorticism', PhD thesis, University of Wisconsin, 1966

—, *David Bomberg: A Critical Study of His Life and Work* (London, 1967)

MacDougall, Sarah, and Rachel Dickson, *Bomberg* (London, 2017)

Meyers, Jeffrey, *The Enemy: A Biography of Wyndham Lewis* (London, 1980)

—, 'Kate Lechmere's "Wyndham Lewis from 1912"', *Journal of Modern Literature*, X/1 (March 1983), pp. 158–66

Nevinson, C.R.W., *Paint and Prejudice* (London, 1937)

O'Keeffe, Paul, *Some Sort of Genius: A Life of Wyndham Lewis* (London, 2001)

—, *Gaudier-Brzeska: An Absolute Case of Genius* (London, 2004)

Orchard, Karin, '"A Laugh Like a Bomb": The History and the Ideas of Vorticism', in *Blast: Vorticism 1914–1918* (London, 2000), pp. 14–23

Peppin, Brigid, *Helen Saunders, 1885–1963* (Oxford and Sheffield, 1996)

—, 'Helen Saunders (1885–1963): Mapping a Career', in *Helen Saunders: Modernist Rebel*, exh. cat., The Courtauld Gallery, London, ed. Rachel Sloan (2023)

Peppis, Paul, '"Surrounded by a Multitude of Other Blasts": Vorticism and the Great War', *Modernism/Modernity*, IV/2 (April 1997), pp. 39–66

Pound, Ezra, *The Letters of Ezra Pound, 1907–1941*, ed. D. D. Paige (London, 1951)

—, *Guide to Kulchur* (London, 1968)

—, *Gaudier-Brzeska: A Memoir* (New York, 1970)

Roberts, William, *A Reply to My Biographer Sir John Rothenstein* (London, 1956)

—, *The Resurrection of Vorticism and the Apotheosis of Wyndham Lewis at the Tate* (London, 1956)

—, *Memories of the War to End War, 1914–18* (London, 1974)

—, *William Roberts: Early Years* (London, 1982)

—, *Five Posthumous Essays and Other Writings* (Valencia, 1990)

Robins, Anna Gruetzner, *Modern Art in Britain, 1910–1914* (London, 1997)

Rose, June, *Demons and Angels: A Life of Jacob Epstein* (New York, 2002)

Rothenstein, John, *Modern English Painters*, 2 vols (London, 1952–6)

Rothenstein, William, *Men and Memories, 1900–1922* (London, 1922)

Schwabe, Randolph, 'Three Teachers: Brown, Tonks and Steer', *Burlington Magazine* LXXXII/483 (June 1943), pp. 141–6

Silber, Evelyn, *The Sculpture of Epstein: With a Complete Catalogue* (Lewisburg, PA, 1986)

Sloan, Rachel, ed., *Helen Saunders: Modernist Rebel*, exh. cat., The Courtauld Gallery, London (2023)

Spalding, Frances, *British Art since 1900* (London, 1986)

—, *The Real and the Romantic: English Art Between Two World Wars* (London, 2022)

Tickner, Lisa, 'The Popular Culture of Kermesse: Lewis, Painting, and Performance, 1912–13', *Modernism/Modernity*, IV/2 (April 1997), pp. 67–120

—, *Modern Life and Modern Subjects: British Art in the Early Twentieth Century* (New Haven, CT, and London, 2000)

Tippett, Maria, *Art at the Service of War: Canada, Art, and the Great War* (Toronto, 1984)

Wadsworth, Barbara, *Edward Wadsworth: A Painter's Life* (Salisbury, 1989)

Walsh, Michael J. K., *C.R.W. Nevinson: The Cult of Violence* (London, 2002)

Wees, William C., *Vorticism and the English Avant-Garde* (Toronto, 1972)

Williams, Andrew Gibbon, *William Roberts: An English Cubist* (London, 2004)

Wood, Jonathan, 'Ornament, Talismans and Toys: The Hand-Held Sculptures of Henri Gaudier-Brzeska', in *Blasting the Future! Vorticism in Britain, 1920–1920* (London, 2004), pp. 41–7

Woolf, Leonard, *Beginning Again* (New York, 1964)

Woolf, Virginia, *Moments of Being* (New York, 2002)

Yu, Menting, *London's Women Artists, 1900–1914: A Talented and Decorative Group* (Singapore, 2020)

ACKNOWLEDGEMENTS

In researching and writing about Vorticism, I have learned a great deal from the outstanding scholarship of Christopher Adams, Mark Antliff, Rebecca Beasley, Jonathan Black, Paul Edwards, Vivien Greene, Miranda Hickman, Scott W. Klein, William Lipke, Paul O'Keeffe, Karin Orchard, Lisa Tickner, Michael J. K. Walsh and William C. Wees. I am particularly grateful to Alicia Foster and Brigid Peppin for their insights, assistance and perceptive writings and to Nathan Flis for excellent guidance. Richard Cork's magisterial series of books on Vorticism has set a high bar for anyone writing on the subject. I wish to thank him for much-appreciated support.

PHOTO ACKNOWLEDGEMENTS

The author and publishers wish to express their thanks to the sources listed below for illustrative material and/or permission to reproduce it. Some locations of artworks are also given below, in the interest of brevity:

Alamy: pp. 42 (Zuri Swimmer), 44 (Historic Collection), 60 (Arthur DAmario III), 64 (Pictorial Press Ltd), 77 (Chronicle), 89 (Chroma Collection), 122 (Archive PL); *Blast 1* (1914): pp. 54, 83 top, 90, 117 top left, top right, bottom left and bottom right; *Blast 2* (1915): pp. 137, 141, 142, 143 top left, top right, bottom left and bottom right, 144, 145, 146, 151 left, 155; courtesy of Ivor Braka: p. 109 bottom; Bridgeman Images: pp. 28 (private collection), 32 top (private collection), 47 (© Wyndham Lewis Memorial Trust. All rights reserved 2024); British Council: p. 76; © Christie's Images Limited: p. 83 bottom; The Courtauld Gallery, London: pp. 97 top and bottom, 154; *Daily Mirror*, 30 March 1914: p. 94; Harvard Art Museums: p. 68 bottom; Imperial War Museum, London: pp. 179, 198 bottom; Leeds Art Gallery: p. 150; Manchester Art Gallery: p. 84 (© Frederick Etchells, Licenced by DACS/CARCC Ottawa 2024); Musée National d'Art Moderne, Centre Georges Pompidou, Paris: p. 68 top; Musée Roubaix la Piscine, France: p. 43; The Museum of Fine Arts, Houston: p. 184; National Gallery of Art, Washington, DC: p. 113 right; National Gallery of Canada: pp. 168, 187, 198 top; National Portrait Gallery, London: pp. 12, 20, 40, 56; courtesy of Brigid Peppin: pp. 36, 37, 193; Private Collections: pp. 41, 53, 93 left and right; Smart Museum of Art, The University of Chicago: p. 164; Stapleton Collection: p. 79 (© Vanessa Bell, Licenced by DACS/CARCC Ottawa 2024); Tate Gallery, London: pp. 17, 25 top and bottom, 32 bottom, 50 top, 59, 61, 62, 70 top and bottom, 100, 109 top, 110, 111, 112, 113 left, 132, 136, 151 right, 158, 172, 173, 176, 177, 180, 181, 192, 195, 196, 202; Victoria and Albert Museum, London: pp. 72, 75, 157, 188; Yale Center for British Art: p. 50 bottom.

INDEX